Portuguese
Phrasebook

LAROUSSE

Editors
Laura Bocco, Daniel Grassi, Mike Harland

with
José A. Gálvez, Valerie Grundy, Christy Johnson, Donald Watt

Supplement on Portuguese language and Brazilian culture
Bill Martin

Publishing manager
Janice McNeillie

Design and typesetting
Sharon McTeir

© Larousse 2006
21, rue du Montparnasse
75283 Paris Cedex 06

ISBN: 2-03-542154-3

Sales: Houghton Mifflin Company, Boston

Achevé d'imprimer en Mai 2006 sur les presses de « La Tipografica Varese S.p.A. » à Varese (Italie)

Introduction

This phrasebook is the ideal companion for your trip. It gets straight to the point, helping you to understand and make yourself understood so that you don't miss a thing. Use it like a dictionary to find the exact word you're looking for right away. And at each word we've provided a selection of key phrases that will help you in any situation, no matter how tricky things may have gotten.

The English–Portuguese section contains all those essential expressions that you'll need to get by in Brazil. And because you need to be able to pronounce the words you see on the page properly, we've provided a simple and straightforward phonetic transcription that will enable you to make yourself understood with ease.

The Portuguese–English section provides all the most important words and expressions that you might read or hear while on vacation.

And that's not all: we've added practical and cultural tips for getting by, a supplement on Brazil and its language, life and culture – everything, in fact, to make your trip go as smoothly as possible.

Boa viagem!

Pronunciation

The sound of Portuguese in Brazil can vary according to the different regions. The form used in this phrasebook is that of Rio de Janeiro, which is also used in many dictionaries.

So that you can say what you want to say in Portuguese without running any risk of being misunderstood, we have devised a simple and straightforward phonetic transcription to show how every Portuguese word or phrase used in this phrasebook is pronounced. This phonetic transcription, which is shown in brackets after each Portuguese word or phrase, uses as many standard English sounds as possible, so that it is virtually self-explanatory. The following list provides further clarification:

[a] as in father
[ang] as in bang, but more nasal
[ay] as in say
[e] like the 'e' in hey
[ee] as in see
[eeng] as in sing, but with an 'ee' sound and more nasal
[eng] as in length, but more nasal
[ew] as in hey with a 'w' added
[j] like the 's' in pleasure
[ly] as in million
[ny] as in canyon
[o] as in so
[oing] as in boing, the bouncy sound, but more nasal
[ong] as in song, but more nasal
[oo] as in too
[oom] as in boom, but more nasal
[ow] as in now
[owng] as in town, but more nasal
[oy] as in boy
[tch] as in switch
[y] as in eye

Abbreviations

abbr	abbreviation
adj	adjective
adv	adverb
art	article
conj	conjunction
excl	exclamation
f	feminine
m	masculine
n	noun
num	numeral
pl	plural
prep	preposition
pron	pronoun
v	verb

English–Portuguese phrasebook

able

- to be able to ... poder... [podeh]
- I'm not able to come tonight não vou poder vir hoje à noite [nowng vo podeh veer ojee a noy-tchee]

about aproximadamente [aprosseemada-mentchee]

- I think I'll stay for about an hour acho que vou ficar aproximadamente uma hora [ashoo kee vo feekah aprosseemada-mentchee ooma ora]

abroad *(live)* no exterior [noo eeshteree-oh]; *(travel)* para o exterior [para oo eeshteree-oh]

- I've never been abroad before nunca fui para o exterior antes [noonka fwee para oo eeshteree-oh antcheesh]

absolutely totalmente [totow-mentchee]

- you're absolutely right você está coberto de razão [vosse eeshta kobeh-too djee hazowng]

accept aceitar [assay-tah]

- do you accept traveler's checks? vocês aceitam cheques de viagem? [vossez assay-towng shekeesh djee vee-ajeng]

access o acesso [assessoo]

- is there disabled access? tem acesso para deficientes? [teng assessoo para defeess-yentcheesh]

accident o acidente [asseedentchee]

- there's been an accident houve um acidente [ovee oom asseedentchee]

according to de acordo com [djee akoh-doo kong]

- it's well worth seeing, according to the guidebook vale a pena ver, de acordo com este guia [valee a pena veh, djee akoh-doo kong esh-tchee ghee-a]

address *(details of place)* o endereço [enderessoo] ◆ *(speak to)* dirigir-se a [deeree-jeeh-see a]

---

addressing people

Use *Senhora, Senhor, Senhorita* to say 'Mrs./Ms.' or 'm'am,' 'Mr.' or 'sir,' and 'Miss.' *Senhorita* is not used very much. Note that after these forms of address you normally use the first name, and not the last name. *Dona* and *Seu* are very common forms of address for older people, e.g. *Seu Antônio* and *Dona Maria*.

- could you write down the address for me? **você poderia anotar o endereço para mim?** [vosse poderee-a anotar oo enderessoo para meeng]
- here is my address and phone number **aqui estão o meu endereço e número de telefone** [akee eeshtowng oo mew enderessoo ee noomeroo djee telefonee]

adult o adulto [adoow-too], a adulta [adoow-ta]
- two adults and one student, please **dois adultos e um estudante, por favor** [doyz adoow-tooz ee oom eeshtoodantchee, poh favoh]

advance *(money)* o adiantamento [adjee-antamento] • **in advance** *(pay, reserve)* adiantado [adjee-antadoo]
- do you have to book in advance? **é preciso reservar adiantado?** [eh presseezoo hezeh-vah adjee-antadoo]

after depois [depoysh]
- the stadium is just after the traffic lights **o estádio fica logo depois do semáforo** [oo eeshtad-yoo feeka logoo depoysh doo semaforoo]
- it's twenty after eight **são oito e vinte** [sowng oytoo ee veentchee]

afternoon a tarde [tah-djee]
- is the museum open in the afternoons? **o museu abre de tarde?** [oo moozew abree djee tah-djee]

aftershave a loção pós-barba [lossowng posh-bah-ba]
- a bottle of aftershave **um frasco de loção pós-barba** [oom frashkoo djee lossowng posh-bah-ba]

afterwards mais tarde [mysh tah-djee]
- join us afterwards **junte-se a nós mais tarde** [joontchee-see a nosh mysh tah-djee]

again novamente [novamentchee]
- the bus is late again **o ônibus está atrasado novamente** [oo oneeboosh eeshta atrazadoo novamentchee]

age a idade [eedadjee]
- what ages are your children? **que idade têm seus filhos?** [ke eedadjee tayeng sewsh feel-yoosh]
- we've been waiting for ages! **estamos esperando há séculos!** [eeshtamooz eeshperandoo a sekooloosh]

agency a agência [ajenss-ya]
- what is the contact number for the agency? **qual é o número de contato da agência?** [kwal eh o noomeroo djee kontatoo da ajenss-ya]

ago atrás [atrash]
- I've been before, several years ago **já estive lá, vários anos atrás** [ja eesh-tcheevee la var-yooz anooz-atrash]

agreement o acordo [akoh-doo]
- we need to come to some agreement about where we're going next **precisamos chegar a um acordo sobre para onde vamos agora** [presseezamoosh shegar a oom akoh-doo sobree para ondjee vamooz agora]

agreement/disagreement

- absolutely! sem dúvida! [seng dooveeda]
- that's fine by me por mim está ótimo [poh meeng eeshta otcheemoo]
- you're right você tem razão [vosse teng hazowng]
- go on, then pode continuar, então [podjee konteen-war entowng]
- I'm not at all convinced não estou nada convencido [nowng eeshto nada konvenseedoo]
- I disagree discordo [djeesh-koh-doo]

---

ahead à frente [a frentchee]
- is the road ahead clear? a estrada à frente está livre? [a eeshtrada a frentchee eeshta leevree]

air *(wind)* o ar [ah]
- the air is much fresher in the mountains o ar é muito mais fresco nas montanhas [oo ar eh mweentoo freshkoo nash montan-yash]

air-conditioning o ar-condicionado [ah-kondeess-yonadoo]
- do you have air-conditioning? você tem ar-condicionado? [vosse teng ah-kondeess-yonadoo]

airline a companhia aérea [kompan-yee-a a-eree-a]
- no, we're traveling with a different airline não, estamos viajando com uma companhia aérea diferente [nowng eeshtamoosh vee-ajandoo kong ooma kompan-yee-a a-eree-a]

airmail o correio aéreo [kohayoo a-eree-oo]
- I'd like to send it airmail gostaria de enviar pelo correio aéreo [goshtaree-a djee envee-ah peloo kohayoo a-eree-oo]

airport o aeroporto [a-eropoh-too]
- how long does it take to get to the airport? quanto tempo leva para chegar no aeroporto? [kwantoo tempoo leva para shegah noo a-eropoh-too]

at the airport

- where is gate number 2? onde fica o portão número dois? [ondjee feeka oo poh-towng noomeroo doysh]
- where is the check-in desk? onde fica o balcão de check-in? [ondjee feeka oo bowkowng djee shekin]
- I'd like an aisle seat gostaria de uma poltrona no corredor [goshtaree-a djee ooma powtrona noo kohedoh]
- where is the baggage claim? onde é a área de recolhimento da bagagem? [ondjee eh a aree-a djee hekol-yeementoo da bagajeng]

airport shuttle o serviço de microônibus do aeroporto [seh-veessoo djee meekro-oneeboosh doo a-eropoh-too]
- is there an airport shuttle? tem algum serviço de microônibus no aeroporto? [teng owgoom seh-veessoo djee meekro-oneeboosh noo a-eropoh-too]

air pressure a pressão do ar [pressowng do ah]
- could you check the air pressure in the tires? você poderia verificar a pressão do ar nos pneus? [vosse poderee-a vereefeekar a pressowng doo ah noosh pnewsh]

airsick enjoado(da) [enjwadoo(da)]
- can I have an airsick bag? poderia me conseguir um saco para enjôo? [poderee-a mee konsegeer oom sakoo para enjo-oo]

aisle o corredor [kohedoh]
- two seats, please: one window and one aisle duas poltronas, por favor: uma na janela e outra no corredor [doo-ash powtronash poh favoh ooma na janela ee otra noo kohedoh]

aisle seat a poltrona no corredor [powtrona noo kohedoh]
- I'd like an aisle seat gostaria de uma poltrona no corredor [goshtaree-a djee ooma powtrona noo kohedoh]

alarm (clock) o despertador [deshpeh-tadoh]
- I set the alarm for nine o'clock coloquei o despertador para as nove horas [kolokay oo deshpeh-tadoh para ash novee orash]

alcohol o álcool [owkwow]
- I don't drink alcohol não bebo álcool [nowng beboo owkwow]

alcohol-free sem álcool [seng owkwow]
- what kind of alcohol-free drinks do you have? que tipo de bebida sem álcool você tem? [ke tcheepoo djee bebeeda seng owkwow vosse teng]

all todo(da) [todoo(da)] ♦ *(the whole amount)* tudo [toodoo]; *(everybody)* todos(das) [todoosh(dash)]
- all the time todo o tempo [todoo oo tempoo]
- will that be all? isso é tudo? [eessoo eh toodoo]

allergic alérgico(ca) [aleh-jeekoo(ka)]
- I'm allergic to aspirin/nuts/wheat/dairy products sou alérgico a aspirina/nozes/trigo/laticínios [so aleh-jeekoo a ashpeereena/nozeesh/treegoo/latchee-seenyoosh]

allow permitir [peh-meetcheeh]
- how much luggage are you allowed? quanta bagagem você pode levar? [kwanta bagajeng vosse podjee levah]
- are you allowed to smoke here? dá para fumar aqui? [da para foomar akee]

almost quase [kwazee]
- it's almost one o'clock é quase uma hora [eh kwazee ooma ora]

alone sozinho(nha) [sozeen-yoo(ya)]
- leave us alone! nos deixe em paz! [nosh day-shee eng paj]

along ao longo de [ow longoo djee]
- along the river ao longo do rio [ow longoo doo hee-oo]

altogether *(in total)* no total [noo totow]
- how much does it cost altogether? quanto custa no total? [kwantoo kooshta noo totow]

always sempre [sempree]
- it's always the same thing é sempre a mesma coisa [eh sempree a mejma koyza]

ambulance a ambulância [amboolanss-ya]
- could you send an ambulance right away to...? você poderia enviar imediatamente uma ambulância para...? [vosse poderee-a envee-ar eemedjee-atamentchee ooma amboolanss-ya para]

ambulance service o serviço de ambulância [seh-veessoo djee amboolanss-ya]
- what's the number for the ambulance service? qual é o número do serviço de ambulância? [kwal eh oo noomeroo doo seh-veessoo djee amboolanss-ya]

America os Estados Unidos [eeshtadooz ooneedoosh]
- I'm from America sou dos Estados Unidos [so dooz eeshtadooz ooneedoosh]
- I live in America moro nos Estados Unidos [moroo nooz eeshtadooz ooneedoosh]
- have you ever been to America? você já foi para os Estados Unidos? [vosse ja foy para ooz eeshtadooz ooneedoosh]

American americano(na) [amereekanoo(na)]
- I'm American sou americano/americana [so amereekanoo/amereekana]
- we're Americans somos americanos/americanas [somooz amereekanoosh/amereekanash]

ankle o tornozelo [toh-nozeloo]
- I've sprained my ankle torci o tornozelo [toh-see oo toh-nozeloo]

announcement o aviso [aveezoo]
- was that an announcement about the São Paulo flight? esse era o aviso para o vôo de São Paulo? [essee era oo aveezoo para oo vo-oo djee sowng powloo]

another outro(tra) [otroo(tra)]
- another coffee, please outro café, por favor [otroo kaffe poh favoh]
- (would you like) another drink? (gostaria de) outra bebida? [(goshtaree-a djee) otra bebeeda]

answer a resposta [hesh-poshta] ♦ responder [hesh-pondeh]
- I didn't understand your answer não entendi sua resposta [nowng entendjee soo-a hesh-poshta]
- there's no answer ninguém atende [neengeng atendjee]
- I phoned earlier but nobody answered telefonei mais cedo, mas ninguém atendeu [telefonay mysh sedoo myj neengeng atendjew]

answering machine a secretária eletrônica [sekretar-ya eletroneeka]
- I left a message on your answering machine deixei uma mensagem na sua secretária eletrônica [day-shay ooma mensajeng na soo-a sekretar-ya eletroneeka]

anti-dandruff shampoo o xampu anticaspa [shampoo anteekashpa]
- do you have anti-dandruff shampoo? você tem xampu anticaspa? [vosse teng shampoo anteekashpa]

anybody, anyone alguém [ow-geng]
- is there anybody there? tem alguém aí? [teng ow-geng a-ee]

anything *(indeterminate)* alguma coisa [owgooma koyza]; *(in negatives)* nada [nada]
- is there anything I can do? tem alguma coisa que eu possa fazer? [teng owgooma koyza kee ew possa fazeh]

anywhere algum lugar [owgoom loogah]
- I can't find my room key anywhere não acho a chave do quarto em nenhum lugar [nowng ashoo a shavee do kwah-too eng nen-yoong loogah]
- do you live anywhere near here? você mora em algum lugar perto daqui? [vosse mora eng owgoong loogah peh-too dakee]

apartment o apartamento [apah-tamentoo]
- we'd like to rent an apartment for one week gostaríamos de alugar um apartamento por uma semana [goshtaree-amoosh djee aloogar oom apah-tamentoo por ooma semana]

apologize pedir desculpas [pedjeeh deshkoow-pash]
- there's no need to apologize não precisa pedir desculpas [nowng presseeza pedjeeh deshkoow-pash]

appetizer o aperitivo [aperee-tcheevoo]
- which of the appetizers would you recommend? qual dos aperitivos você recomendaria? [kwow dooz apereetcheevoosh vosse hekomendaree-a]

apple a maçã [massang]
- could I have a kilo of apples, please? você me daria um quilo de maçãs, por favor? [vosse mee daree-a oom keeloo djee massangsh poh favoh]

apple juice o suco de maçã [sookoo djee massang]
- I'd like some apple juice eu queria um suco de maçã [ew keree-a oom sookoo djee massang]

---

apologizing

- excuse me! desculpe! [deshkoow-pee]
- I'm sorry, I can't come on Saturday sinto muito, não vou poder vir no sábado [seentoo mweentoo nowng vo podeh veeh noo sabadoo]
- that's OK tudo bem [toodoo beng]
- it doesn't matter não tem importância [nowng teng eempoh-tanss-ya]
- don't mention it não tem de quê [nowng teng djee ke]

appointment a hora marcada [ora mah-kada]
- could I get an appointment for tomorrow morning? **posso marcar hora para amanhã de manhã** [possoo mah-kar ora para aman-yang djee man-yang]
- I have an appointment with Doctor ... **tenho hora marcada com o médico...** [tenyoo ora mah-kada kong oo medjeekoo]

April abril [abreew]
- April 6th **seis de abril** [saysh djee abreew]

area a área [aree-a]; *(region)* a região [hej-yowng]
- I'm visiting the area **estou visitando a área** [eeshto veezeetandoo a aree-a]
- what walks can you recommend in the area? **que passeios você recomenda na região?** [ke passayoosh vosse hekomenda na hej-yowng]

area code *(for telephoning)* o código de área [kodjeegoo djee aree-a]
- what's the area code for Rio? **qual é o código de área para o Rio?** [kwal eh oo kodjeegoo djee aree-a para oo hee-o]

arm o braço [brassoo]
- I can't move my arm **não consigo mexer o braço** [nowng konseegoo mesher oo brassoo]

around *(in all directions)* por todas as partes [poh todaz ash pah-tcheesh]; *(nearby)* por perto [poh peh-too]; *(here and there)* por aí [por a-ee] ◆ *(encircling)* ao redor de [ow hedoh djee]; *(through)* por todo(da) [poh todoo(da)]; *(approximately)* cerca de [seh-ka djee]
- we've been traveling around Europe **estamos viajando por toda a Europa** [eeshtamoosh vee-ajando poh toda a ew-ropa]
- I don't know my way around yet **ainda não estou bem situado** [a-eenda nowng eeshto beng seetwadoo]
- I arrived around two o'clock **cheguei lá pelas duas horas** [shegay la pelash doo-az orash]
- I'd like something for around 15 reais **queria algo que custasse cerca de 15 reais** [keree-a owgoo kee kooshtassee seh-ka djee keenzee hee-ysh]

arrive chegar [shegah]
- my luggage hasn't arrived **minha bagagem não chegou** [meenya bagajeng nowng shego]
- we arrived late **chegamos tarde** [shegamoosh tah-djee]
- we just arrived **acabamos de chegar** [akabamoosh djee shegah]

art a arte [ah-tchee]
- I'm not really interested in art **não me interesso muito por arte** [nowng mee eenteressoo mweentoo por ah-tchee]

as *(while)* enquanto [enkwantoo]; *(like, since)* como [komoo] ◆ *(in comparisons)* como [komoo]
- the lights went out just as we were about to eat **as luzes se apagaram bem quando íamos comer** [ash loozesh see apagarowng beng kwandoo ee-amoosh komeh]

- as I said before como eu disse antes [komoo ew deessee antchesh]
- leave it as it is deixe como está [dayshee komoo eeshta]
- as... as tão... quanto [towng kwantoo]
- as much as tanto quanto [tantoo kwantoo]
- as many as tantos quanto [tantoosh kwantoo]

ashtray o cinzeiro [seenzayroo]

- could you bring us an ashtray? você poderia nos trazer um cinzeiro? [vosse poderee-a nosh trazer oom seenzayroo]

ask *(question)* perguntar [peh-goontah]; *(time)* pedir [pedjeeh]

- can I ask you a question? posso fazer uma pergunta? [possoo fazer ooma peh-goonta]

aspirin a aspirina [ashpeereena]

- I'd like some aspirin eu queria uma aspirina [ew keree-a ooma ashpeereena]

asthma a asma [ajma]

- I have asthma tenho asma [tenyoo ajma]

at *(indicating place, position)* em [eng]; *(indicating time)* a [a]

- our bags are still at the airport nossas malas ainda estão no aeroporto [nossash malaz a-eenda eeshtowng noo a-eropoh-too]
- we arrive at midnight chegamos à meia-noite [shegamooz a maya noytchee]

ATM o caixa automático [kysha owto-matcheekoo]

- I'm looking for an ATM estou procurando um caixa automático [eeshto prokoorandoo oom kysha owto-matcheekoo]
- the ATM has eaten my card o caixa automático engoliu meu cartão [oo kysha owto-matcheekoo engol-yoo mew kah-towng]

attack *(of illness)* o ataque [atakee] ♦ *(person)* atacar [atakah]

- he had a heart attack ele teve um ataque do coração [elee tevee oom atakee doo korassowng]
- I've been attacked fui atacado [fwee atakadoo]

---

asking questions

- is this seat free? este lugar está livre? [esh-tchee loogah eeshta leevree]
- where is the station? onde fica a estação? [ondjee feeka a eeshtassowng]
- could you help me get my suitcase down, please? você poderia me ajudar a descer minha mala? [vosse poderee-a mee ajoodah desseh meenya mala]
- could you give me a hand? pode me dar uma mãozinha? [podjee mee dar ooma mowng-zeenya]
- could you lend me ten reals? você poderia me emprestar dez reais? [vosse poderee-a mee empreshtah desh hee-ysh]

ATMs

There are ATMs (*caixas eletrônicos*) pretty much everywhere. To withdraw money, search for *Banco 24 Horas* ATMs. You can pay by credit card in most shops, hotels and restaurants as long as you show some ID.

---

attention a atenção [atensowng]
▸ may I have your attention for a moment? você poderia me dar atenção por um momento? [vosse poderee-a mee dar atensowng por oom momentoo]

attractive atraente [atra-entchee]
▸ I find you very attractive eu acho você muito atraente [ew ashoo vosse mweentoo atra-entchee]

August o agosto [agoshtoo]
▸ we're arriving on August 29th vamos chegar dia vinte e nove de agosto [vamoosh shegah djee-a veentchee novee djee agoshtoo]

automatic automático(ca) [owtomatcheekoo(ka)]
▸ I want a car with automatic transmission quero um carro com transmissão automática [keroo oom kahoo kong tranj-meessowng owtomatcheeka]
▸ is it a manual or an automatic? tem marcha manual ou automática? [teng mah-sha man-wow o owtomatcheeka]

available disponível [djeesh-poneevew]
▸ you don't have a table available before then? antes disso não tem uma mesa disponível? [antchesh djeessoo nowng teng ooma meza djeesh-poneevew]

average médio(dia) [medjoo(dja)]
▸ what's the average price of a meal there? qual é o preço médio de uma refeição aí? [kwal eh oo pressoo medjoo djee ooma hefay-sowng a-ee]

avoid evitar [eveetah]
▸ is there a route that would help us avoid the traffic? tem alguma rota alternativa para a gente evitar o trânsito? [teng owgooma hota owteh-natcheeva para a jentchee eveetar oo tranzeeto]

away
▸ the village is ten kilometers away a vila fica a dez quilômetros daqui [a veela feeka a desh keelometroosh dakee]
▸ how far away is Rio? a que distância fica o Rio? [a ke djeeshtanss-ya feeka oo hee-o]
▸ we're looking for a cottage far away from the town estamos procurando uma casa de campo que fique longe da cidade [eeshtamoosh prokoorandoo ooma kaza djee kampoo kee feeka lonjee da seedadjee]
▸ do you have any rooms away from the main road? você tem algum quarto longe da estrada principal? [vosse teng owgoom kwah-too lonjee da eeshtrada preenseepow]

b

baby bottle a mamadeira [mamadayra]
- I need to sterilize a baby bottle preciso esterilizar uma mamadeira [presseezoo eeshtereeleezar ooma mamadayra]

back atrás [atrash] ♦ *(part of body)* as costas [koshtash]; *(of room)* a parte de trás [pah-tchee djee trash]
- I'll be back in 5 minutes volto em cinco minutos [vowtoo eng seenkoo meenootoosh]
- I've got a bad back estou mal das costas [eeshto mow dash koshtash]
- I prefer to sit at the back prefiro sentar atrás [prefeeroo sentar atrash]

backache a dor nas costas [doh nash koshtash]
- I've got a backache estou com dor nas costas [eeshto kong doh nash koshtash]

backpack a mochila [mosheela]
- my passport's in my backpack meu passaporte está na mochila [mew passapoh-tchee eeshta na mosheela]

back up dar marcha a ré [dah mah-sha a re]
- I think we have to back up and turn right acho que a gente tem que dar marcha a ré e dobrar à direita [ashoo kee a jentchee teng kee dah mah-sha a re ee dobrar a djeerayta]

bad ruim [hoo-eeng]
- the weather's bad today o tempo está ruim hoje [oo tempoo eeshta hoo-eeng ojee]

bag o saco [sakoo]; *(suitcase)* a mala [mala]; *(purse)* a bolsa [bowsa]
- are these the bags from flight 502? essas são as malas do vôo cinco zero dois? [essash sowng ash malash doo vo-oo seenkoo zeroo doysh]
- can someone take our bags up to the room, please? alguém pode levar as malas para o quarto, por favor? [owgoom podjee levar ash malash para oo kwah-too poh favoh]

baggage a bagagem [bagajeng]
- my baggage hasn't arrived a minha bagagem ainda não chegou [a meenya bagajeng a-eenda nowng shego]
- I'd like to report the loss of my baggage eu queria informar que a minha bagagem foi extraviada [ew keree-a eemfoh-mah kee a meenya bagajeng foy eeshtravee-ada]

baggage cart o carrinho de bagagem [kaheenyoo djee bagajeng]

‣ I'm looking for a baggage cart estou procurando um carrinho de bagagem [eeshto prokoorandoo oom kaheenyoo djee bagajeng]

bakery a padaria [padaree-a]

‣ is there a bakery nearby? tem alguma padaria por aqui? [teng owgooma padaree-a por akee]

balcony a sacada [sakada]

‣ do you have any rooms with a balcony? vocês têm quartos com sacada? [vossesh tayeng kwah-toosh kong sakada]

banana a banana [banana]

‣ a kilo of bananas, please? um quilo de banana, por favor [oom keeloo djee banana poh favoh]

bandage a atadura [atadoora]

‣ I need a bandage for my ankle preciso de uma atadura para o meu tornozelo [presseezoo djee ooma atadoora para oo mew toh-nozeloo]

Band-Aid® o Band-Aid® [band aidj]

‣ can I have a Band-Aid®? você tem Band-Aid®? [vosse teng band aidj]

bank *(finance)* o banco [bankoo]

‣ is there a bank nearby? tem um banco aqui perto? [teng oom bankoo akee peh-too]

‣ are banks open on Saturdays? os bancos abrem aos sábados? [oosh bankooz abreng owsh sabadoosh]

bank card o cartão do banco [kah-towng doo bankoo]

‣ I've lost my bank card perdi meu cartão do banco [peh-djee mew kah-towng doo bankoo]

---

at the bank

‣ I'd like to change 200 dollars into reais eu gostaria de trocar duzentos dólares por reais [ew goshtaree-a djee trokah doozentoosh dolaresh por hee-ysh]

‣ in small bills, please em trocado, por favor [eng trokadoo poh favoh]

‣ what is the exchange rate for the real? qual é a taxa de câmbio do real? [kwal eh a tasha djee kamb-yoo doo hee-ow]

‣ how much is that in reais? quanto dá isso em reais? [kwantoo da eessoo eng hee-ysh]

‣ do you take traveler's checks? vocês aceitam cheque de viagem? [vossesh assay-towng shekee djee vee-ajeng]

‣ do you charge a commission? vocês cobram comissão? [vossesh kobrowng komeessowng]

bars

At night you can go to *um bar* (also called *um barzinho*), where you can drink a beer, have a snack or even have a complete dinner. If you prefer somewhere with dancing, *uma boate* or *uma casa noturna* (club) is the best option. During the day you can go to *um bar*, *um botequim*, or *um boteco* to buy sodas, alcoholic drinks and snacks.

bar *(establishment serving alcohol)* o bar [bah]; *(counter)* o balcão [bowkowng]; *(of chocolate, soap)* a barra [baha]
 ▸ are there any good bars around here? tem bares bons por aqui? [teng bareesh bongsh por akee]

base a base [bazee]
 ▸ the base of the lamp got broken a base da lâmpada quebrou [a bazee da lampada kebro]
 ▸ we're going to use the village as our base to explore the area vamos usar a aldeia como base para explorar a região [vamooz oozar a owdaya komoo bazee para eeshplorar a hej-yowng]

basic básico(ca) [bazeekoo(ka)]
 ▸ do the staff all have a basic knowledge of English? toda a equipe tem um conhecimento básico de inglês? [toda a ekeepee teng oom konyessee-mentoo bazeekoo djee eenglesh]
 ▸ the basics os fundamentos (básicos) [foondamentoosh (bazeekoosh)]
 ▸ I know the basics, but no more than that conheço os fundamentos, mas não mais do que isso [konyessoo oosh foondamentoosh myj nowng mysh doo kee eessoo]

basis a base [bazee]
 ▸ the price per night is on a double-occupancy basis o preço por pernoite é para duas pessoas [oo pressoo poh peh-noytchee eh para doo-ash pesso-ash]

bat *(for table tennis)* a raquete [haketchee]
 ▸ can you rent bats? dá para alugar uma raquete? [da para aloogar ooma haketchee]

bath o banho [banyoo]
 ▸ to take a bath tomar um banho [tomar oom banyoo]

bathroom *(with toilet and bathtub or shower)* o banheiro [ban-yayroo]; *(with toilet)* o toalete [twaletchee]
 ▸ where's the bathroom? onde fica o banheiro? [ondjee feeka oo ban-yayroo]

bathtub a banheira [ban-yayra]
 ▸ there's no plug for the bathtub não tem tampa para a banheira [nowng teng tampa para a ban-yayra]

battery *(for radio, flashlight)* a pilha [peel-ya]; *(in car)* a bateria [bateree-a]
 ▸ I need new batteries preciso de pilhas novas [presseezoo djee peel-yash novash]

▸ the battery needs to be recharged a bateria precisa ser recarregada [a bateree-a presseeza seh heka-hegada]

▸ the battery's dead acabou a bateria [akabo a bateree-a]

be *(with adj, n)* ser [seh]; *(referring to health, movement, weather)* estar [eeshtah]; *(referring to age)* ter [teh]; *(referring to prices, measurements)* custar [kooshtah]

▸ where are you from? de onde você é? [djee ondjee vosse eh]

▸ I'm a teacher sou professor/professora [so professoh/professora]

▸ I'm happy estou feliz [eeshto feleej]

▸ what day is it? que dia é hoje? [ke djee-a eh ojee]

▸ it's eight o'clock são oito horas [sowng oytoo orash]

▸ how are you? como você está? [komoo vosse eeshta]

▸ I'm fine estou bem [eeshto beng]

▸ where is terminal 1? onde fica o terminal um? [ondjee feeka oo teh-meenow oong]

▸ could you show me where I am on the map? você poderia me mostrar no mapa onde eu estou? [vosse poderee-a mee moshtrah noo mapa ondjee ew eeshto]

▸ have you ever been to the United States? você já foi para os Estados Unidos? [vosse ja foy para ooz eeshtadooz ooneedoosh]

▸ it's the first time I've been here é a primeira vez que venho aqui [eh a preemay-ra vesh kee ven-yoo akee]

▸ how old are you? quantos anos você tem? [kwantooz anoosh vosse teng]

▸ I'm 18 (years old) tenho dezoito anos [ten-yoo dezoytoo anoosh]

▸ it was over thirty-five degrees estava fazendo mais de trinta e cinco graus [eeshtava fazendoo mysh djee treenta ee seenkoo growsh]

▸ it's cold in the evenings faz frio durante a noite [fash free-oo doorantchee a noytchee]

▸ how much is it? quanto custa? [kwantoo kooshta]

▸ I'm 1.68 meters tall tenho um metro e sessenta e oito de altura [tenyoo oom metroo ee sessenta ee oytoo djee owtoora]

beach a praia [pry-a]

▸ it's a sandy beach é uma praia de areia [eh ooma pry-a djee araya]

▸ is it a quiet beach? é uma praia tranqüila? [eh ooma pry-a trankweela]

beach umbrella o guarda-sol [gwah-da sow]

▸ can you rent beach umbrellas? dá para alugar guarda-sóis? [da para aloogah gwah-da soysh]

beautiful bonito(ta) [boneetoo(ta)]

▸ isn't the weather beautiful today? o tempo não está bonito hoje? [oo tempoe nowng eeshta boneetoo ojee]

bed a cama [kama]

▸ is it possible to add an extra bed? é possível colocar uma cama extra? [eh posseevew kolokar ooma kama eshtra]

- do you have a children's bed? **tem cama para criança?** [teng kama para kree-ansa]
- to go to bed **ir para a cama** [eer para a kama]
- I went to bed late **fui dormir tarde** [fwee doh-meeh tah-djee]
- I need to put my children to bed now **tenho que colocar as crianças para dormir agora** [tenyoo kee kolokar ash kree-ansash para doh-meer agora]

bedroom o quarto [kwah-too]
- how many bedrooms does the apartment have? **quantos quartos tem o apartamento?** [kwantoosh kwah-toosh teng oo apah-tamentoo]

bedside lamp o abajur [abajooh]
- the bedside lamp doesn't work **o abajur não funciona** [oo abajooh nowng foonss-yona]

beef a carne de vaca [kah-nee djee vaka]
- I don't eat beef **não como carne de vaca** [nowng komoo kah-nee djee vaka]

beer a cerveja [seh-veja]
- two beers, please **duas cervejas, por favor** [doo-ash seh-vejash poh favoh]

begin *(start)* **começar** [komessah]
- when does the performance begin? **a que horas começa a apresentação?** [a kee orash komessa a aprezenta-sowng]

beginner o principiante, a principiante [preenseep-yantchee]
- I'm a complete beginner **sou um principiante completo** [so oom preenseep-yantchee kompletoo]

behind atrás [atrash]
- from behind **por trás** [poh trash]
- the rest of our party is in the car behind **o resto do grupo está no carro de trás** [oo heshtoo doo groopoo eeshta noo kahoo djee trash]

berth *(on ship)* **o beliche** [beleeshee]
- I'd prefer the upper berth **prefiro a cama de cima** [prefeeroo a kama djee seema]

beside ao lado de [ow ladoo djee]
- is there anyone sitting beside you? **tem alguém sentado do seu lado?** [teng owgeng sentadoo doo sew ladoo]

best melhor [mel-yoh]
- what's the best restaurant in town? **qual é o melhor restaurante da cidade?** [kwal eh oo mel-yoh heshtow-rantchee da seedadjee]

better melhor [mel-yoh]
- I've been on antibiotics for a week and I'm not any better **estou tomando antibióticos há uma semana e ainda não estou melhor** [eeshto tomandoo antcheebee-otcheekooz a ooma semana ee a-eenda nowng eeshto mel-yoh]
- the better situated of the two hotels **o hotel mais bem situado dos dois** [oo otew mysh beng seetwadoo doosh doysh]

between entre [entree]

▸ I traveled between Rio and São Paulo **viajei entre o Rio e São Paulo** [vee-ajay entree o hee-o ee sowng powloo]

bicycle a bicicleta [beessee-kleta]

▸ is there a place to leave bicycles? **tem um lugar para deixar as bicicletas?** [teng oom loogah para day-shar ash beessee-kletash]

bicycle lane a ciclovia [seeklovee-a]

▸ are there any bicycle lanes? **tem ciclovias aqui?** [teng seeklovee-az akee]

bicycle pump a bomba (de bicicleta) [bomba (djee beessee-kleta]

▸ do you have a bicycle pump? **você tem uma bomba de bicicleta?** [vosse teng ooma bomba djee beessee-kleta]

big grande [grandjee]

▸ do you have it in a bigger size? **tem num tamanho maior?** [teng noom taman-yoo my-oh]

▸ it's too big **é muito grande** [eh mweentoo grandjee]

bike a bicicleta [beessee-kleta]

▸ I'd like to rent a bike for an hour **eu gostaria de alugar uma bicicleta por uma hora** [ew goshtaree-a djee aloogar ooma beessee-kleta por ooma ora]

▸ I'd like to do a bike tour **eu gostaria de fazer um passeio de bicicleta** [ew goshtaree-a djee fazer oom passayoo djee beessee-kleta]

bill *(in restaurant, hotel)* a conta [konta]; *(for goods)* a nota [nota]; *(paper money)* a cédula [sedoola]

▸ the bill, please! **a conta, por favor!** [a konta poh favoh]

▸ I think there's a mistake with the bill **acho que tem um erro na conta** [ashoo kee teng oom ehoo na konta]

▸ put it on my bill **coloca na minha conta** [koloka na meenya konta]

▸ can you write up my bill, please? **você poderia discriminar a minha conta, por favor?** [vosse poderee-a deeshkreemeenar a meenya konta poh favoh]

birthday o aniversário [aneeveh-sar-yoo]

▸ happy birthday! **feliz aniversário!** [feleez aneeveh-sar-yoo]

bite *(of animal)* a mordida [moh-djeeda]; *(of insect)* a picada [peekada] ◆ *(animal)* morder [moh-deh]; *(insect)* picar [peekah]

▸ do you have a cream for mosquito bites? **você tem repelente para mosquito?** [vosse teng hepelentchee para moshkeetoo]

▸ I've been bitten by a mosquito **fui picado por um mosquito** [fwee peekadoo por oom moshkeetoo]

black preto(ta) [pretoo(ta)]

▸ I'm looking for a little black dress **estou procurando um vestido escuro e pequeno** [eeshtoo prokoorandoo oom vesh-tcheedoo eeshkooroo ee pekenoo]

black-and-white em preto-e-branco [em pretoo-ee-brankoo]

▸ I'd like to see a black-and-white movie **eu gostaria de ver um filme em preto-e-branco** [ew goshtaree-a djee ver oom feewmee em pretoo ee brankoo]

blanket o cobertor [kobeh-toh]
> I'd like an extra blanket gostaria de mais um cobertor [goshtaree-a djee myz oom kobeh-toh]

bleed sangrar [sangrah]
> it won't stop bleeding não pára de sangrar [nowng para djee sangrah]

blind *(on window)* a persiana [peh-see-ana]
> can we pull down the blinds? podemos baixar as persianas? [podemoosh by-shar ash peh-see-anash]

blister a bolha [bol-ya]
> I got a blister tenho uma bolha [tenyoo ooma bol-ya]

block bloquear [blokee-ah]
> the toilet's blocked a descarga está trancada [a deshkah-ga eeshta trankada]
> my ears are completely blocked meus ouvidos estão completamente fechados [mewz oveedoosh eeshtowng kompletamentchee feshadoosh]

blond loiro(ra) [loyroo(ra)]
> I have blond hair tenho cabelo loiro [tenyoo kabeloo loyroo]

blood o sangue [sangee]
> traces of blood restos de sangue [heshtoosh djee sangee]

blood pressure a pressão sangüínea [pressowng sangweenee-a]
> I have high blood pressure tenho pressão alta [tenyoo pressowng owta]

blood type o tipo sangüíneo [tcheepoo sangweenee-oo]
> my blood type is A positive meu tipo sangüíneo é A positivo [mew tcheepoo sangweenee-oo eh a pozeetcheevoo]

blue azul [azoow]
> the blue one o azul [oo azoow]

board *(plane)* embarcar em [embah-kar eng] ◆ embarcar [embah-kah]
> what time will the plane be boarding? a que horas será o embarque? [a kee orash sera oo embah-kee]
> where is the flight to New York boarding? de onde se embarca para o vôo para Nova lorque? [djee ondjee see embah-ka para oo vo-oo para nova yorkee]

boarding pass o cartão de embarque [kah-towng djee embah-kee]
> I can't find my boarding pass não consigo achar meu cartão de embarque [nowng konseegoo ashah mew kah-towng djee embah-kee]

boat o barco [bah-koo]
> can we get there by boat? dá para ir de barco? [da para eeh djee bah-koo]

boat trip o passeio de barco [passayoo djee bah-koo]
> are there boat trips on the river? há passeios de barco pelo rio? [a passayoosh djee bah-koo peloo hee-oo]

book *(for reading, stamps)* o livro [leevroo]; *(of tickets)* o talão [talowng]; *(of matches)* a caixa [ky-sha] ◆ *(ticket, room)* reservar [hezeh-vah]

- do you sell English–language books? vocês vendem livros em inglês? [vossesh vendeng leevrooz eng eenglesh]
- is it more economical to buy a book of tickets? sai mais barato comprar um talão de entradas? [sy mysh baratoo komprar oom talowng djee entradash]
- I'd like to book a ticket queria reservar uma entrada [keree-a hezeh-var ooma entrada]
- do you need to book in advance? precisa reservar com antecedência? [presseeza hezeh-vah kong antessedenss-ya]

born
- to be born nascer [nasseh]
- I was born on March 3rd, 1985 nasci no dia três de março de mil, novecentos e oitenta e cinco [nassee no djee-a tresh djee mah-soo djee meew novee-sentooz ee oytenta ee seenkoo]

bottle a garrafa [gahafa]
- a bottle of red wine, please uma garrafa de vinho tinto, por favor [ooma gahafa djee veenyoo tcheentoo poh favoh]

bottle opener o abridor de garrafas [abreedoh djee gahafash]
- can you pass me the bottle opener? pode me alcançar o abridor de garrafas? [podjee mee owkansar oo abreedoh djee gahafash]

bottom *(of a well, of a box)* o fundo [foondoo]
- my passport's at the bottom of my suitcase o meu passaporte está no fundo da mala [oo mew passapoh-tchee eeshta noo foondoo da mala]

box a caixa [ky-sha]
- could I have a box of matches, please? eu queria uma caixa de fósforos, por favor [ew keree-a ooma ky-sha djee foshforoosh poh favoh]

boy *(young male)* o menino [meneenoo]; *(son)* o filho [feel-yoo]
- he seems like a nice boy parece um menino ótimo [paressee oom meneenoo otcheemoo]
- she has two boys ela tem dois filhos [ella teng doysh feel-yoosh]

boyfriend o namorado [namoradoo]
- my boyfriend is a biologist meu namorado é biólogo [mew namoradoo eh bee-ologoo]

brake o freio [frayoo]
- the brakes aren't working properly os freios não estão funcionando direito [oosh frayoosh nowng eeshtowng foonss-yonandoo djeeraytoo]

brake fluid o fluido de freio [floo-eedoo djee frayoo]
- could you check the brake fluid? você poderia verificar o fluido de freio? [vosse poderee-a vereefeekar oo floo-eedoo djee frayoo]

branch *(of bank)* a agência [ajenss-ya]
- which branch should I visit to get the replacement traveler's checks? a que agência eu devo ir para substituir os cheques de viagem? [a ke ajenss-ya ew devoo eeh para soob-shteetweer oosh shekeesh djee vee-ajeng]

breakfast

Breakfast (*o café da manhã*) is usually light: some *pão francês* (white bread) or *pão integral* (whole-wheat bread) with cheese and butter and white coffee. It's eaten early, between 7 and 8 o'clock. Since people don't stop for a snack in the morning, they eat lunch between about midday and 1 p.m.

bread o pão [powng]
- do you have any bread? tem pão? [teng powng]
- could I have some more bread? poderia me alcançar mais pão? [poderee-a mee owkansah mysh powng]

break *(pause)* a pausa [powza] ◆ quebrar [kebrah]
- should we take a break? vamos fazer uma pausa? [vamoosh fazer ooma powza]
- be careful you don't break it tenha cuidado para não quebrar [tenya kweedadoo para nowng kebrah]
- I think I've broken my ankle acho que quebrei o tornozelo [ashoo ke kebray oo toh-nozeloo]

break down estragar [eeshtragah]
- my car has broken down meu carro estragou [mew kahoo eeshtrago]

breakdown o estrago [eeshtragoo]
- we had a breakdown on the freeway o carro estragou na estrada [oo kahoo eeshtrago na eeshtrada]

breakfast o café da manhã [kaffe da man-yang]
- to have breakfast tomar o café da manhã [tomar oo kaffe da man-yang]
- what time is breakfast served? a que horas é servido o café da manhã? [a kee oraz eh seh-veedoo oo kaffe da man-yang]

bridge a ponte [pontchee]
- do you have to pay a toll to use the bridge? tem que pagar pedágio para usar a ponte? [teng kee pagah pedaj-yoo para oozar a pontchee]

bring trazer [trazeh]
- what should we bring to drink? o que a gente traz para beber? [oo kee a jentchee trash para bebeh]

bring down *(bags, luggage)* descer [desseh]
- could you get someone to bring down our luggage, please? você conseguiria alguém para descer nossa bagagem, por favor? [vosse konseg-eeree-a owgeng para desseh nossa bagajeng poh favoh]

bring in *(bags, luggage)* trazer [trazeh]
- can you bring in my bags, please? você poderia trazer minhas malas, por favor? [vosse poderee-a trazeh meenyash malash poh favoh]

broken quebrado(da) [kebradoo(da)]

- ▸ the lock is broken **a fechadura está quebrada** [a feshadoora eeshta kebrada]
- ▸ I think I've got a broken leg **acho que quebrei a perna** [ashoo kee kebray a peh-na]

bronchitis a bronquite [bronkeetchee]

- ▸ do you have anything for bronchitis? **tem alguma coisa para bronquite?** [teng owgooma koyza para bronkeetchee]

brother o irmão [eeh-mowng]

- ▸ I don't have any brothers or sisters **não tenho irmãos nem irmãs** [nowng tenyoo eeh-mowngsh neng eeh-mangsh]

brown marrom [mahong]

- ▸ he has brown hair **ele tem cabelos castanhos** [elee teng kabeloosh kashtan-yoosh]
- ▸ I'm looking for a brown leather belt **estou procurando um cinto de couro marrom** [eeshto prokoorando oom seentoo djee koroo mahong]

brush *(for hair, clothes, with short handle)* a escova [eeshkova]; *(broom)* a vassoura [vassora] ◆ *(hair)* escovar [eeshkovah]

- ▸ can I borrow a brush? **me empresta uma escova?** [mee empreshta ooma eeshkova]
- ▸ where are the brush and dustpan? **onde estão a vassoura e a pá de lixo?** [ondjee eeshtowng a vassora ee a pa djee leeshoo]
- ▸ to brush one's teeth **escovar os dentes** [eeshkovar oosh dentcheesh]

bulb *(light)* a lâmpada [lampada]

- ▸ the bulb's out in the bathroom **a lâmpada do banheiro queimou** [a lampada doo ban-yayroo kay-mo]

bunk beds o beliche [beleeshee]

- ▸ are there bunk beds for the children? **tem beliche para as crianças?** [teng beleeshee para ash kree-ansash]

burn queimado(da) [kaymadoo(da)]

- ▸ the food's completely burnt **a comida queimou toda** [a komeeda kaymo toda]
- ▸ I've burned my hand **queimei a mão** [kaymay a mowng]

burst *(tire)* furar [foorah]

- ▸ one of my tires burst **um dos pneus do meu carro furou** [oom doosh pnewsh do mew kahoo fooro], **furou um pneu** [fooro oom pnew]

bus o ônibus [oneeboosh]

- ▸ does this bus go downtown? **esse ônibus vai para o centro?** [essee oneeboosh vy para oo sentroo]
- ▸ which bus do I have to take to go to...? **que ônibus que eu tenho que pegar para ir para...?** [ke oneeboosh kee ew tenyoo kee pegah para eeh para]
- ▸ when is the next bus to Sao Paulo? **quando é o próximo ônibus para São Paulo?** [kwandoo eh oo prosseemoo oneeboosh para sowng powloo]
- ▸ I'd like a round-trip ticket for the 9 a.m. bus to Vitoria tomorrow, please **eu queria uma passagem de ida e volta para o ônibus das nove da manhã de**

bus

For long-distance travel, Brazilians use the bus. When buying a ticket, you will have to choose *com ou sem seguro* (with or without travel insurance), in *um direto* (a direct bus, with no stops) or a *pinga-pinga* or *semidireto* (a bus that stops in some or most towns on the way to pick up passengers). When traveling at night, you may choose *um ônibus comum* (with non-reclining seats), *semileito* (with semi-reclining seats) or *leito* (with fully-reclining seats). Remember, Brazil is huge and the journey might take days...

amanhã para Vitória, por favor [ew keree-a ooma passajeng djee eeda ee vowta para oo oneeboosh dash novee da manyang para veetorya poh favoh]

▶ do you have reduced-price bus tickets for seniors? tem passagem com preço reduzido para aposentados? [teng passajeng kong pressoo hedoozeedoo para apozentadoosh]

▶ the bus was fifteen minutes late o ônibus estava quinze minutos atrasado [oo oneeboosh eeshtava keenzee meenootooz atrazadoo]

bus driver o motorista(de ônibus) [motoreeshta (djee oneeboosh)]

▶ can you buy tickets from the bus driver? dá para comprar passagem com o motorista? [da para komprah passajeng kong oo motoreeshta]

business *(commerce)* os negócios [negoss-yoosh]; *(company)* a empresa [empreza]; *(concern)* o assunto [assoontoo]; *(affair, matter)* a conta [konta]

▶ it's none of your business não é da sua conta [nowng eh da soo-a konta]

business card o cartão (de visitas) [kah-towng (djee veezeetash)]

▶ here's my business card aqui está o meu cartão [akee eeshta oo mew kah-towng]

business class a classe executiva [klassee ezekoo-tcheeva] ◆ de classe executiva [djee klassee ezekoo-tcheeva]

▶ are there any seats in business class? há alguma poltrona na classe executiva? [a owgooma powtrona na klassee ezekoo-tcheeva]

▶ I prefer to travel business class prefiro viajar na classe executiva [prefeeroo vee-ajah na klassee ezeko-tcheeva]

business hours

In Brazil most stores open at about 8 a.m., close at noon, open again at 2 p.m. and close again at 6 p.m. Some do not close at lunchtime. Banks are open from 10 a.m. to 4 p.m. In shopping malls, the stores open at 10 a.m. and close at 10 p.m., Saturdays and Sundays included.

bus station a (estação) rodoviária [(eeshtassowng) hodovee-aree-a]
▶ I'm looking for the bus station estou procurando a (estação) rodoviária [eeshto prokoorando a (eeshtassowng) hodovee-aree-a]

bus stop a parada de ônibus [parada djee oneeboosh]
▶ where's the nearest bus stop? onde fica a parada de ônibus mais próxima? [ondjee feeka a parada djee oneeboosh mysh prosseema]

busy *(person, phone line)* ocupado(da) [okoopadoo(da)]; *(town, beach, street)* movimentado(da) [moveementadoo(da)]; *(period)* agitado(da) [ajeetadoo (da)]
▶ I'm afraid I'm busy tomorrow acho que vou estar ocupado amanhã [ashoo kee vo eeshtar okoopadoo aman-yang]
▶ the line's busy a linha está ocupada [a leenya eeshta okoopada]

butter a manteiga [mantayga]
▶ could you pass the butter please? você poderia me passar a manteiga, por favor? [vosse poderee-a mee passar a mantayga poh favoh]

buy comprar [komprah]
▶ where can I buy tickets? onde posso comprar as entradas? [ondjee possoo komprar az entradash]
▶ can I buy you a drink? posso lhe pagar um drinque? [possool-yee pagar oom dreenkee]

bye tchau [tchow]
▶ bye, see you tomorrow! tchau, até amanhã! [tchow a-te aman-yang]

C

cab o táxi [taksee]
▶ can you order me a cab to the airport? você pode pedir um táxi para me levar até o aeroporto? [vosse podjee pedjeer oom taksee para mee levar a-te oo a-eropoh-too]

cab driver o motorista de táxi [motoreeshta djee taksee]
▶ does the cab driver speak English? o motorista do táxi fala inglês? [oo motoreeshta doo taksee fala eenglesh]

cabin *(on boat)* o camarote [kamarotchee]; *(on plane)* a cabine [kabeenee]
▶ can I have breakfast in my cabin? posso tomar o café da manhã na cabine? [possoo tomar oo kaffe da man-yang na kabeenee]

cable o cabo [kaboo]
▶ does the hotel have cable? tem cabo no hotel? [teng kaboo noo otew]

café o café [kaffe]
- is there a café near here? **tem um café aqui por perto?** [teng oom kaffe akee poh peh-too]

cake o bolo [boloo]
- a piece of that cake, please **um pedaço de esse bolo, por favor** [oom pedassoo djee essee boloo poh favoh]

call *(on phone)* a ligação [leegassowng] ◆ *(name)* chamar [shamah]; *(on phone)* ligar [leegah]
- I have to make a call **tenho que fazer uma ligação** [tenyoo kee fazer ooma leegassowng]
- what is this called? **como se chama isso?** [komoo see shama eessoo]
- who's calling? **quem fala?** [keng fala]

call back ligar de volta [leegah djee vowta]
- could you ask her to call me back? **poderia pedir para ela me ligar depois?** [poderee-a pedjeeh para ella mee leegah depoysh]
- I'll call her back (later) **ligo de volta para ela (depois)** [leegoo djee vowta para ella (depoysh)]

calm calmo(ma) [kowmoo(ma)]
- keep calm! **fique calmo!** [feekee kowmoo]

camera *(for taking photos)* a câmera [kamera]; *(for filming)* a filmadora [feewmadora]
- can I use my camera here? **posso usar a câmera aqui?** [possoo oozar a kamera akee]

camper o trailer [trayler]
- do you have a space left for a camper? **tem espaço para um trailer?** [teng eeshpassoo para oom trayler]
- I'd like to book space for a camper for the night of August 15th **gostaria de reservar espaço para um trailer na noite do dia quinze de agosto** [goshtaree-a djee hezeh-var eeshpassoo para oom trayler na noytchee doo djee-a keenzee djee agoshtoo]

campground o camping [kampeeng]
- I'm looking for a campground **estou procurando um camping** [eeshto prokoorandoo oom kampeeng]

---

in a café

- is this table free? **essa mesa está desocupada?** [essa meza eeshta dezokoopada]
- excuse me! **desculpe!** [djeeshkoowpee]
- two black coffees/coffees with cream, please **dois cafés pretos/cafés com creme, por favor** [doysh kaffesh pretoosh/kaffesh kong kremee poh favoh]
- can I have another beer, please? **pode me trazer outra cerveja?** [podjee mee trazeh otra seh-veja]

camping

In Brazil, it's best to go camping in designated areas (*campings*), which can be found in the main tourist spots. Most of them are equipped with bathroom facilities, electricity, and a snack bar.

camping o acampamento [akampamentoo]
  ▸ I love going camping **adoro ir acampar** [adoroo eer akampah]

can a lata [lata]
  ▸ a can of oil, please **uma lata de óleo, por favor** [ooma lata djee olee-oo poh favoh]

can *(be able to)* **poder** [podeh]; *(know how to)* **saber** [sabeh]
  ▸ can I help you? **posso ajudar?** [possoo ajoodah]
  ▸ can you speak English? **você sabe falar inglês?** [vosse sabee falar eenglesh]

Canada o Canadá [kanada]
  ▸ I'm from Canada **sou do Canadá** [so doo kanada]
  ▸ I live in Canada **moro no Canadá** [moroo noo kanada]
  ▸ have you ever been to Canada? **você já foi para o Canadá?** [vosse ja foy para oo kanada]

Canadian canadense [kanadensee]
  ▸ I'm Canadian **sou canadense** [so kanadensee]
  ▸ we're Canadians **somos canadenses** [somoosh kanadenseesh]

cancel cancelar [kanselah]
  ▸ is it possible to cancel a reservation? **é possível cancelar uma reserva?** [eh posseevew kanselar ooma hezeh-va]

canoeing a canoagem [kan-wajeng]
  ▸ I was told we could go canoeing **me disseram que a gente poderia praticar canoagem** [mee deesserowng kee a jentchee poderee-a pratcheekah kan-wajeng]

car o carro [kahoo]
  ▸ I'd like to rent a car for a week **gostaria de alugar um carro por uma semana** [goshtaree-a djee aloogar oom kahoo por ooma semana]
  ▸ I've just crashed my car **acabei de bater o carro** [akabay djee bater oo kahoo]

renting a car

  ▸ with comprehensive insurance **com seguro total** [kong segooroo totow]
  ▸ can I leave the car at the airport? **posso deixar o carro no aeroporto?** [possoo day-shar oo kahoo noo a-eropoh-too]
  ▸ can I see your driver's license, please? **posso ver a sua carteira de motorista, por favor?** [possoo ver a soo-a kah-tayra djee motoreeshta poh favoh]

‣ can you help us push the car? você pode nos ajudar a empurrar o carro? [vosse podjee noz ajoodar a empoohar oo kahoo]

‣ my car's been towed away meu carro foi rebocado [mew kahoo foy hebokadoo]

‣ my car's broken down meu carro pifou [mew kahoo peefo]

carafe a garrafa [gahafa]

‣ a large carafe of water, please uma garrafa grande de água, por favor [ooma gahafa grandjee djee agwa poh favoh]

‣ a carafe of house wine uma garrafa de vinho da casa [ooma gahafa djee veenyoo da kaza]

car crash o acidente de carro [asseedentchee djee kahoo]

‣ he's been killed in a car crash ele morreu num acidente de carro [elee mohew noom asseedentchee djee kahoo]

card o cartão [kah-towng]

‣ the waiter hasn't brought my card back o garçom não me devolveu o cartão [oo gah-song nowng mee devow-vew oo kah-towng]

‣ can I give you my card? posso lhe dar o meu cartão? [possool-yee dar oo mew kah-towng]

cardigan o cardigã [kah-djeegang]

‣ should I take a cardigan for the evening? devo levar um cardigã para a noite? [devoo levar oom kah-djeegang para a noytchee]

carpet o carpete [kah-petchee]

‣ the carpet hasn't been vacuumed não passaram o aspirador no carpete [nowng passarowng oo ashpeeradoh noo kah-petchee]

car rental o aluguel de carro [aloogew djee kahoo]

‣ is car rental expensive? é caro alugar um carro? [eh karoo aloogar oom kahoo]

car rental agency a locadora de automóveis [lokadora djee owtomovaysh]

‣ do you know of any car rental agencies? você conhece alguma locadora de automóveis? [vosse konyessee owgooma lokadora djee owtomovaysh]

carry (baggage) carregar [kahegah]

‣ could you help me carry something? você poderia me ajudar a carregar uma coisa? [vosse poderee-a mee ajoodar a kahegah ooma koyza]

carry-on bag a mala de mão [mala djee mowng]

‣ am I only allowed one carry-on bag? posso levar só uma mala de mão? [possoo levah so ooma mala djee mowng]

cart o carrinho [kaheenyoo]

‣ where can I get a cart? onde eu consigo um carrinho? [ondjee ew konseegoo oom kaheenyoo]

carton (of cigarettes) o maço [massoo]

‣ I'd like a carton of cigarettes gostaria de um maço de cigarros [goshtaree-a djee oom massoo djee seegahoosh]

in case caso [kazoo]
- just in case por via das dúvidas [poh vee-a dash dooveedash], só por precaução [so poh prekow-sowng]

cash *(notes and coins)* o dinheiro [djeen-yayroo] ◆ *(check)* descontar [deshkontah]
- I'll pay cash vou pagar em dinheiro [vo pagar eng djeen-yayroo]
- I want to cash this traveler's check quero trocar este cheque de viagem [keroo trokar esh-tche shekee djee vee-ajeng]

castle o castelo [kashteloo]
- is the castle open to the public? o castelo está aberto para visitação? [oo kashteloo eeshta abeh-too para veezeeta-sowng]

catalog o catálogo [katalogoo]
- do you have a catalog? tem um catálogo? [teng oom katalogoo]

catch *(with hands, cold)* pegar [pegah]; *(hear clearly)* compreender [kompree-endeh]
- I've caught a cold peguei um resfriado [pegay oom heshfree-adoo]
- I'm sorry, I didn't quite catch your name desculpe, não entendi direito o seu nome [djeeshkoow-pee nowng entendjee djeeraytoo oo sew nomee]

Catholic católico(ca) [katoleekoo(ka)]
- where is there a Catholic church? onde tem uma igreja (católica)? [ondjee teng ooma eegreja (katoleeka)]

CD o CD [se-de]
- how much does this CD cost? quanto custa esse CD? [kwantoo kooshta essee se-de]

cellphone o (telefone) celular [(telefonee) seloolah]
- what's your cellphone number? qual é o número do seu celular? [kwal eh oo noomeroo doo sew seloolah]

center o centro [sentroo]
- we want to be based near the center of the region queremos ficar no centro da região [keremoosh feekah noo sentroo da hej-yowng]

chair a cadeira [kadayra]
- could we have another chair in our room? daria para colocar outra cadeira no meu quarto? [daree-a para kolokar otra kadayra noo mew kwah-too]

change a mudança [moodanssa]; *(money)* o troco [trokoo] ◆ mudar [moodah]; *(baby)* trocar [trokah]
- do you have any change? você tem troco? [vosse teng trokoo]
- keep the change fique com o troco [feekee kong oo trokoo]
- I don't have exact change não tenho o troco exato [nowng tenyoo oo trokoo ezatoo]
- is it possible to change a reservation? tem como mudar uma reserva? [teng komoo moodar ooma hezeh-va]
- I'd like to change 200 dollars into reais gostaria de trocar duzentos dólares em reais [goshtaree-a djee trokah doozentoosh dolaresh eng hee-ysh]

- I'd like to change these traveler's checks eu queria trocar esseesh shekeesh djee vee-ajeng]

- can you help me change the tire? pode me ajudar a trocar o pneu? [podjee mee ajoodar a trokar oo pnew]

- the oil needs to be changed tem que trocar o óleo [teng kee trokar oo olee-oo]

changing table o trocador [trokadoh]

- is there a changing table? tem um trocador? [teng oom trokadoh]

charge *(cost)* o preço [pressoo]

- is there a charge for the parking lot? tem que pagar para usar o estacionamento? [teng kee pagah para oozar oo eeshtass-yonamentoo]

- is there a charge for using the facilities? tem taxa de utilização das instalações? [teng tasha djee ooteeleeza-sowng daz eenshtala-soyngsh]

- is there a charge for cancellations? tem taxa para cancelar? [teng tasha para kanselah]

- I'd like to speak to the person in charge gostaria de falar com o responsável [goshtaree-a djee falah kong oo heshponsavew]

charter flight o vôo fretado [vo-oo fretadoo]

- where do we board the charter flight to Rio? onde é o embarque para o vôo fretado para o Rio? [ondjee eh oo embah-kee para oo vo-oo fretadoo para oo hee-oo]

cheap barato(ta) [baratoo(ta)]

- that's cheap! que barato! [ke baratoo]

- I'm trying to find a cheap flight home estou tentando achar um vôo mais em conta para voltar para casa [eeshto tentandoo ashar oom vo-oo myz eng konta para vowtah para kaza]

check *(for paying)* o cheque [shekee] ◆ *(test, verify)* verificar [veree-feekah]

- can I pay by check? posso pagar com cheque? [possoo pagah kong shekee]

- can you check the oil? pode verificar o óleo? [podjee veree-feekar oo olee-oo]

checkbook o talão de cheques [talowng djee shekeesh]

- my checkbook's been stolen roubaram meu talão de cheques [hobarowng mew talowng djee shekeesh]

check in *(baggage)* despachar [deshpashah] ◆ *(at airport)* fazer check-in [fazeh shekin]; *(at hotel)* registrar-se [hejeesh-trah-see]

- I'd like to check in both these bags, please eu gostaria de despachar essas duas malas, por favor [ew goshtaree-a djee deshpashar essash doo-ash malash poh favoh]

- what time do you have to be at the airport to check in? a que horas tem que estar no aeroporto para fazer check-in? [a kee orash teng kee eeshtah noo a-eropoh-too para fazeh shekin]

check-in desk *(at airport)* o balcão de check-in [bowkowng djee shekin]

- where is the United Airlines check-in desk? onde fica o balcão de check-in da United Airlines? [ondjee feeka oo bowkowng djee shekin da United Airlines]

check out *(from hotel)* a saída [sa-eeda]

▶ what time do you have to check out by? até que horas a gente pode fechar a conta? [a-te kee oraz a jentchee podjee feshar a konta]

cheers saúde [sa-oodjee]

▶ cheers and all the best! saúde para todos! [sa-oodjee para todoosh]

cheese o queijo [kayjoo]

▶ what are the best local cheeses? quais são os melhores queijos da região? [kwysh sowng oosh mel-yoreesh kayjoosh da hej-yowng]

chicken *(bird)* a galinha [galeenya]; *(food)* o frango [frangoo]

▶ half a roast chicken, please meio frango assado, por favor [mayoo frangoo assadoo poh favoh]

▶ a chicken sandwich and fries um sanduíche de frango e batatas fritas [oom sandweeshee djee frangoo ee batatash freetash]

child *(boy, girl)* a criança [kree-ansa]; *(son, daughter)* o filho [feel-yoo], a filha [feel-ya]

▶ do you have children? você tem filhos? [vosse teng feel-yoosh]

▶ two adults and two children, please dois adultos e duas crianças, por favor [doyz adoow-tooz ee doo-ash kree-ansash poh favoh]

▶ do you have discounts for children? tem desconto para criança? [teng djeeshkontoo para kree-ansa]

children's menu o menu para criança [menoo para kree-ansa]

▶ do you have a children's menu? tem menu para criança? [teng menoo para kree-ansa]

chilled *(wine)* gelado(da) [jeladoo(da)]

▶ this wine isn't chilled enough esse vinho não está gelado o suficiente [essee veenyoo nowng eeshta jeladoo oo soofeess-yentchee]

checking

▶ is it right and then left? primeiro à direita e depois à esquerda? [preemayroo a djeerayta ee depoyz a eeshkeh-da]

▶ is this the bus for São Paulo? este é o ônibus para São Paulo? [esh-tchee eh oo oneeboosh para sowng powloo]

▶ could you tell me where to get off, please? poderia me dizer onde a gente desce, por favor? [poderee-a mee djeezer ondjee a jentchee dessee poh favoh]

▶ is this the right stop for ...? é aqui que tem que descer para ir em...? [eh akee ke teng kee desseh para eer eng]

▶ are you sure that he'll be able to come? tem certeza de que ele vai poder vir? [teng seh-teza djee ee elee vy podeh veeh]

chocolate o chocolate [shokolatchee]
> I'd like a bar of chocolate gostaria de uma barra de chocolate [goshtaree-a djee ooma baha djee shokolatchee]

choose escolher [eeshkol-yeh]
> I don't know which one to choose não sei qual escolher [nowng say kwal eeshkol-yeh]

Christmas o Natal [natow]
> Merry Christmas! feliz Natal! [feleesh natow]
> I wish you a very merry Christmas lhe desejo um feliz Natal [l-yee dezejoo oom feleesh natow]

Christmas Day o dia de Natal [djee-a djee natow]
> we're closed on Christmas Day fechamos no dia de Natal [feshamoosh noo djee-a djee natow]

church a igreja [eegreja]
> how old is the church? a igreja é muito antiga? [a eegreja eh mweetoo antcheega]
> where can we find a Protestant church? onde tem uma igreja protestante? [ondjee teng ooma eegreja protestantchee]
> where is there a Catholic church? onde tem uma igreja (católica)? [ondjee teng ooma eegreja (katoleeka)]

cigarette o cigarro [seegahoo]
> can I ask you for a cigarette? posso lhe pedir um cigarro? [possool-yee pedjeer oom seegahoo]
> where can I buy cigarettes? onde eu posso comprar cigarro? [ondjee ew possoo komprah seegahoo]

cigarette lighter o isqueiro [eeshkayroo]
> do you have a cigarette lighter? você tem um isqueiro? [vosse teng oom eeshkayroo]

city a cidade [seedadjee]
> what's the nearest big city? qual é a cidade grande mais próxima daqui? [kwal eh a seedadjee grandjee mysh prosseema dakee]

class *(on plane)* a classe [klassee]
> which class are your seats in? de que classe são os lugares de vocês? [djee ke klassee sowng oosh loogareesh djee vossesh]

clean limpo(pa) [leempoo(pa)] ♦ limpar [leempah]
> the sheets aren't clean os lençóis não estão limpos [oosh lensoysh nowng eeshtowng leempoosh]
> do we have to clean the apartment before leaving? temos que limpar o apartamento antes de sair? [temoosh kee leempar oo apah-tamentoo antchesh djee sa-eeh]
> could you clean the windshield? daria para limpar o pára-brisas? [daree-a para leempar oo para-breezash]

cleaning a limpeza [leempeza]
- who does the cleaning? quem faz a limpeza? [keng faz a leempeza]

clear *(easily understood)* claro(ra) [klaroo(ra)]; *(way)* livre [leevree] ◆ *(road, path)* desobstruir [dezob-shtroo-eeh]
- is that clear? está claro? [eeshta klaroo]
- is the road ahead clear? a estrada está livre daqui para frente? [a eeshtrada eeshta leevree dakee para frentchee]
- when will the road be cleared? quando a estrada será liberada? [kwandoo a eeshtrada sera leeberada]

climb *(mountaineer)* escalar [eeshkalah]; *(plane, road)* subir [soobeeh]
- the road climbs steadily after you leave the village a estrada sobe o tempo todo depois de sair da cidade [a eeshtrada sobee oo tempoo todoo depoysh djee sa-eeh da seedadjee]

climbing o alpinismo [owpeeneejmoo]
- can you go climbing here? podemos praticar alpinismo aqui? [podemoosh pratcheekar owpeeneejmoo akee]

cloakroom *(in a museum, a theater)* o guarda-volumes [gwah-da-voloomeesh]
- is there a charge for the cloakroom? tem uma taxa para usar o guarda-volumes? [teng ooma tasha para oozar oo gwah-da-voloomeesh]
- I'd like to leave my things in the cloakroom gostaria de deixar as minhas coisas no guarda-volumes [goshtaree-a djee dayshar ash meenyash koyzash noo gwah-da-voloomeesh]

close *(door, window)* fechar [feshah]
- what time do the stores close? a que horas as lojas fecham? [a kee oraz ash lojash feshowng]
- what time do you close? a que hora você fecha? [a kee ora vosse fesha]
- the door won't close a porta não fecha [a poh-ta nowng fesha]

closed fechado(da) [feshadoo(da)]
- are the stores closed on Sundays? as lojas fecham no sábado? [ash lojash feshowng noo sabadoo]

clothes as roupas [hopash]
- where can we wash our clothes? onde podemos lavar nossas roupas? [ondjee podemoosh lavah nossash hopash]

club *(nightclub)* a boate [bwatchee]
- we could go to a club afterwards a gente poderia ir em uma boate depois [a jentchee poderee-a eer eng ooma bwatchee depoysh]

coach o ônibus [oneeboosh]
- what time does the coach leave? a que horas sai o ônibus? [a kee orash sy oo oneeboosh]

coast a costa [koshta]
- an island off the coast of Brazil uma ilha perto da costa do Brasil [ooma eelya peh-too da koshta doo brazeew]

ordering coffee

How do you like your coffee? Black, like a lot of Brazilians? If so, ask for *um cafezinho*. If you like, you can add *açúcar* (sugar) to it. You can also order *um pingado*, which has some milk added. At breakfast time or at dinner it's usually drunk *com leite* (with milk). If you go to a *café* (coffee bar), you can try *um café gelado* (iced coffee), *um café irlandês* (Irish coffee, with rum) or the traditional *cappuccino*.

coffee *(drink, beans)* o café [kaffe]
- coffee with milk or cream **café com leite ou creme** [kaffe kong lay-tchee o kremee]
- black coffee **café preto** [kaffe pretoo]
- I'd like a coffee **eu queria um café** [ew keree-a oom kaffe]
- would you like some coffee? **quer café?** [keh kaffe]

coin a moeda [mweda]
- the machine only takes coins **a máquina só aceita moeda** [a makeena so assayta mweda]

cold frio(fria) [free-oo(free-a)] ◆ *(illness)* a gripe [greepee]; *(low temperature)* o frio [free-oo]
- it's cold today **está frio hoje** [eeshta free-oo ojee]
- I'm very cold **estou com muito frio** [eeshto kong mweentoo free-oo]
- to have a cold **estar gripado(da)** [eeshtah greepadoo(da)]
- I've caught a cold **peguei uma gripe** [pegay ooma greepee]

collect a cobrar [a kobrah]
- I have to call my parents collect **tenho que ligar a cobrar para os meus pais** [tenyoo kee leegar a kobrah para oosh mewsh pysh]

collect call a ligação a cobrar [leegassowng a kobrah]
- to make a collect call **fazer uma ligação a cobrar** [fazer ooma leegassowng a kobrah]

color a cor [koh]
- do you have it in another color? **tem em outra cor?** [teng eng otra koh]

color film o filme colorido [feewmee koloreedoo]
- I'd like a roll of color film **eu queria um rolo de filme colorido** [ew keree-a oom holoo djee feewmee koloreedoo]

come *(move here)* vir [veeh]; *(arrive)* chegar [shegah]; *(pass by)* passar [passah]
- come here! **vem cá!** [veng ka]
- coming! **estou indo!** [eeshto eendoo]
- when does the bus come? **a que horas chega o ônibus?** [a kee orash shega oo oneeboosh]

come from vir de [veeh djee]
- where do you come from? **de onde você vem?** [djee ondjee vosse veng]

come in *(enter)* entrar [entrah]; *(tide)* subir [soobeeh]

- may I come in? posso entrar? [possoo entrah]
- come in! entre! [entree]
- the tide's coming in a maré está subindo [a ma-re eeshta soobeendoo]

come on *(light, heating)* ligar [leegah]

- the heating hasn't come on o aquecimento não ligou [oo akesseementoo nowng leego]
- come on! vamos lá! [vamoosh la]

come with vir com [veeh kong]

- could you come with me to...? você poderia vir comigo para...? [vosse poderee-a veeh komeegoo para]
- what does it come with? vem com o quê? [veng kong oo ke]

comfortable *(person)* confortável [konfoh-tavew]

- we're very comfortable here estamos muito confortáveis aqui [eeshtamoosh mweentoo konfoh-tavewsh akee]

commission a comissão [komeessowng]

- what commission do you charge? quanto você cobra de comissão? [kwantoo vosse kobra djee komeessowng]

company *(firm)* a empresa [empreza]

- is it a big company? é uma empresa grande? [eh ooma empreza grandjee]

compartment o compartimento [kompah-tcheementoo]

- which compartment are our seats in? em que compartimento estão nossos lugares? [eng ke kompah-tcheementoo eeshtowng nossoosh loogareesh]

complain reclamar [heklamah]

- I will be writing to your headquarters to complain estou escrevendo para a direção para reclamar [eeshto eeshkrevendoo para a djeeressowng para heklamah]

---

complaints

- I'd like to see the manager, please eu gostaria de ver o gerente, por favor [ew goshtaree-a djee ver oo jerentchee poh favoh]
- I have a complaint tenho uma reclamação [tenyoo ooma heklamassowng]
- there's a problem with the heating o aquecimento está com algum problema [oo akesseementoo eeshta kong owgoom problema]
- I am relying on you to sort this problem out estou contando com você para resolver este problema [eeshto kontando kong vosse para hessowver esh-tchee problema]
- I expect the cost of the camera to be fully reimbursed espero que o custo da câmera me seja totalmente reembolsado [eeshperoo kee oo kooshtoo da kamera mee seja totow-mentchee hee-embowsadoo]

complaint *(protest)* a queixa [kaysha]; *(in store)* a reclamação [heklamassowng]
- I'd like to make a complaint *(protest)* quero fazer uma queixa [keroo fazer ooma kaysha]; *(in store)* quero fazer uma reclamação [keroo fazer ooma heklamassowng]

complete *(form)* preencher [pre-ensheh]
- here's the completed form aqui está o formulário preenchido [akee eeshta oo fohmoolar-yoo pre-ensheedoo]

comprehensive insurance o seguro total [segooroo totow]
- is the car covered by comprehensive insurance? o carro tem seguro total? [oo kahoo teng segooroo totow]
- how much extra is the comprehensive insurance coverage? tem que pagar mais quanto pela cobertura total? [teng kee pagah mysh kwantoo pela kobeh-toora totow]

computer o computador [kompootadoh]
- is there a computer I could use? tem um computador que eu poderia usar? [teng oom kompootadoh kee ew poderee-a oozah]

concert o concerto [konseh-too]
- did you like the concert? gostou do concerto? [goshto doo konseh-too]

condom a camisinha [kameezeenya]
- do you have any condoms? você tem camisinha? [vosse teng kameezeenya]

confirm confirmar [konfeeh-mah]
- I confirmed my reservation by phone eu confirmei minha reserva por telefone [ew konfeeh-may meenya hezeh-va poh telefonee]
- I'd like to confirm my return flight gostaria de confirmar meu vôo de volta [goshtaree-a djee konfeeh-mah mew vo-oo djee vowta]

congratulations os parabéns [parabengsh]
- congratulations! parabéns! [parabengsh]

connecting flight o vôo de conexão [vo-oo djee koneksowng]
- does the connecting flight leave from the same terminal? o vôo de conexão sai do mesmo terminal? [oo vo-oo djee koneksowng sy doo mejmoo teh-meenow]

connection *(on phone)* a ligação [leegassowng]; *(transportation)* a conexão [koneksowng]
- the connection is very bad: I can't hear very well a ligação está muito ruim: não escuto você muito bem [a leegassowng eeshta mweentoo hoo-eeng nowng eeshkootoo vosse mweentoo beng]
- I've missed my connection perdi a minha conexão [peh-djee a meenya koneksowng]

consulate o consulado [konsooladoo]
- where is the American consulate? onde fica o consulado americano? [ondjee feeka oo konsooladoo ameree-kanoo]

contact *(communication)* o contato [kontatoo] ◆ entrar em contato com [entrar eng kontatoo kong]

▶ I need to contact my family in the States preciso entrar em contato com a minha família nos Estados Unidos [presseezoo entrar eng kontatoo kong a meenya fameel-ya nooz eeshtadooz ooneedoosh]

▶ do you know how to get in contact with him? você sabe como entrar em contato com ele? [vosse sabee komoo entrar eng kontatoo kong elee]

contact lens a lente (de contato) [lentchee (djee kontatoo)]

▶ I've lost a contact (lens) perdi uma lente (de contato) [peh-djee ooma lentchee (djee kontatoo)]

cookie *(food)* o biscoito [beesh-koytoo]

▶ a box of cookies, please um pacote de biscoitos, por favor [oom pakotchee djee beesh-koytoosh poh favoh]

cooking *(activity)* a culinária [kooleenar-ya]; *(type of food)* a cozinha [kozeenya]

▶ we prefer to do our own cooking a gente prefere fazer nossa própria comida [a jentchee preferee fazeh nossa propree-a komeeda]

▶ do you like Brazilian cooking? você gosta da culinária brasileira? [vosse goshta da kooleenar-ya brazee-layra]

cork *(for a bottle)* a rolha [hol-ya]

▶ where's the cork for the bottle? onde está a rolha da garrafa? [ondjee eeshta a hol-ya da gahafa]

corked azedo(da) [azedoo(da)]

▶ this wine is corked esse vinho está azedo [essee veenyoo eeshta azedoo]

corner *(of street)* a esquina [eeshkeena]; *(of table)* o canto [kantoo]; *(spot)* o ponto [pontoo]

▶ stop at the corner pare na esquina [paree na eeshkeena]

coronary o infarto [eenfah-too]

▶ he's had a coronary ele teve um infarto [elee tevee oom eenfah-too]

correct *(check)* correto(ta) [kohetoo(ta)]

▶ that's correct está correto [eeshta kohetoo]

cost custar [kooshtah]

▶ how much will it cost to go to the airport? quanto custa para ir até o aeroporto? [kwantoo kooshta para eer a-te oo a-eropoh-too]

▶ it cost us 150 reais vai nos custar cento e cinqüenta reais [vy nosh kooshtah sentoo ee seenkwenta hee-ysh]

cot o berço [beh-soo]

▶ we can put a cot in the room for you podemos colocar um berço no quarto para você [podemoosh kolokar oom beh-soo noo kwah-too para vosse]

cough a tosse [tossee] ◆ tossir [tosseeh]

▶ I've got a cough estou com tosse [eeshto kong tossee]

▶ I need something for a cough preciso de alguma coisa para tosse [presseezoo djee owgooma koyza para tossee]

could poder [podeh]
- could you help me? você poderia me ajudar? [vosse poderee-a mee ajoodah]

count contar [kontah]
- that doesn't count isso não conta [eessoo nowng konta]

counter *(in store)* o balcão [bowkowng]; *(in bank)* o guichê [gheeshe]
- which counter do I have to go to? em qual guichê eu tenho que ir? [eng kwow gheeshe ew tenyoo kee eeh]
- do you sell this medication over the counter? vocês vendem esse remédio sem receita? [vossesh vendeng essee hemed-yoo seng hessayta]

country o país [pa-eesh]
- what country do you come from? de que país você vem? [djee ke pa-eesh vosse veng]

couple o casal [kazow]
- it's for a couple and two children é para um casal e duas crianças [eh para oom kazow ee doo-ash kree-ansash]

course *(of a meal)* o prato [pratoo]; *(of a ship, a plane)* o rumo [hoomoo]; *(for a race)* o circuito [seeh-kweetoo]; *(in yoga, sailing)* o curso [kooh-soo] ◆ **of course** *(inevitably)* é óbvio [eh obvee-oo]; *(for emphasis)* claro [klaroo]
- is the set meal three courses? o menu do dia inclui três pratos? [oo menoo doo djee-a eenklooy tresh pratoosh]
- how much does the sailing course cost? quanto custa o curso de vela? [kwantoo kooshta oo kooh-soo djee vela]
- of course he'll come claro que ele vai vir [klaroo kee elee vy veeh]

cream *(for the skin)* o creme [kremee]
- I need some cream for my sunburn preciso de um creme para as queimaduras do sol [presseezoo djee oom kremee para ash kayma-doorash doo sow]

credit card o cartão de crédito [kah-towng djee kredjeetoo]
- do you take credit cards? vocês aceitam cartões de crédito? [vossez assaytowng kah-toyngsh djee kredjeetoo]

cross *(street, river)* atravessar [atravessah]; *(border)* cruzar [kroozah]
- how do we cross this street? como a gente atravessa essa rua? [komoo a jentchee atravessa essa hoo-a]

cross-country skiing o esqui de longa distância [eeshkee djee longa djeeshtanss-ya]
- where can I go cross-country skiing around here? onde eu posso praticar esqui de longa distância aqui? [ondjee ew possoo pratcheekar eeshkee djee longa djeeshtanss-ya akee]

crosswalk a faixa de segurança [fy-sha djee segooranssa]
- always cross at the crosswalk sempre atravesse na faixa de segurança [sempree atravessee na fy-sha djee segooranssa]

cruise o cruzeiro [kroozayroo]
▶ how much does a cruise on the Rio Negro cost? quanto custa um cruzeiro para o Rio Negro? [kwantoo kooshta oom kroozayroo para oo hee-oo negroo]

cry chorar [shorah]
▶ don't cry não chore [nowng shoree]

cup a xícara [sheekara]
▶ I'd like a cup of tea eu queria uma xícara de chá [ew keree-a ooma sheekara djee sha]
▶ a coffee cup uma xícara de café [ooma sheekara djee kaffe]

currency *(money)* a moeda [mweda]
▶ how much local currency do you have? quanto dinheiro local você tem? [kwantoo djeen-yayroo lokow vosse teng]

cut cortar [koh-tah]
▶ I cut my finger cortei o dedo [koh-tay oo dedoo]

d

daily diário(ria) [djee-aryoo(arya)] ♦ *(newspaper)* o diário [djee-aryoo]
▶ what's the name of the local daily newspaper? qual é o nome do diário local? [kwal eh oo nomee doo djee-aryoo lokow]

damage danificar [danee-feekah]
▶ my suitcase was damaged in transit no transporte a minha mala foi danificada [noo tranjpoh-tchee a meenya mala foy danee-feekada]

damp úmido(da) [oomeedoo(da)]
▶ it's damp today está úmido hoje [eeshta oomeedoo ojee]

dance dançar [dansah]
▶ shall we dance? vamos dançar? [vamoosh dansah]
▶ I can't dance não sei dançar [nowng say dansah]

dancing o baile [by-lee]
▶ will there be dancing? vai ter um baile? [vy ter oom by-lee]
▶ where can we go dancing? onde a gente pode ir dançar? [ondjee a jentchee podjee eeh dansah]

dandruff a caspa [kashpa]
▶ I have bad dandruff tenho muita caspa [tenyoo mweenta kashpa]

danger o perigo [pereegoo]
▶ hurry! someone's in danger! rápido! tem alguém em perigo! [hapeedoo teng owgeng eng pereegoo]

dangerous perigoso(sa) [pereegozoo(za)]
- this stretch of the river is quite dangerous esse trecho do rio é muito perigoso [essee treshoo do hee-oo eh mweentoo pereegozoo]

dark escuro(ra) [eeshkooroo(ra)]
- it's dark está escuro [eeshta eeshkooroo]
- she has dark hair ela tem cabelo escuro [ella teng kabeloo eeshkooroo]

dark chocolate o chocolate meio amargo [shokolatchee mayoo amah-goo]
- I prefer dark chocolate prefiro chocolate meio amargo [prefeeroo shokolatchee mayoo amah-goo]

date *(in time)* a data [data]; *(appointment)* o encontro [enkontroo]
- I've got a date tonight tenho um encontro hoje à noite [tenyoo oom enkontroo ojee a noytchee]

date-stamp fechar [feshah]
- do I have to date-stamp this ticket? eu tenho que fechar essa entrada? [ew tenyoo kee feshar essa entrada]

daughter a filha [feel-ya]
- this is my daughter esta é a minha filha [eshta eh a meenya feel-ya]

day o dia [djee-a]
- what day is it? que dia é hoje? [ke djee-a eh ojee]
- I arrived three days ago cheguei há três dias [shegay a tresh djee-ash]
- I'd like to do a round trip in a day eu gostaria de fazer uma viagem de ida e volta em um dia [ew goshtaree-a djee fazer ooma vee-ajeng djee eeda ee vowta eng oom djee-a]
- how much is it per day? quanto custa por dia? [kwantoo kooshta poh djee-a]

dead morto(ta) [moh-too(ta)]
- he was pronounced dead at the scene ele foi declarado morto no local [elee foy deklaradoo moh-too noo lokow]
- the battery's dead acabou a bateria [akabo a bateree-a]

dead end a rua sem saída [hoo-a seng sa-eeda]
- it's a dead end é uma rua sem saída [eh ooma hoo-a seng sa-eeda]

deal *(business agreement)* o negócio [negoss-yoo]
- I got a good deal on the room fiz um bom negócio pelo quarto [feez oom bong negoss-yoo peloo kwah-too]

death a morte [moh-tchee]
- there were two deaths houve duas mortes [ovee doo-ash moh-tcheesh]

decaf, decaffeinated descafeinado(da) [djeesh-kafaynadoo(da)]
- a decaf(feinated coffee), please um café descafeinado, por favor [oom kaffe djeesh-kafaynadoo poh favoh]

December dezembro [dezembroo]
- December 10th dez de dezembro [desh djee dezembroo]

decide decidir [desseedjeeh]
▸ we haven't decided yet ainda não decidimos [a-eenda nowng dessee-djeemoosh]

deck *(of ship)* o convés [konvesh]; *(of cards)* o baralho [baralyoo]
▸ how do I get to the upper deck? como eu faço para subir ao convés superior? [komoo ew fassoo para soobeer ow konvesh sooperee-oh]

deckchair a espreguiçadeira [eeshpregeeessa-dayra]
▸ I'd like to rent a deckchair eu queria alugar uma espreguiçadeira [ew keree-a aloogar ooma eeshpregeeessa-dayra]

declare declarar [deklarah]
▸ I have nothing to declare não tenho nada a declarar [nowng tenyoo nada a deklarah]
▸ I have a bottle of spirits to declare tenho para declarar uma garrafa de licor [tenyoo para deklarar ooma gahafa djee leekoh]

definitely definitivamente [defeeneetcheeva-mentchee]
▸ we'll definitely come back here com certeza vamos voltar aqui [kong seh-teza vamoosh vowtar akee]

degree o grau [grow]
▸ it's 5 degrees below freezing está cinco graus abaixo de zero [eeshta seenko growsh a-by-shoo djee zeroo]

delay o atraso [atrazoo]
▸ is there a delay for this flight? tem algum atraso nesse vôo? [teng owgoom atrazoo nessee vo-oo]

delayed atrasado(da) [atrazadoo(da)]
▸ how long will the flight be delayed? quanto tempo vai atrasar o vôo? [kwantoo tempoo vy atrazar oo vo-oo]

delighted contente [kontentchee]
▸ we're delighted you could make it estamos muito contentes de que você tenha chegado a tempo [eeshtamoosh mweentoo kontentcheesh djee ke vosse tenya shegadoo a tempoo]

dentist o(a) dentista [dentcheeshta]
▸ I need to see a dentist urgently preciso ir ao dentista urgentemente [presseezoo eer ow dentcheeshta ooh-jentchee-mentchee]

department *(in store)* o departamento [depah-tamentoo], a seção [sessowng]
▸ I'm looking for the menswear department estou procurando a seção de roupas masculinas [eeshto prokoorandoo a sessowng djee hopash mashkoo-leenash]

department store a loja de departamentos [loja djee depah-tamentoosh]
▸ where are the department stores? onde ficam as lojas de departamentos? [ondjee feekowng ash lojash djee depah-tamentoosh]

departure o embarque [embah-kee]
▸ 'departures' *(in airport)* 'embarque' [embah-keee]

departure lounge a sala de embarque [sala djee embah-kee]
▸ where's the departure lounge? onde é a sala de embarque? [ondjee eh a sala djee embah-kee]

deposit *(against loss or damage)* a caução [kow-sowng]; *(down payment)* o depósito [depozeetoo]
▸ is there a deposit to pay on the equipment? tem que pagar caução pelo equipamento? [teng kee pagah kow-sowng peloo ekeepa-mentoo]
▸ how much is the deposit? de quanto é a caução? [djee kwantoo eh a kow-sowng]

desk *(in office, home)* a escrivaninha [eeshkreeva-neenya]; *(at hotel)* a recepção [hessep-sowng]; *(for cashier)* o caixa [ky-sha]; *(at airport)* o balcão [bow-kowng]
▸ where can I find the American Airlines desk ? onde fica o balcão da American Airlines? [ondjee feeka oo bow-kowng da American Airlines]

dessert a sobremesa [sobreemeza]
▸ what desserts do you have? que sobremesa vocês têm? [ke sobreemeza vossesh tayeng]

dessert wine o vinho doce [veenyoo dossee]
▸ can you recommend a good dessert wine? você poderia me recomendar um bom vinho doce? [vosse poderee-a mee hekomendar oom bong veenyoo dossee]

detour o desvio [djeej-vee-oo]
▸ is there a detour ahead? tem algum desvio aí na frente? [teng owgoom djeej-vee-oo a-ee na frentchee]

develop revelar [hevelah]
▸ how much does it cost to develop a roll of 36 photos? quanto custa para revelar trinta e seis fotos? [kwantoo kooshta para hevelah treenta ee saysh fotoosh]

diabetic diabético(ca) [djee-abetcheekoo(ka)]
▸ I'm diabetic and I need a prescription for insulin sou diabético e preciso de uma receita para comprar insulina [so djee-abetcheekoo ee presseezoo djee ooma hessayta para komprar eensooleena]

diarrhea a diarréia [djee-ahaya]
▸ I'd like something for diarrhea eu queria algo para diarréia [ew keree-a owgoo para djee-ahaya]

difference *(in price, cost)* a diferença [djeeferenssa]
▸ will you pay the difference? você vai pagar a diferença? [vosse vy pagar a djeeferenssa]

difficult difícil [djeefeesseew]
▸ I find some sounds difficult to pronounce alguns sons são difíceis de pronunciar [owgoonsh songsh sowng djeefeessaysh djee pronoonss-yah]

difficulty a dificuldade [djeefee-koowdadjee]
▸ I'm having difficulty finding the place estou tendo alguma dificuldade para encontrar o lugar [eeshto tendoo owgooma djeefee-koowdadjee para enkontrar oo loogah]

dinner

In Brazil, most families have dinner between 7 and 8 p.m., and this may be either a whole meal, similar to lunch, or just some *café com leite* (white coffee), bread, cheese and jam, more like breakfast.

digital camera a câmera digital [kamera djeejeetow]
> my digital camera's been stolen roubaram minha câmera digital [hobarowng meenya kamera djeejeetow]

dining room a sala de jantar [sala djee jantah]
> do you have to have breakfast in the dining room? tem que tomar o café da manhã na sala de jantar? [teng kee tomar oo kaffe da manyang na sala djee jantah]

dinner a janta [janta]
> up to what time do they serve dinner? até que horas servem a janta? [a-te kee orash seh-veng a janta]

direct direto(ta) [djeeretoo(ta)]
> is this bus direct? esse ônibus é direto? [essee oneeboosh eh djeeretoo]

direction *(heading)* a direção [djeeressowng]
> am I going in the right direction for the bus station? esta é a direção certa para a rodoviária? [eshta eh a djeeressowng seh-ta para a hodovee-aree-a]

directory assistance o auxílio à lista [owseelyoo a leeshta]
> what's the number for directory assistance? qual é o número do auxílio à lista? [kwal eh oo noomeroo doo owseelyoo a leeshta]

dirty *(room, tablecloth)* sujo(ja) [soojoo(ja)]
> the sheets are dirty os lençóis estão sujos [oosh lensoyz eeshtowng soojoosh]

disability a deficiência (física) [defeess-yensee-a (feezeeka]
> do you have facilities for people with disabilities? vocês têm instalações para deficientes? [vossesh tayeng eenshtala-soyngsh para defeess-yentcheesh]

disabled deficiente [defeess-yentchee]
> where's the nearest disabled parking spot? onde fica o estacionamento para deficientes mais próximo? [ondjee feeka oo eeshtass-yonamentoo para defeess-yentcheesh mysh prosseemoo]

disco *(club)* a discoteca [djeeshkoteka]
> are there any discos around here? tem alguma discoteca por aqui? [teng owgooma djeeshkoteka por akee]

discount o desconto [djeeshkontoo]
> is there any chance of a discount? teria como me dar algum desconto? [teree-a komoo mee dar owgoom djeeshkontoo]

dish o prato [pratoo] ◆ **dishes** a louça [lo-sa]
- what's the dish of the day? qual é o prato do dia? [kwal eh oo pratoo doc djee-a]
- can I help you with the dishes? posso ajudar com a louça? [possoo ajoodah kong a lo-sa]

disposable descartável [djeeshkah-tavew]
- I need some disposable razors preciso de algumas lâminas de barbear descartáveis [presseezoo djee owgoomash lameenash djee bah-bee-ah djeeshkah-tavaysh]
- do you sell disposable cameras? vocês vendem câmeras descartáveis? [vossesh vendeng kamerash djeeshkah-tavaysh]

distance a distância [djeeshtanss-ya]
- the hotel is only a short distance from here o hotel fica a uma distância bem pequena daqui [oo otew feeka a ooma djeeshtanss-ya beng pekena dakee]

district (of town) o bairro [by-hoo]
- which district do you live in? em que bairro você mora? [eng ke by-hoo vosse mora]

dive mergulhar [meh-goolyah] ◆ o mergulho [meh-goolyoo]
- can we do a night dive? (scuba diving) podemos dar um mergulho de noite? [podemoosh dar oom meh-goolyoo djee noytchee]

diving (scuba diving) o mergulho [meh-goolyoo]
- what's the diving like around here? dá para mergulhar por aqui? [da para meh-goolyah por akee]
- I'd like to take diving lessons eu gostaria de ter aulas de mergulho [ew goshtaree-a djee ter owlash djee meh-goolyoo]
- do you rent out diving equipment? vocês alugam equipamento de mergulho? [vossez aloogowng ekeepamentoo djee meh-goolyoo]

diving board o trampolim [trampoleeng]
- is there a diving board? tem trampolim? [teng trampoleeng]

dizzy spell a tontura [tontoora]
- I've been having dizzy spells ando tendo tonturas [andoo tendoo tontoorash]

do fazer [fazeh]
- what do you do for a living? no que você trabalha? [noo kee vosse trabal-ya]
- is there anything I can do (to help)? há algo que eu possa fazer (para ajudar)? [a owgoo kee ew possa fazeh (para ajoodah)]
- what are you doing tonight? o que você vai fazer hoje de noite? [oo kee vosse vy fazer ojee djee noytchee]
- what is there to do here on Sundays? o que tem para fazer nos domingos? [oo kee teng para fazeh noosh domeengoosh]

doctor o médico [medjeekoo], a médica [medjeeka]
- I have to see a doctor preciso ver um médico [presseezoo ver oom medjeekoo]

doctor

If you need to see a doctor, go to a *posto de saúde* (a local medical center) or to a *hospital* (a hospital). If you are in need of urgent medical attention, you should go to a hospital emergency room (*emergência* or *pronto-socorro*). Dial 192 to call an ambulance.

dollar o dólar [dolah]
- I'd like to change some dollars into reais queria trocar alguns dólares em reais [keree-a trokar owgoonsh dolareesh eng hee-ysh]

door a porta [poh-ta]
- do you want me to answer the door? quer que eu atenda a porta? [keh kee ew atenda a poh-ta]

dormitory *(in youth hostel)* o dormitório [doh-meetoryoo]; *(for students)* a casa de estudantes [kaza djee eeshtoo-dantcheesh]
- are you staying in the dormitory? você está na casa de estudantes? [vosse eeshta na kaza djee eeshtoo-dantcheesh]

double duplo(pla) [dooploo(pla)] ◆ o dobro [dobroo] ◆ dobrar [dobrah]
- it's spelled with a double 'l' se escreve com dois 'l' [see eeshkrevee kong doyz elee]
- prices have doubled since last year os preços dobraram desde o ano passado [oosh pressoosh dobrarowng dejdjee oo anoo passadoo]

double bed a cama de casal [kama djee kazow]
- does the room have a double bed? o quarto tem cama de casal? [oo kwah-too teng kama djee kazow]

double room o quarto para duas pessoas [kwah-too para doo-ash pesso-ash]
- I'd like a double room for 5 nights, please eu gostaria de um quarto para duas pessoas por cinco noites, por favor [ew goshtaree-a djee oom kwah-too para doo-ash pesso-ash poh seenkoo noytcheesh poh favoh]

downtown do centro [doo sentroo] ◆ no centro [ow sentroo] ◆ o centro [sentroo]
- we're looking for a good downtown hotel estamos procurando um bom hotel no centro [eeshtamoosh prokoorandoo oom bong otew noo sentroo]
- does this bus go downtown? esse ônibus vai até o centro? [essee oneeboosh vy a-te oo sentroo]

draft beer o chope [shopee]
- a draft beer, please um chope, por favor [oom shopee poh favoh]

dream o sonho [sonyoo] ◆ sonhar [sonyah]
- to have a dream ter um sonho [ter oom sonyoo]
- I dreamt (that)... sonhei que... [sonyay ke]

ordering drinks

If you ask for *uma cerveja* (a beer) you'll get a bottle of beer. If you don't want as much as that, ask for *uma long neck* or *uma lata de cerveja* (a can of beer). You can also ask for *um chope* (a draft beer), or *uma malzbier*, which is a sweet black beer. If you prefer wine, ask for *uma taça de vinho*. If you'd rather have a soft drink, you might want to try *um Guaraná*, which is a typical Brazilian soda.

drink a bebida [bebeeda], o drinque [dreenkee] ◆ beber [bebeh]

> I'll have a cold drink eu queria uma bebida gelada [ew keree-a ooma bebeeda jelada]

> I could do with a drink não me cairia mal um drinque [nowng mee ka-eeree-a mow oom dreenkee]

> what kind of hot drinks do you have? que bebida quente vocês têm? [ke bebeeda kentchee vossesh tayeng]

> shall we go for a drink? vamos tomar um drinque? [vamoosh tomar oom dreenkee]

> can I buy you a drink? posso lhe pagar um drinque? [possool-yee pagar oom dreenkee]

drinking water a água potável [agwa potavew]

> I'm looking for bottled drinking water estou procurando uma garrafa de água potável [eeshto prokoorando ooma gahafa djee agwa potavew]

drive *(in vehicle)* o passeio (de carro) [passayoo djee kahoo] ◆ *(vehicle)* dirigir [djeereejeeh]

> could you drive me home? poderia me levar para casa? [poderee-a mee levah para kaza]

> she was driving too close ela estava dirigindo muito perto [ella eeshtava djeereejeendoo mweentoo peh-too]

driver *(gen)* o(a) motorista [motoreeshta]; *(of taxi)* o(a) taxista [takseeshta]

> the other driver wasn't looking where he was going o outro motorista não estava olhando para onde ia [oo otroo motoreeshta nowng eeshtava ol-yandoo para ondjee ee-a]

driver's license a carteira de motorista [kah-tayra djee motoreeshta]

> can I see your driver's license? posso ver sua carteira de motorista? [possoo veh soo-a kah-tayra djee motoreeshta]

drop a gota [gota] ◆ *(let fall)* deixar cair [dayshah ka-eeh]; *(let out of vehicle)* deixar [dayshah]

> could I just have a drop of milk? poderia me colocar um pouquinho de leite? [poderee-a mee kolokar oom pokeenyoo djee laytchee]

> I dropped my scarf deixei cair o xale [dayshay ka-eer oo shalee]

drop off *(let out of vehicle)* deixar [dayshah]

- could you drop me off here? você poderia me deixar aqui? [vosse poderee-a mee dayshar akee]

drown afogar-se [afogah-see]

- he's drowning: somebody call for help ele está se afogando: alguém peça ajuda [elee eeshta see afogandoo owgeng pessa ajooda]

drugstore a farmácia [fah-massya]

- where is the nearest drugstore? qual é a farmácia mais próxima? [kwal eh a fah-massya mysh prosseema]

drunk bêbado(da) [bebadoo(da)]

- he's very drunk ele está muito bêbado [elee eeshta mweentoo bebadoo]

dry seco(ca) [sekoo(ka)] ◆ secar [sekah]

- a small glass of dry white wine um copo pequeno de vinho branco seco [oom kopoo pekenoo djee veenyoo brankoo sekoo]
- where can I put my towel to dry? onde eu coloco a toalha para secar? [ondjee ew kolokoo a twalya para sekah]

dry cleaner's a tinturaria [tcheentooraree-a]

- is there a dry cleaner's nearby? tem uma tinturaria aqui por perto? [teng ooma tcheentooraree-a akee poh peh-too]

dryer *(for laundry)* a secadora [sekadora]

- is there a dryer? tem uma secadora? [teng ooma sekadora]

dub *(movie)* dublar [dooblah]

- do they always dub English-language movies? eles sempre dublam os filmes em inglês? [eleesh sempree dooblowng oosh feewmeez eng eenglesh]

during durante [doorantchee]

- is there restricted parking during the festival? dá para estacionar normalmente durante o festival? [da para eeshtass-yonah noh-mow-mentchee doorantchee oo feshteevow]

---

at the drugstore

- I'd like something for a headache/a sore throat/diarrhea eu queria alguma coisa para dor de cabeça/dor de garganta/diarréia [ew keree-a owgooma koyza para doh djee kabessa/doh djee gah-ganta/djee-ahaya]
- I'd like some aspirin/some Band-Aids® eu queria uma aspirina/um Band-Aid® [ew keree-a ooma ashpeereena/oom band aidj]
- could you recommend a doctor? você poderia me recomendar um médico? [vosse poderee-a mee hekomendar oom medjeekoo]

duty *(tax)* o imposto [eemposhtoo]
- do I have to pay duty on this? tem que pagar imposto por isso? [teng kee pagar eemposhtoo por eessoo]
- I want to see the doctor on duty quero ver o médico de plantão [keroo ver oo medjeekoo djee plantowng]

duty-free shop o duty-free [duty-free]
- where are the duty-free shops? onde ficam os duty-free? [ondjee feekowng oosh duty-free]

DVD o DVD [de-ve-de]
- which region is this DVD coded for? qual é a região desse DVD? [kwal eh a hej-yowng dessee de-ve-de]

ear o ouvido [oveedoo]
- I have a ringing in my ears os meus ouvidos estão zunindo [oosh mewz oveedooz eeshtowng zooneendoo]

earache a dor de ouvido [doh djee oveedoo]
- he has an earache ele está com dor de ouvido [elee eeshta kong doh djee oveedoo]

ear infection a infecção no ouvido [eenfeksowng noo oveedoo]
- I think I have an ear infection acho que estou com uma infecção no ouvido [ashoo kee eeshto kong ooma eenfeksowng noo oveedoo]

early cedo [sedoo]
- is there an earlier flight? tem um vôo mais cedo? [teng oom vo-oo mysh sedoo]
- we arrived early chegamos cedo [shegamoosh sedoo]
- I'll be leaving early in the morning vou sair cedo da manhã [vo sa-eeh sedoo da manyang]

Easter a Páscoa [pashkwa]
- Happy Easter! feliz Páscoa! [feleej paskwa]

easy fácil [fasseew]
- is it easy to use? é fácil de usar [eh fasseew djee oozah]
- I'd like something easy to carry eu queria algo fácil de carregar [ew keree-a owgoo fasseew djee kahegah]

eat comer [komeh]
- I'm afraid I don't eat meat eu não como carne [ew nowng komoo kah-nee]
- where can we get something to eat? onde a gente pode comer alguma coisa? [ondjee a jentchee podjee komer owgooma koyza]

economy (class) a classe econômica [klassee ekonomeeka]

▸ are there any seats in economy class? ainda tem lugar na classe econômica? [a-eenda teng loogah na klassee ekonomeeka]

▸ I'd prefer to go economy prefiro viajar na classe econômica [prefeeroo vee-ajah na klassee ekonomeeka]

▸ I'd like an economy-class ticket eu queria uma passagem na classe econômica [ew keree-a ooma passajeng na klassee ekonomeeka]

egg o ovo [ovoo]

▸ I'd like my eggs sunny side up, please eu queria os ovos com a gema para cima, por favor [ew keree-a ooz ovoosh kong a jema para seema poh favoh]

eight oito [oytoo]

▸ there are eight of us somos oito [somooz oytoo]

electric heater o aquecedor elétrico [akessedor eletreekoo]

▸ do you have an electric heater? vocês têm um aquecedor elétrico? [vossesh tayeng oom akessedor eletreekoo]

electricity a eletricidade [eletreessee-dadjee]

▸ there's no electricity in the room não tem luz no quarto [nowng teng loosh noo kwah-too]

electric razor, electric shaver o barbeador elétrico [bah-bee-ador eletreekoo]

▸ where can I plug in my electric razor? onde eu posso ligar o meu barbeador (elétrico)? [ondjee ew possoo leegar oo mew bah-bee-adoh (eletreekoo)]

elevator o elevador [elevadoh]

▸ is there an elevator? tem elevador? [teng elevadoh]

▸ the elevator is out of order o elevador não funciona [oo elevadoh nowng foonss-yona]

eleven onze [onshee]

▸ there are eleven of us somos onze [somoosh onshee]

e-mail o email [email]

▸ I'd like to send an e-mail eu queria enviar um email [ew keree-a envee-ar oom email]

▸ where can I check my e-mail? onde eu posso verificar meu email? [ondjee ew possoo vereefeekah mew email]

e-mail address o endereço de email [enderessoo djee email]

▸ do you have an e-mail address? você tem um endereço de email? [vosse teng oom enderessoo djee email]

emergency a emergência [emeh-jenss-ya]

▸ it's an emergency! é uma emergência! [eh ooma emeh-jenss-ya]

▸ what number do you call in an emergency? que número tem que ligar em caso de emergência? [ke noomeroo teng ke leegar eng kazoo djee emeh-jenss-ya]

emergency brake o freio de mão [frayoo djee mowng]
 ▸ I'm sure I put the emergency brake on tenho certeza de que puxei o freio de mão [tenyoo seh-teza djee ke pooshay oo frayoo djee mowng]

emergency cord a corda de emergência [koh-da djee emeh-jenss-ya]
 ▸ someone's pulled the emergency cord alguém puxou a corda de emergência [owgeng poosho a koh-da djee emeh-jenss-ya]

emergency exit a saída de emergência [sa-eeda djee emeh-jenss-ya]
 ▸ remember that the nearest emergency exit may be behind you *(on plane)* lembre-se de que a saída de emergência mais próxima pode estar atrás de você [lembree-see djee ke a sa-eeda djee emeh-jenss-ya mysh prosseema podjee eeshtar atrash djee vosse]

emergency room a emergência [emeh-jenss-ya]
 ▸ I need to go to the emergency room right away preciso ir para a emergência imediatamente [presseezoo eeh para a emeh-jenss-ya eemedjee-atamentchee]

emergency services os serviços de emergência [seh-veessoosh djee emeh-jenss-ya]
 ▸ do you a have a listing of emergency services numbers? você tem uma lista com o número dos serviços de emergência? [vosse teng ooma leeshta kong oo noomeroo doosh seh-veessoosh djee emeh-jenss-ya]

end *(conclusion, finish)* o final [feenow]
 ▸ at the end of July no final de julho [noo feenow djee joolyoo]

engine o motor [motoh]
 ▸ the engine is making a funny noise o motor está fazendo um barulho engraçado [oo motor eeshta fazendoo oom bahool-yoo engrassadoo]

English inglês(esa) [eenglesh(eza) ♦ *(language)* o inglês [eenglesh]
 ▸ I'm English sou inglês/inglesa [so eenglesh/eengleza]
 ▸ that's not how you say it in English não é assim que se diz em inglês [nowng eh asseeng ke see deesh eng eenglesh]
 ▸ do you understand English? você entende inglês? [vosse entendjee eenglesh]

enjoy gostar [goshtah]
 ▸ to enjoy oneself desfrutar [djeesh-frootah]
 ▸ enjoy your meal! bom proveito! [bong provaytoo]
 ▸ did you enjoy your meal? você gostou da comida? [vosse goshto da komeeda]

enough suficiente [soofeess-yentchee]
 ▸ I don't have enough money não tenho dinheiro suficiente [nowng tenyoo djeen-yayroo soofeess-yentchee]
 ▸ that's enough! chega! [shega]
 ▸ no thanks, I've had quite enough não, obrigado, estou satisfeito [nowng obreegadoo eeshto sateesh-faytoo]

enter *(go in)* entrar [entrah]; *(type in)* inserir [eensereeh]
▸ do I enter my PIN number now? insiro meu número de identificação agora? [eenseeroo mew noomeroo djee eedentchee-feekassowng agora]

entrance a entrada [entrada]
▸ where's the entrance to the subway? onde fica a entrada para o metrô? [ondjee feeka a entrada para oo metro]

entry *(to place)* a entrada [entrada]
▸ entry to the exhibit is free a entrada para a exposição é grátis [a entrada para a eeshpozee-sowng eh gratcheesh]

envelope o envelope [envelopee]
▸ I'd like a pack of envelopes eu queria um pacote de envelopes [ew keree-a oom pakotchee djee envelopeesh]

equipment o equipamento [ekeepamentoo]
▸ do you provide the equipment? você fornece o equipamento? [vosse foh-nessee oo ekeepamentoo]

escalator a escada rolante [eeshkada holantchee]
▸ is there an escalator? tem escada rolante? [teng eeshkada holantchee]

evening a tarde [tah-djee]
▸ why don't we meet up this evening? por que a gente não se encontra esta tarde? [poh ke a jentchee nowng see enkontra eshta tah-djee]
▸ in the evening *(of every day)* às tardes [ash tah-djeesh]

event *(cultural)* a atividade [atcheevee-dadjee]
▸ what's the program of events? qual é o programa de atividades? [kwal eh oo programa djee atcheevee-dadjeesh]

ever *(at any time)* sempre [sempree]; *(before now)* já [ja]
▸ have you ever been to Boston? você já foi a Boston? [vosse ja foy a Boston]

everything tudo [toodoo]
▸ that's everything, thanks isso é tudo, obrigado [eessoo eh toodoo obreegadoo]
▸ we didn't have time to see everything não tivemos tempo de ver tudo [nowng tcheevemoosh tempoo djee veh toodoo]

excess baggage o excesso de bagagem [essessoo djee bagajeng]
▸ what's your policy on excess baggage? qual é a política de vocês para excesso de bagagem? [kwal eh a poleetcheeka djee vossesh para essessoo djee bagajeng]

exchange trocar [trokah]
▸ I'd like to exchange this T-shirt eu queria trocar essa camiseta [ew keree-a trokar essa kameezeta]

exchange rate a taxa de câmbio [tasha djee kamb-yoo]
▸ what is today's exchange rate? qual é a taxa de câmbio de hoje? [kwal eh a tasha djee kamb-yoo djee ojee]

excuse me!

If you want to get someone's attention politely or ask them a question, say *desculpe* or *com licença*; to say thank you, say *obrigado*; and when someone says thank you to you, say *de nada* or *não tem de quê* (you're welcome). If someone says *desculpe* to you, you can reply *não foi nada* (don't mention it).

excursion a excursão [eeshkooh-sowng]
- I'd like to sign up for the excursion on Saturday eu queria me inscrever para a excursão no sábado [ew keree-a mee eenshkreveh para a eeshkooh-sowng noo sabadoo]

excuse *(behavior, person)* desculpar [djeeshkoowpah]
- excuse me? *(asking for repetition)* como? [komoo]
- excuse me! *(to get attention, when interrupting, leaving, to get by)* com licença! [kong leessensa]; *(to apologize)* desculpe! [djeeshkoowpee]; *(expressing disagreement)* sinto muito! [seentoo mweentoo]
- you'll have to excuse my (poor) Portuguese não leva em conta o meu português (ruim)! [nowng leva eng konta oo mew poh-toogesh (hoo-eeng)]

exhaust o cano de descarga [kanoo djee djeeshkah-ga]
- the exhaust is making a strange noise o cano de descarga está fazendo um barulho estranho [oo kanoo djee djeeshkah-ga eeshta fazendoo oom baroolyoo eeshtranyoo]

exhausted *(tired)* exausto(ta) [ezowshtoo(ta)]
- I'm exhausted estou exausto [eeshto ezowshtoo]

exhibit a exposição [eeshpozeessowng]
- I'd like a ticket for the temporary exhibit eu queria uma entrada para a exposição temporária [ew keree-a ooma entrada para a eeshpozeessowng temporar-ya]
- is this ticket valid for the exhibit too? essa entrada vale para a exposição também? [essa entrada valee para a eeshpozeessowng tambeng]

exit a saída [sa-eeda]
- where's the exit? onde é a saída? [ondjee eh a sa-eeda]

expect *(baby, letter)* esperar [eeshperah]
- I'll be expecting you at eight o'clock at... vou te esperar às oito horas no... [vo tchee eeshperar az oytoo orash noo]
- when do you expect it to be ready? quando você imagina que vai estar pronto? [kwandoo vosse eemajeena ke vy eeshtah prontoo]

expensive caro(ra) [karoo(ra)]
- do you have anything less expensive? tem algo menos caro? [teng owgoo menoosh karoo]

expire *(visa)* expirar [eeshpeerah]
- my passport has expired meu passaporte expirou [mew passapoh-tchee eeshpeero]

explain explicar [eeshpleekah]
- please explain how to get to the airport teria como me explicar como se chega ao aeroporto? [teree-a komoo mee eeshpleekah komoo see shega ow a-eropoh-too]
- can you explain what this means? você pode explicar o que isso significa? [vosse podjee eeshpleekar oo ke eessoo seegneefeeka]

extension *(phone line)* o ramal [hamow]; *(cord)* a extensão [eeshtensowng]
- could I have extension 358, please? ramal três cinco oito, por favor [hamow tresh seenkoo oytoo poh favoh]

extra extra [eeshtra]
- is it possible to add an extra bed? tem como acrescentar uma cama extra? [teng komoo akressentar ooma kama eshtra]
- would it be possible to stay an extra night? teria como ficar mais uma noite? [teree-a komoo feekah myz ooma noytchee]

extra charge a taxa extra [tasha eshtra]
- what would the extra charge be for this service? qual seria a taxa extra para este serviço? [kwow seree-a a tasha eshtra para esh-tchee seh-veessoo]
- at no extra charge sem custo extra [seng kooshtoo eshtra]

eye o olho [ol-yoo]
- she has blue eyes ela tem olhos azuis [ella teng ol-yooz azweesh]
- can you keep an eye on my bag for a few minutes? você poderia cuidar da minha bagagem por alguns minutos? [vosse poderee-a kweedah da meenya bagajeng por owgoonsh meenootoosh]

eye drops o colírio [koleeryoo]
- do you have any eye drops? você tem algum colírio? [vosse teng owgoom koleeryoo]

eye shadow a sombra (para os olhos) [sombra (para ooz ol-yoosh)]
- is this the only eye shadow you've got? essa é a única sombra (para os olhos) que vocês têm? [essa eh a ooneeka sombra (para ooz ol-yoosh) ke vossesh tayeng]

eyesight a visão [veezowng]
- I don't have very good eyesight eu não tenho uma visão muito boa [ew nowng tenyoo ooma veezowng mweentoo boa]

face *(of person)* o rosto [hoshtoo]
- the attacker had a broad face o agressor tinha um rosto grande [oo agressoh tcheenya oom hoshtoo grandjee]

facilities as instalações [eenshtala-soyngsh]
- what kind of exercise facilities do you have here? vocês têm algum tipo de sala de ginástica? [vossesh tayeng owgoom tcheepoo djee sala djee jeenash-tcheeka]
- do you have facilities for people with disabilities? vocês têm instalações para deficientes? [vossesh tayeng eenshtala-soyngsh para defeess-yentcheesh]
- are there facilities for children? tem sala de recreação para crianças? [teng sala djee hekree-assowng para kree-ansash]

faint desmaiar [djeej-my-ah]
- I fainted twice last week desmaiei duas vezes na semana passada [djeej-my-ay doo-ash vezeesh na semana passada]

fair *(person, situation)* bom(boa) [bong(boa)]; *(price)* justo(ta) [jooshtoo(ta)]; *(hair)* loiro(ra) [loyroo(ra)]; *(skin, complexion)* claro(ra) [klaroo(ra)]
- this isn't a fair price não é um preço justo [nowng eh oom pressoo jooshtoo]
- it's not fair! não é justo! [nowng eh jooshtoo]

fall cair [ka-eeh]
- I fell on my back caí de costas [ka-ee djee koshtash]

family a família [fameelya]
- do you have any family in the area? você tem família que mora por aqui? [vosse teng fameelya kee mora por akee]

fan o ventilador [ventcheeladoh]
- how does the fan work? como funciona o ventilador? [komoo foonss-yona oo ventcheeladoh]

far longe [lonjee]
- am I far from the village? estou longe da vila? [eeshto lonjee da veela]
- is it far to walk? é longe para ir caminhando? [eh lonjee para eeh kameen-yandoo]
- is it far by car? é longe para ir de carro? [eh lonjee para eeh djee kahoo]
- how far is the market from here? o mercado fica longe daqui? [oo meh-kadoo feeka lonjee dakee]
- far away/off muito longe [mweentoo lonjee]
- so far até aqui [towng lonjee]

fast rápido(da) [hapeedoo(da)]
- please don't drive so fast por favor dirija mais devagar [poh favoh djeereeja mysh djeevagah]

▸ to be fast *(watch, clock)* estar adiantado [eeshtar adjee-antadoo]
▸ my watch is five minutes fast meu relógio está cinco minutos adiantado [mew heloj-yoo eeshta seenkoo meenootooz adjee-antado]

fat *(in diet)* a gordura [goh-doora]
▸ it's low in fat tem baixo teor de gordura [teng by-shoo te-oh djee goh-doora]

father o pai [py]
▸ this is my father este é o meu pai [esh-tchee eh oo mew py]

fault *(responsibility)* a culpa [koowpa]
▸ it was my fault foi minha culpa [foy meenya koowpa]

favor *(kind act)* o favor [favoh]
▸ can I ask you a favor? posso lhe pedir um favor? [possool-yee pedjeer oom favoh]

favorite favorito(ta) [favoreetoo(ta)]
▸ it's my favorite book é o meu livro favorito [eh oo mew leevroo favoreetoo]

feather a pena [penna]
▸ are these feather pillows? esses travesseiros são de pena? [esseesh travessayr-oosh sowng djee penna]

February fevereiro [feverayroo]
▸ February 8th oito de fevereiro [oytoo djee feverayroo]

feed dar de comer [dah djee komeh]
▸ where can I feed the baby? onde eu posso dar de comer para o bebê? [ondjee ew possoo dah djee komeh para oo be-be]

feel *(touch)* tocar [tokah]; *(sense)* sentir [sentcheeh] ◆ *(physically)* sentir-se [sentcheeh-see]
▸ I can't feel my feet não sinto os pés [nowng seentoo oosh pesh]
▸ I don't feel well não me sinto bem [nowng mee seentoo beng]

ferry a balsa [bowsa]
▸ when does the next ferry leave? quando sai a próxima balsa? [kwandoo sy a prosseema bowsa]

ferry terminal o terminal da balsa [teh-meenow da bowsa]
▸ which way is the ferry terminal? como se chega ao terminal da balsa? [komoo see shega ow teh-meenow da bowsa]

fever a febre [febree]
▸ the baby's got a fever o bebê está com febre [oo be-be eeshta kong febree]

few poucos(cas) [pokoosh(kash)] ◆ **a few** alguns(algumas) [owgoonsh(owgoomash)]
▸ there are few sights worth seeing around here há poucos lugares que vale a pena visitar por aqui [a pokoosh loogareesh ke valee a pena veezeetah por akee]
▸ we're thinking of staying a few more days estamos pensando em ficar mais alguns dias [eeshtamoosh pensandoo eng feekah myz owgoonsh djee-ash]
▸ I spent a month in Recife a few years ago fiquei um mês em Recife há alguns anos [feekay oom mesh eng hesseefee a owgoonz anoosh]

fifth quinto(ta) [keentoo(ta)] ♦ *(gear)* a quinta [keenta]
  ▸ I can't get it into fifth não consigo engatar a quinta [nowng konseegoo engatar a keenta]

filling *(in a tooth)* a obturação [obtoorassowng]
  ▸ one of my fillings has come out caiu uma obturação [kayoo ooma obtoorassowng]

fill up encher [ensheh]
  ▸ fill it up, please encha, por favor [ensha poh favoh]

film *(for camera)* o filme [feewmee] ♦ filmar [feewmah]
  ▸ I'd like to have this film developed eu queria revelar este filme [ew keree-a hevelah esh-tchee feewmee]
  ▸ do you have black-and-white film? tem filme preto-e-branco? [teng feewmee pretoo-ee-brankoo]
  ▸ is filming allowed in the museum? dá para filmar no museu? [da para feewmah noo moozew]

find encontrar [enkontrah]; *(lost object)* achar [ashah]
  ▸ has anyone found a watch? ninguém achou um relógio? [neengeng asho oom heloj-yoo]
  ▸ where can I find a doctor on a Sunday? onde eu encontro um médico num domingo? [ondjee ew enkontroo oom medjeekoo noom domeengoo]

find out descobrir [djeeshkobreeh]
  ▸ I need to find out the times of trains to Sao Paulo eu preciso descobrir o horário dos trens para São Paulo [ew presseezoo djeeshkobreer oo oraryoo doosh trensh para sowng powloo]

fine *(in health etc.)* bem [beng] ♦ a multa [moowta]
  ▸ fine thanks, and you? bem, obrigado, e você? [beng obreegadoo ee vosse]
  ▸ how much is the fine? de quanto é a multa? [djee kwantoo eh a moowta]

finger o dedo [dedoo]
  ▸ I've cut my finger cortei o dedo [koh-tay oo dedoo]

finish terminar [teh-meenah]
  ▸ can we leave as soon as we've finished our meal? podemos sair assim que terminarmos de comer? [podemoosh sa-eer asseeng ke teh-meenah-moosh djee komeh]

fire *(gen)* o fogo [fogoo]; *(out of control)* o incêndio [eensendyoo]
  ▸ to make a fire fazer um fogo [fazer oom fogoo]
  ▸ on fire *(forest, house)* em chamas [eng shamash]

fire department os bombeiros [bombayroosh]
  ▸ call the fire department! chamem os bombeiros! [shameng oosh bombayroosh]

fireworks (display) os fogos de artifício [fogoosh djee ah-tcheefeess-yoo]
  ▸ what time do the fireworks start? a que horas começam os fogos de artifício? [a kee orash komessowng oosh fogoosh djee ah-tcheefeess-yoo]

‣ where is the fireworks display being held? onde vão ser os fogos de artifício? [ondjee vowng ser oosh fogoosh djee ah-tcheefeess-yoo]

first primeiro(ra) [preemayroo(ra)]

‣ it's the first time I've been here é a primeira vez que eu venho aqui [eh a preemayra vesh kee ew venyoo akee]

‣ you have to take the first left after the lights tem que dobrar na primeira à esquerda depois do semáforo [teng kee dobrah na preemayra a eeshkeh-da depoysh doo semaforoo]

‣ put it into first coloque a primeira [kolokee a preemayra]

first-aid kit o kit de primeiros socorros [keetchee djee preemayrroosh sokohoosh]

‣ do you have a first-aid kit? você tem um kit de primeiros socorros? [vosse teng oom keetchee djee preemayrroosh sokohoosh]

first class a primeira classe [preemayra klassee]

‣ are there any seats in first class? tem algum assento na primeira classe? [teng owgoom assentoo na preemayra klassee]

‣ I'd like to send this first class eu queria mandar pelo correio mais rápido [ew keree-a mandah peloo kohayoo mysh hapeedoo]

‣ I prefer to travel first class eu prefiro viajar de primeira classe [ew prefeeroo vee-ajah djee preemayra klassee]

‣ how much is it for a first-class ticket? quanto custa uma passagem de primeira classe? [kwantoo kooshta ooma passajeng djee preemayra klassee]

fish o peixe [payshee]

‣ I don't eat fish eu não como peixe [ew nowng komoo payshee]

fishing permit a licença de pesca [leessensa djee peshka]

‣ do you need a fishing permit to fish here? precisa de uma licença (de pesca) para pescar aqui? [presseeza djee ooma leessensa (djee peshka) para peshkar akee]

fit *(of laughter)* o ataque [atakee]; *(of tears)* a crise [kreezee] ‣ *(be correct size for)* ficar [feekah] ‣ *(be correct size)* encaixar [enkyshah]

‣ I think she's having some kind of fit acho que ela está tendo um ataque [ashoo kee ella eeshta tendoo oom atakee]

‣ those pants fit you better essas calças ficam bem em ti [essash kalsash feekowng beng eng tchee]

‣ the key doesn't fit in the lock a chave não encaixa na fechadura [a shavee nowng enkysha na feshadoora]

‣ we won't all fit around one table não vamos caber todos na mesa [nowng vamoosh kabeh todoosh na meza]

fit in *(go in)* colocar [kolokah] ‣ *(put in)* entrar [entrah]

‣ I can't get everything to fit in my suitcase não consigo colocar tudo na mala [nowng konseegoo kolokah toodoo na mala]

‣ how many people can you fit in this car? quantas pessoas entram nesse carro? [kwantash pesso-az entrowng nessee kahoo]

fitting room o provador [provadoh]
  ▸ where are the fitting rooms? onde ficam os provadores? [ondjee feekowng oosh provadoreesh]

five cinco [seenkoo]
  ▸ there are five of us somos cinco [somoosh seenkoo]

fix consertar [konseh-tah]
  ▸ where can I find someone to fix my bike? onde eu consigo alguém para consertar minha bicicleta? [ondjee ew konseegoo owgeng para konseh-tah meenya beesseekleta]

fixed price o preço fixo [pressoo feeksoo]
  ▸ do taxis to the airport charge a fixed price? os táxis para o aeroporto cobram um preço fixo? [oosh takseesh para oo a-eropoh-too kobrowng oom pressoo feeksoo]

flash o flash [flash]
  ▸ I'd like some batteries for my flash preciso de pilha para o flash [presseezoo djee peelya para oo flash]

flash photography a foto com flash [fotoo kong flash]
  ▸ is flash photography allowed here? dá para bater foto com flash aqui? [da para bateh fotoo kong flash akee]

flat *(tire)* vazio(zia) [vazee-oo(zee-a)]
  ▸ the tire's flat o pneu está vazio [oo pnew eeshta vazee-oo]

flavor o sabor [saboh]
  ▸ I'd like to try a different flavor of ice cream eu queria provar um sabor diferente de sorvete [ew keree-a provar oom saboh djeeferentchee djee soh-vetchee]

flight o vôo [vo-oo]
  ▸ how many flights a day are there? há quantos vôos diários? [a kwantoosh vo-oosh djee-aryoosh]
  ▸ what time is the flight? a que horas é o vôo? [a kee oraz eh oo vo-oo]

flight of stairs o lance de escadas [lansee djee eeshkadash]
  ▸ your room's up that flight of stairs o seu quarto fica depois desse lance de escadas [oo sew kwah-too feeka depoysh dessee lansee djee eeshkadash]

floor *(story)* o piso [peezoo]
  ▸ which floor is it on? em que piso fica? [eng ke peezoo feeka]
  ▸ it's on the top floor fica no último piso [feeka noo oowtcheemoo peezoo]

flower a flor [floh]
  ▸ do you sell flowers vocês vendem flores? [vossesh vendeng floreesh]

flu a gripe [greepee]
  ▸ I'd like something for the flu eu queria alguma coisa para gripe [ew keree-a owgooma koyza para greepee]

flush a descarga [djeeeshkah-ga] ◆ *(toilet)* puxar a descarga [pooshar a djeeshkah-a] ◆ *(person)* ficar vermelho(lha) [feekah vermelyoo(lya)]; *(toilet)* dar a descarga [dar a djeeshkah-ga]

▸ the toilet won't flush o vaso não dá descarga [oo vazoo nowng da djeeshkah-ga]

fog o nevoeiro [nev-wayroo]

▸ is there a lot of fog today? tem muito nevoeiro hoje? [teng mweentoo nev-wayroo ojee]

food a comida [komeeda]

▸ is there some place to buy food nearby? tem algum lugar para comprar comida por aqui? [teng owgoom loogah para komprah komeeda por akee]

▸ the food here is excellent a comida aqui é excelente [a komeeda akee eh esselentchee]

food section *(in store)* a seção de comida [sessowng djee komeeda]

▸ where's the food section? onde fica a seção de comida? [ondjee feeka a sessowng djee komeeda]

foot o pé [pe]

▸ on foot a pé [ape]

for *(expressing purpose, function)* para [para]; *(indicating direction, destination)* de [djee]; *(indicating duration)* por [poh]; *(showing preference)* a favor [a favoh]

▸ what's that for? para o que é? [para oo ke eh]

▸ the flight for Boston o vôo de Boston [oo vo-oo djee Boston]

▸ is this the right bus for Rio? é este o ônibus do Rio? [eh esh-tchee oo oneeboosh do hee-oo]

▸ I'm staying for two months vou ficar dois meses [vo feekah doysh mezeesh]

▸ I've been here for a week estou aqui há uma semana [eeshto akee a ooma semana]

▸ I need something for a cough preciso de alguma coisa para tosse [presseezoo djee owgooma koyza para tossee]

foreign *(country, language)* estrangeiro(ra) [eeshtran-jayroo(ra)]

▸ I don't speak any foreign languages não falo nenhum idioma estrangeiro [nowng faloo nenyoom eedjoma eeshtran-jayroo]

foreign currency a moeda estrangeira [mweda eeshtran-jayra]

▸ do you change foreign currency? vocês trocam moeda estrangeira? [vossesh trokowng mweda eeshtran-jayra]

foreigner o estrangeiro [eeshtran-jayroo], a estrangeira [eeshtran-jayra]

▸ as a foreigner, this custom seems a bit strange to me sendo eu estrangeiro, esse costume parece um pouco estranho para mim [sendoo ew eeshtran-jayroo essee koshtoomee paressee oom pokoo eeshtranyoo para meeng]

forever para sempre [para sempree]

▸ our money won't last forever o nosso dinheiro não vai durar para sempre [oo nossoo djeenyayroo nowng vy doorah para sempree]

fork o garfo [gah-foo]
> could I have a fork? poderia me trazer um garfo? [poderee-a mee trazeh oom gah foo]

forward encaminhar [enkameenyah]
> can you forward my mail? você pode encaminhar o meu correio? [vosse podje enkameenyar oo mew kohayoo]

four quatro [kwatroo]
> there are four of us somos quatro [somoosh kwatroo]

fourth quarto(ta) [kwah-too(ta)] ◆ (gear) a quarta [kwah-ta]
> it's hard to get it into fourth é difícil colocar em quarta [eh djeefeesseew koloka eng kwah-ta]

four-wheel drive o quatro por quatro [kwatroo poh kwatroo]
> I'd like a four-wheel drive eu queria um quatro por quatro [ew keree-a oor kwatroo poh kwatroo]

fracture a fratura [fratoora]
> is it a fracture? é uma fratura? [eh ooma fratoora]

free (offered at no charge) grátis [gratcheesh]; (not occupied) desocupado(da) [djeezokoo-padoo(da)]; (available) livre [leevree]
> is it free? é grátis? [eh gratcheesh]
> is this seat free? esse lugar está desocupado? [essee loogar eeshta djeezokoo padoo]
> are you free on Thursday evening? você está livre na quinta de tarde? [vosse eeshta leevree na keenta djee tah-djee]

freeway a auto-estrada [owto-eeshtrada]
> what is the speed limit on freeways? qual é o limite de velocidade nas auto-estradas? [kwal eh oo leemeetchee djee velossee-dadjee naz owto-eeshtradash]
> how do I get onto the freeway? como eu chego na auto-estrada? [komoo ew shegoo na owto-eeshtrada]

freezing (cold) (room, day) gelado(da) [jeladoo(da)]
> I'm freezing (cold) estou congelando [eeshto konjelando]

frequent freqüente [frekwentchee]
> how frequent are the trains to the city? com que freqüência os trens vão para a cidade? [kong ke frekwenss-ya ozz trengsh vowng para a seedadjee]

fresh (food) fresco(ca) [freshkoo(ka)]
> I'd like some fresh orange juice eu queria um suco de laranja feito na hora [ew keree-a oom sookoo djee laranja faytoo na ora]

freshly (ironed) recentemente [hessentchee-mentchee]
> freshly squeezed orange juice suco de laranja feito na hora [sookoo djee laranja faytoo na ora]

Friday a sexta-feira [seshta-fayra], a sexta [seshta]
- we're arriving/leaving on Friday estamos chegando/saindo na sexta [eeshta-moosh shegandoo/sa-eendoo na seshta]

fried egg o ovo frito [ovoo freetoo]
- I'd prefer a fried egg eu prefiro ovo frito [ew prefeeroo ovoo freetoo]

friend o amigo [ameegoo], a amiga [ameega]
- are you with friends? você está com amigos? [vosse eeshta kong ameegoosh]
- I've come with a friend vim com um amigo [veeng kong oom ameegoo]
- I'm meeting some friends vou encontrar alguns amigos [vo enkontrar owgoonz ameegoosh]

from de [djee]
- I'm from the United States sou dos Estados Unidos [so dooz eeshtadooz ooneedoosh]
- how many flights a day are there from Belém to Rio? quantos vôos por dia saem de Belém com destino ao Rio? [kwantoosh vo-oosh poh djee-a sa-eng djee beleng kong desh-tcheenoo ow hee-oo]

front *(of bus)* a parte da frente [pah-tchee da frentchee] • **in front** da frente [da frentchee] • **in front of** em frente de [eng frentchee djee]
- I'd like a seat toward the front of the bus eu queria um lugar na parte da frente do ônibus [ew keree-a oom loogah na pah-tchee da frentchee doo oneeboosh]
- the car in front braked suddenly o carro da frente freou de repente [oo kahoo da frentchee free-o djee hepentchee]
- I'll meet you in front of the museum encontro você na frente do museu [enkontroo vosse na frentchee doo moozew]

front door a porta da frente [poh-ta da frentchee]
- which is the key to the front door? qual é a chave da porta da frente? [kwal eh a shavee da poh-ta da frentchee]
- the front door is closed a porta da frente está fechada [a poh-ta da frentchee eeshta feshada]

frozen congelado(da) [konjelado(da)]
- I'm absolutely frozen estou simplesmente congelado [eeshto sempleesh-mentchee konjelado]

frozen food a comida congelada [komeeda konjelada]
- is that all the frozen food you have? essa é toda a comida congelada que você tem? [essa eh toda a komeeda konjelada ke vosse teng]

fruit juice o suco de frutas [sookoo djee frootash]
- what types of fruit juice do you have? que tipo de suco de frutas vocês têm? [ke tcheepoo djee sookoo djee frootash vossesh tayeng]

full cheio(a) [shayoo(ya)]; *(with food)* satisfeito(ta) [satcheesh-faytoo(ta)]
- is it full? está cheio? [eeshta shayoo]

▸ I'm quite full, thank you estou satisfeito, obrigado [eeshto satcheesh-faytoo obreegadoo]

full up *(with food)* satisfeito(ta) [satcheesh-faytoo(ta)]

▸ I'm full up estou satisfeito [eeshto satcheesh-faytoo]

fun *(pleasure, amusement)* a diversão [djeeveh-sowng]

▸ to have fun divertir-se [djeeveh-tcheeh-see-a]

g

gallery *(for art)* a galeria [galeree-a]

▸ what time does the gallery open? a que horas abre a galeria? [a kee oraz abree a galeree-a]

game *(fun activity)* o jogo [jogoo]; *(of sport)* a partida [pah-tcheeda]

▸ do you want to play a game of tennis tomorrow? quer jogar uma partida de tênis amanhã? [keh jogar ooma pah-tcheeda djee teneesh amanyang]

garage *(for car repair)* a oficina [ofeesseena]

▸ is there a garage near here? tem uma oficina por aqui? [teng ooma ofeesseena por akee]

▸ could you tow me to a garage? você pode me rebocar até uma oficina? [vosse podjee mee hebokar a-te ooma ofeesseena]

garbage can a lata de lixo [lata djee leeshoo]

▸ where is the garbage can? onde está a lata de lixo? [ondjee eeshta a lata djee leeshoo]

gas *(for vehicle)* a gasolina [gazoleena]; *(for domestic and medical use)* o gás [gash]

▸ where can I get gas? onde eu posso achar gasolina? [ondjee ew possoo ashah gazoleena]

▸ I've run out of gas estou sem gasolina [eeshto seng gazoleena]

gas pump a bomba de gasolina [bomba djee gazoleena]

▸ how do you use this gas pump? como se usa essa bomba de gasolina? [komoo see ooza essa bomba djee gazoleena]

gas station o posto de gasolina [poshtoo djee gazoleena]

▸ where can I find a gas station? onde tem um posto de gasolina? [ondjee teng oom poshtoo djee gazoleena]

gas stove a estufa a gás [eeshtoofa a gash]

▸ do you have a gas stove we could borrow? você poderia nos emprestar uma estufa a gás? [vosse poderee-a nooz empreshtar ooma eeshtoofa a gash]

gas tank o tanque de gasolina [tankee djee gazoleena]

▸ the gas tank is leaking o tanque de gasolina está vazando [oo tankee djee gazoleena eeshta vazandoo]

gate *(a town)* o pórtico [poh-tcheekoo]; *(of a garden, at an airport)* o portão [poh-towng]

▸ where is Gate 2? onde fica o Portão 2? [ondjee feeka oo poh-towng doysh]

gear *(of a car, a bike)* a marcha [mah-sha]

▸ how many gears does the bike have? quantas marchas tem a bicicleta? [kwantash mah-shash teng a besseekleta]

get *(obtain)* conseguir [konsegeeh], obter [obteh]; *(understand)* entender [entendeh] ♦ *(make one's way)* chegar [shegah]

▸ where can we get something to eat this time of night? onde a gente pode conseguir alguma coisa para comer a essa hora da noite? [ondjee a jentchee podjee konsegeer owgooma koyza para komer a essa ora da noytchee]

▸ I can't get it into reverse não consigo engatar a ré [nowng konseegoo engatar e re]

▸ now I get it agora eu entendi [agora ew entendjee]

▸ I got here a month ago cheguei aqui faz um mês [shegay akee faz oom mesh]

▸ can you get there by car? dá para chegar lá de carro? [da para shegah la djee kahoo]

▸ how can I get to... como eu faço para ir até... [komoo ew fasso para eer a-te]

▸ could you tell me the best way to get to Salvador? você poderia me dizer qual é o melhor caminho para Salvador? [vosse poderee-a mee djeezeh kwal eh oo melyoh kameenyoo para sow-vadoh]

▸ how do we get to Terminal 2? como a gente chega no Terminal 2? [komoo a jentchee shega noo teh-meenow doysh]

get back *(money)* recobrar [hekobrah]

▸ I just want to get my money back eu só quero o meu dinheiro de volta [ew so keroo oo mew djeen-yayroo djee vowta]

get back onto *(road)* voltar [vowtah]

▸ how can I get back onto the freeway? como eu faço para voltar para a auto-estrada? [komoo fasso para vowtah para a owto-eeshtrada]

get in *(arrive)* chegar [shegah]; *(gain entry)* entrar [entrah]

▸ what time does the bus get in to Sao Paulo? a que horas chega o ônibus a São Paulo? [a kee orash shega oo oneeboosh a sowng powloo]

▸ what time does the flight get in? a que horas chega o vôo? [a kee orash shega o vo-oo]

▸ do you have to pay to get in? tem que pagar para entrar? [teng kee pagah para entrah]

get off *(bus, bike)* descer de [desseh djee]; *(road)* sair de [sa-eeh djee] ♦ descer [desseh]

▸ where do we get off the bus? onde a gente desce do ônibus? [ondjee a jentchee dessee doo oneeboosh]

▸ where do I get off the freeway? onde eu saio da auto-estrada? [ondjee ew sy-oo da owto-eeshtrada]

get on subir [soobeeh]
▸ which bus should we get on to go downtown? que ônibus a gente tem que pegar para ir para o centro? [ke oneeboosh a jentchee teng kee pegah para eeh para oo sentroo]

get past passar [passah]
▸ sorry, can I get past, please? desculpe, posso passar? [djeesh-koowpee possoo passah]

get up (in morning) levantar-se [levantah-see]
▸ I get up very early levanto muito cedo [levantoo mweentoo sedoo]

gift-wrap embrulhar para presente [embroolyah para prezentchee]
▸ could you gift-wrap it for me? você poderia embrulhar para presente? [vosse poderee-a embroolyah para prezentchee]

girl (young female) a menina [meneena]; (daughter) a filha [feelya]
▸ who is that girl? quem é aquela menina? [keng eh akella meneena]
▸ I've got two girls tenho duas filhas [tenyoo doo-ash feel-yash]

girlfriend a namorada [namorada]
▸ is she your girlfriend? ela é sua namorada? [ella eh soo-a namorada]

give dar [dah]
▸ I can give you my e-mail address posso lhe dar meu endereço de email [possool-yee dah mew enderessoo djee email]
▸ can you give me a hand? você pode me dar uma mão? [vosse podjee mee dar ooma mowng]

glass (material) o vidro [veedroo]; (for drinking) o copo [kopoo] ◆ **glasses** os óculos [okooloosh]
▸ can I have a clean glass? poderia me alcançar um copo limpo? [poderee-a mee owkansar oom kopoo leempoo]
▸ would you like a glass of champagne? quer um copo de champanha? [ker oom kopoo djee shampanya]
▸ I've lost my glasses perdi meus óculos [peh-djee mewz okooloosh]

glove a luva [loova]
▸ I've lost a brown glove perdi uma luva marrom [peh-djee ooma loova mahong]

go (move, travel, vehicle) ir [eeh]; (depart) ir embora [eer embora]; (lead) levar [levah]
▸ let's go to the beach vamos para a praia [vamoosh para a pry-a]
▸ where can we go for breakfast? onde podemos tomar café da manhã? [ondjee podemoosh tomah kaffe da manyang]
▸ where does this path go? onde vai dar esse caminho? [ondjee vy dar essee kameenyoo]
▸ I must be going tenho que ir (embora) [tenhoo ke eeh (embora)]

▸ we're going home tomorrow vamos para casa amanhã [vamoosh para kaza amanyang]

go away *(person)* ir embora [eer embora]; *(pain)* passar [passah]

▸ go away and leave me alone! vá embora e me deixe em paz! [va embora ee mee dayshee eng paj]

go back *(return)* voltar [vowtah]

▸ we're going back home tomorrow voltamos para casa amanhã [vowtamoosh para caza amanyang]

go down descer [desseh]

▸ go down that street and turn left at the bottom desça essa rua e vire à esquerda no final [dessa essa hoo-a ee veeree a eeskeh-da noo feenow]

gold *(metal)* o ouro [oroo]

▸ is it made of gold? é feito de ouro? [eh faytoo djee oroo]

golf o golfe [gowfee]

▸ I play golf eu jogo golfe [ew jogoo gowfee]

golf club o taco de golfe [takoo djee gowfee]

▸ where can I rent golf clubs? onde eu posso alugar tacos de golfe? [ondjee ew possoo aloogah takoosh djee gowfee]

golf course o curso de golfe [kooh-soo djee gowfee]

▸ is there a golf course nearby? tem algum curso de golfe por aqui? [teng owgoom kooh-soo djee gowfee por akee]

good bom(boa) [bong(boa)]

▸ this isn't a very good restaurant não é um restaurante muito bom [nowng eh oom heshtow-rantchee mweentoo bong]

▸ you're really good at surfing! você é muito bom no surfe! [vosse eh mweentoo bong noo sooh-fee]

▸ we had a good time nos divertimos muito [nosh djeeveh-tcheemoosh mweentoo]

good afternoon boa tarde [boa tah-djee]

▸ good afternoon! isn't it a beautiful day? boa tarde! não é um dia maravilhoso? [boa tah-djee nowng eh oom djee-a maraveel-yozoo]

goodbye tchau [tchow]

▸ I'd better say goodbye now é melhor eu me despedir agora [eh mel-yor ew mee djeesh-pedjeeh agora]

good evening *(earlier)* boa tarde [boa tah-djee]; *(later)* boa noite [boa noytchee]

▸ good evening! how are you tonight? boa noite! como vai? [boa noytchee komoo vy]

good morning bom dia [bong djee-a]

▸ good morning! how are you today? bom dia! como vai? [bong djee-a komoo vy]

good night boa noite [boa noytchee]

▸ I'll say good night, then vou dar boa noite [vo dah boa noytchee]

guesthouses

Pensões, casas de família or *residências* are all names for the same thing: small, family-run guesthouses. You should ask to look at the room before you take it, as standards can vary considerably. Be warned that prices can double in the high season. In places geared toward tourists, you can try *uma pousada* instead of a hotel: these are plainer and less expensive, as well as much cozier.

---

go out *(leave house, socially, on date)* sair [sa-eeh]; *(tide)* baixar [by-shah]
- what's a good place to go out for a drink? onde a gente pode ir para tomar um drinque? [ondjee a jentchee podjee eeh para tomar oom dreenkee]
- the tide's going out a maré está baixando [a ma-re eeshta by-shandoo]

grapefruit o pomelo [pomeloo]
- I'll just have the grapefruit eu vou comer só o pomelo [ew vo komeh so oo pomeloo]

great *(very good)* ótimo(ma) [otcheemoo(ma)]
- that's great! que ótimo! [ke otcheemoo]
- it was really great! foi muito bom! [foy mweentoo bong]

green verde [veh-djee]
- the green one o verde [oo veh-djee]

grocery store o armazém [ah-mazeng]
- is there a grocery store around here? tem um armazém por aqui? [teng oom ah-mazeng por akee]

ground cloth o pano de chão [panoo djee showng]
- I brought a ground cloth trouxe um pano de chão [trossee oom panoo djee showng]

group o grupo [groopoo]
- there's a group of 12 of us somos um grupo de doze [somooz oom groopoo djee dozee]
- are there reductions for groups? há descontos para grupo? [a djeeshkontoosh para groopoo]

group rate o preço para grupo [pressoo para groopoo]
- are there special group rates? há preços especiais para grupo? [a pressooz eeshpessee-ysh para groopoo]

guarantee *(for purchased product)* a garantia [garantchee-a]
- it's still under guarantee ainda está na garantia [a-eenda eeshta na garantchee-a]

guesthouse a pousada [pozada]
- we're looking for a guesthouse for the night estamos procurando uma pousada para passar a noite [eeshtamoosh prokoorandoo ooma pozada para passar a noytchee]

guide *(person)* o(a) guia [ghee-a]; *(book)* o guia [ghee-a]
- does the guide speak English? o guia fala inglês? [oo ghee-a fala eenglesh]

guidebook o guia [ghee-a]
- do you have a guidebook in English? você tem um guia em inglês? [vosse teng oom ghee-a eng eenglesh]

guided tour a visita guiada [veezeeta ghee-ada]
- what time does the guided tour begin? a que horas começa a visita guiada? [a kee orash komessa a veezeeta ghee-ada]
- is there a guided tour in English? tem uma visita guiada em inglês? [teng ooma veezeeta ghee-ada eng eenglesh]
- are there guided tours of the museum? há visitas guiadas no museu? [a veezeetash ghee-adash noo moozew]

h

hair o cabelo [kabeloo]
- she has short hair ela tem cabelo curto [ella teng kabeloo kooh-too]
- he has red hair ela tem cabelo ruivo [ella teng kabeloo hweevoo]

hairbrush a escova de cabelo [eeshkova djee kabeloo]
- do you sell hairbrushes? vocês vendem escova de cabelo? [vossesh vendeng eeshkova djee kabeloo]

hairdryer o secador de cabelo [sekadoh djee kabeloo]
- do the rooms have hairdryers? tem secador de cabelo no quarto? [teng sekadoh djee kabeloo noo kwah-too]

hair salon o salão de beleza [salowng djee beleza]
- does the hotel have a hair salon? o hotel tem salão de beleza? [oo otew teng salowng djee beleza]

half meio(a) [mayoo(a)] ◆ na metade [na metadjee] ◆ a metade [metadjee]
- shall we meet in half an hour? nos encontramos em meia hora? [noz enkontramooz eng maya ora]
- it's half past eight são oito e meia [sowng oytoo ee maya]

half-bottle a meia garrafa [maya gahafa]
- a half-bottle of red wine, please meia garrafa de vinho tinto, por favor [maya gahafa djee veenyoo tcheentoo poh favoh]

ham o presunto [prezoontoo]
- I'd like five slices of ham eu quero cinco fatias de presunto [ew keroo seenkoo fatchee-ash djee prezoontoo]

hand a mão [mowng]
 ▶ where can I wash my hands? onde eu posso lavar as mãos? [ondjee ew possoo lavar ash mowngsh]

handbag a bolsa [bowsa]
 ▶ someone's stolen my handbag roubaram a minha bolsa [hobarowng a meenya bowsa]

hand baggage a bagagem de mão [bagajeng djee mowng]
 ▶ I have one suitcase and one piece of hand baggage tenho uma mala e uma bagagem de mão [tenyoo ooma mala ee ooma bagajeng djee mowng]

handkerchief o lenço [lensoo]
 ▶ do you have a spare handkerchief? você tem um lenço sobrando? [vosse teng oom lensoo sobrandoo]

handle *(of a door)* a maçaneta [massaneta]; *(of a suitcase)* a alça [owsa]
 ▶ the handle's broken quebrou a alça [kebro a owsa]

handmade feito(ta) à mão [faytoo(ta) a mowng]
 ▶ is this handmade? isso foi feito à mão? [eessoo foy faytoo a mowng]

happen *(occur)* acontecer [akontesseh]
 ▶ what happened? o que aconteceu? [oo ke akontessew]
 ▶ these things happen essas coisas acontecem? [essash koyzaz akontesseng]

happy *(not sad)* feliz [feleej]; *(satisfied)* contente [kontentchee]
 ▶ I'd be happy to help eu adoraria ajudar [ew adoraree-a ajoodah]
 ▶ Happy Birthday! feliz aniversário! [feleez aneeveh-saryoo]
 ▶ Happy New Year! feliz Ano Novo! [feleez anoo novoo]

hat o chapéu [shapew]
 ▶ I think I left my hat here acho que deixei meu chapéu aqui [ashoo kee dayshay mew shapew akee]

hate odiar [odyah], detestar [deteshtah]
 ▶ I hate golf odeio golfe [odayoo gowfee]

have *(possess, as characteristic)* ter [teh]; *(drink)* tomar [tomah]; *(meal)* comer [komeh] ◆ *(be obliged)* ter que [teh kee]
 ▶ do you have any bread? tem pão? [teng powng]
 ▶ do you have them in red? tem vermelho? [teng veh-melyoo]
 ▶ he has brown hair ele tem cabelo castanho [elee teng kabeloo kashtanyoo]
 ▶ where should we go to have a drink? onde devemos ir para tomar alguma coisa? [ondjee devemooz eeh para tomar owgooma koyza]
 ▶ I have to be at the airport by six (o'clock) tenho que estar no aeroporto às seis (horas) [tenyoo kee eeshtah noo a-eropoh-too ash saysh (orash)]
 ▶ we have to go temos que ir [temoosh kee eeh]

head *(of a person)* a cabeça [kabessa]; *(of a shower)* o espalhador [eeshpal-yadoh]
 ▶ I hit my head when I fell bati a cabeça quando caí [batchee a kabessa kwandoo ka-ee]

▸ the shower head is broken o espalhador do chuveiro está quebrado [oo eeshpal-yadoh doo shoovayroo eeshta kebradoo]

headache a dor de cabeça [doh djee kabessa]
▸ I've got a headache estou com dor de cabeça [eeshto kong doh djee kabessa]
▸ do you have anything for a headache? tem alguma coisa para dor de cabeça? [teng owgooma koyza para doh djee kabessa]

headlight o farol [farow]
▸ one of my headlights got smashed um dos faróis quebrou [oom doosh faroysh kebro]

headphones os fones (de ouvido) [foneesh (djee oveedoo)]
▸ did you find my headphones? você achou meus fones (de ouvido)? [vosse asho mewsh foneesh (djee oveedoo)]

health a saúde [sa-oodjee]
▸ in good/poor health em boas/más condições de saúde [eng boash/mash kondjee-soyngsh djee sa-oodjee]

hear ouvir [oveeh]; *(learn of)* ficar sabendo [feekah sabendoo]
▸ I've heard a lot about you eu ouvi muitas coisas a seu respeito [ew ovee mweentash koyzash a sew heshpaytoo]

heart o coração [korassowng]
▸ he's got a weak heart ele está mal do coração [elee eeshta mow doo korassowng]

heart attack o ataque do coração [atakee doo korassowng]
▸ he had a heart attack ele teve um infarto [elee tevee oom eenfan-too]
▸ I nearly had a heart attack! quase tive um ataque! [kwazee tcheevee oom atakee]

heart condition a doença do coração [dwensa doo korassowng]
▸ to have a heart condition sofrer do coração [sofreh doo korassowng]

heat *(hot quality, weather)* o calor [kaloh]; *(for cooking)* o fogo [fogoo]
▸ there's no heat from the radiator in my room não sai calor do aquecedor no meu quarto [nowng sy kaloh doo akessedoh noo mew kwah-too]

heating o aquecimento [akesseementoo]
▸ how does the heating work? como funciona o aquecimento? [komoo foonss-yona oo akesseementoo]

heavy pesado(da) [pezadoo(da)]
▸ my bags are very heavy minhas malas estão muito pesadas [meenyash malash eeshtowng mweentoo pezadash]

heel *(of a foot)* o calcanhar [kowkanyah]; *(of a shoe)* o salto [sowtoo]
▸ can you put new heels on these shoes? você pode colocar saltos novos nesses sapatos? [vosse podjee kolokah sowtoosh novoosh nesseesh sapatoosh]

saying hello

Oi! and *olá!* are the equivalents of 'hi!' and are used by young and old alike. If you want to be formal, say *bom dia* (in the morning, including lunchtime), *boa tarde* (in the afternoon) or *boa noite* (in the evening). *Tudo bem?* or *tudo bom?* (how are things?) is another very common way of saying hello.

hello *(as a greeting)* olá [o-la]; *(on the phone)* alô [allo]
▸ hello, is this ...? alô, é ...? [allo eh]

helmet o capacete [kapassetchee]
▸ do you have a helmet you could lend me? tem um capacete para me emprestar? [teng oom kapassetchee para mee empreshtah]

help *(assistance)* a ajuda [ajooda]; *(emergency aid)* o socorro [sokohoo] ◆ ajudar [ajoodah]
▸ help! socorro! [sokohoo]
▸ go and get help quickly! vai e consegue ajuda rápido! [vy ee konsegee ajooda hapeedoo]
▸ thank you for your help obrigado pela ajuda [obreegadoo pela ajooda]
▸ could you help me? você poderia me ajudar? [vosse poderee-a mee ajoodah]
▸ could you help us push the car? poderia nos ajudar a empurrar o carro? [poderee-a noz ajoodar a empoohar oo kahoo]
▸ let me help you with that deixe que eu ajudo você com isso [dayshee kee ew ajoodoo vosse kong eessoo]
▸ could you help me with my bags? você poderia me ajudar com as malas? [vosse poderee-a mee ajoodah kong ash malash]

herbal tea o chá de ervas [sha djee eh-vash]
▸ I'd like an herbal tea eu queria um chá de ervas [ew keree-a oom sha djee eh-vash]

here aqui [akee]
▸ I've been here two days estou aqui há dois dias [eeshto akee a doysh djee-ash]
▸ I came here three years ago vim aqui faz três anos [veeng akee fash trez anoosh]
▸ are you from around here? você é da região? [vosse eh da hej-yowng]
▸ I'm afraid I'm a stranger here myself acho que também sou um estranho no ninho aqui [ashoo kee tambeng so oom eeshtranyoo noo neenyoo akee]
▸ it's five minutes from here fica a cinco minutos daqui [feeka a seenkoo meenootoosh dakee]
▸ here is/are... eis... [aysh]
▸ here are my passport and ticket aqui estão meu passaporte e a passagem [akee eeshtowng mew passapoh-tchee ee a passajeng]

hi oi [oy]
  ▸ hi, I'm Julia oi, meu nome é Julia [oy mew nomee eh joolya]

high beam a luz alta [looz owta]
  ▸ put your lights on high beam coloque luz alta [kolokee looz owta]

high chair a cadeirinha [kadereenya]
  ▸ could we have a high chair for the baby? teria como conseguir uma cadeirinha para o bêbê? [teree-a komoo konsegeeh ooma kadereenya para oo be-be]

high season a alta estação [owta eeshtassowng]
  ▸ is it very expensive in the high season? é muito caro na alta estação? [eh mweentoo karoo na owta eeshtassowng]

high tide a maré alta [ma-re owta]
  ▸ what time is high tide? a que horas a maré sobe? [a kee oraz a ma-re sobee]

hike a caminhada [kameenyada]
  ▸ are there any good hikes around here? dá para fazer boas caminhadas por aqui? [da para fazeh boash kameenyadash por akee]

hiking a trilha [treelya]
  ▸ to go hiking fazer trilha [fazeh treelya]
  ▸ are there any hiking trails? tem caminhos para praticar trilha? [teng kameenyoosh para pratcheekah treelya]

hiking boot as botas de trilha [botash djee treelya]
  ▸ do you need to wear hiking boots? precisa usar botas de trilha? [presseeza oozah botash djee treelya]

hitchhike pegar carona [pegah karona]
  ▸ we hitchhiked here pegamos carona aqui [pegamoosh karona akee]

holiday o feriado [feree-adoo]
  ▸ is tomorrow a holiday? amanhã é feriado? [amanyang eh feree-adoo]

home *(house)* a casa [kaza] ◆ em casa [eng kaza]
  ▸ to stay at home ficar em casa [feekar eng kaza]
  ▸ we're going home tomorrow vamos para casa amanhã [vamoosh para kaza amanyang]

homemade feito(ta) em casa [faytoo(ta) eng kaza]
  ▸ is it homemade? é feito em casa? [eh faytoo eng kaza]

hood *(car)* o capô [kapo]
  ▸ I've dented the hood o capô do carro abaulou [oo kapo doo kahoo abowlo]

horrible horrível [oheevew]
  ▸ what horrible weather! que tempo horrível! [ke tempoo oheevew]

horseback riding a equitação [ekeetassowng]
  ▸ can we go horseback riding? podemos ir montar a cavalo? [podemooz eeh montar a kavaloo]

hotel rooms

If you're traveling with your partner, ask for *um quarto com uma cama de casal* (a room with a double bed). Otherwise, it's better to specify *um quarto com duas camas de solteiro* (a room with with two single beds).

hospital o hospital [oshpeetow]
> where is the nearest hospital? onde fica o hospital mais próximo? [ondjee feeka oo oshpeetow mysh prosseemoo]

hot *(in temperature)* quente [kentchee]; *(spicy)* picante [peekantchee]
> I'm too hot estou com muito calor [eeshto kong mweentoo kaloh]
> this dish is really hot esse prato é muito picante [essee pratoo eh mweentoo peekantchee]
> there's no hot water não tem água quente [nowng teng agwa kentchee]

hotel o hotel [otew]
> do you have a list of hotels in this area? você tem uma lista de hotéis da região? [vosse teng ooma leeshta djee otaysh da hej-yowng]
> are there any reasonably priced hotels near here? tem algum hotel com preços razoáveis aqui na região? [teng owgoom otew kong pressoosh hazwavayz akee na hej-yowng]
> is the hotel downtown? o hotel fica no centro? [oo otew feeka noo sentroo]
> could you recommend another hotel? você poderia recomendar outro hotel? [vosse poderee-a hekomendar otroo otew]

hour a hora [ora]
> I'll be back in an hour volto em uma hora [vowtoo eng ooma ora]

at the hotel

> we'd like a double room/two single rooms queremos um quarto de casal/dois quartos de solteiro [keremooz oom kwah-too djee kazow/doysh kwah-toosh djee sowtayroo]
> I have a reservation in the name of Kennedy tenho uma reserva em nome de Kennedy [tenyoo ooma hezeh-va eng nomee djee Kennedy]
> what time is breakfast/dinner served? a que horas é o café da manhã/a janta? [a kee oraz eh oo kaffe da manyang/a janta]
> could I have a wake-up call at 7 a.m.? seria possível me acordar às sete horas? [seree-a posseevew mee akoh-dar ash setchee orash]

how are you?

If you want to ask your friend Pedro how he is, you say *oi, Pedro, e aí?* (how are you, Pedro?). If it's someone you don't know so well, say *como vai?* Alternatively you can say *oi, tudo bem?*, to people you know well, or *como vai o senhor/a senhora?*, which is more formal, to people you've just met or who are just acquaintances.

- the flight takes three hours o vôo leva três horas [o vo-oo leva trez orash]

house a casa [kaza]
- is this your house? esta é a sua casa? [eshta eh a soo-a kaza]

house wine o vinho da casa [veenyoo da kaza]
- a bottle of house wine, please uma garrafa de vinho da casa, por favor [ooma gahafa djee veenyoo da kaza poh favoh]

how como [komoo]
- how are you? como vai você? [komoo vy vosse]
- how do you spell it? como se escreve? [komoo see eeshkrevee]
- how about a drink? que tal um drinque? [ke tal oom dreenkee]

humid úmido(da) [oomeedoo(da)]
- it's very humid today está muito úmido hoje [eeshta mweentoo oomeedoo ojee]

hungry
- to be hungry estar com fome [eeshtah kong fomee]
- I'm starting to get hungry estou começando a ficar com fome [eeshto komessando a feekah kong fomee]

hurry
- to be in a hurry estar com pressa [eeshtah kong pressa]

hurry up apressar-se [apressah-see]
- hurry up! depressa! [djeepressa]

hurt *(to cause physical pain)* machucar [mashookah]
- you're hurting me! você está me machucando! [vosse eeshta mee mashookandoo]
- to hurt oneself machucar-se [mashookah-see]
- I hurt myself me machuquei [mee mashookay]
- I hurt my hand machuquei a mão [mashookay a mowng]
- it hurts (isso) machuca [(eessoo) mashooka]

ice o gelo [jeloo]
- a Diet Coke® without ice, please uma Diet Coke® sem gelo, por favor [ooma diet coke seng jeloo poh favoh]

ice cream o sorvete [soh-vetchee]
- I'd like some ice cream eu queria um sorvete [ew keree-a oom soh-vetchee]

ice cube o cubo de gelo [kooboo djee jeloo]
- could I have a carafe of water with no ice cubes in it? eu queria uma jarra de água sem cubos de gelo, por favor [ew keree-a ooma jaha djee agwa seng kooboosh djee jeloo poh favoh]

iced coffee o café gelado [kaffe jeladoo]
- I'd like an iced coffee eu queria café gelado [ew keree-a kaffe jeladoo]

ID card o cartão de identificação [kah-towng djee eedentchee-feekassowng]
- I don't have an ID card: will a passport work? não tenho cartão de identificação: serve um passaporte? [nowng tenyoo kah-towng djee eedentchee-feekassowng seh-vee oom passapoh-tchee]

if se [see]
- we'll go if you want podemos ir se você quiser [podemooz eeh see vosse keezeh]

ill doente [dwentchee]
- my son is ill meu fiho está doente [mew feelyoo eeshta dwentchee]

immediately imediatamente [eemedjee-atamentchee]
- can you do it immediately? dá para fazer isso imediatamente? [da para fazer eessoo eemedjee-atamentchee]

improve melhorar [melyorah]
- I'm hoping to improve my Portuguese while I'm here espero melhorar meu português enquanto estiver aqui [eeshperoo melyorah mew poh-toogez enkwantoo eesh-tcheever akee]

in em [eng]
- our bags are still in the room nossas malas ainda estão na sala [nossash malash a-eenda eeshtowng na sala]
- do you live in Rio? você mora em Rio? [vosse mora eng hee-oo]

included incluído(da) [eenklweedoo(da)]
- is breakfast included? inclui café da manhã? [eenklooy kaffe da manyang]
- is sales tax included? o IVA está incluído? [oo eeva eeshta eenklweedoo]
- is the tip included? com a gorjeta incluída? [kong a goh-jeta eenklweeda]

indoor coberto(ta) [kobeh-too(ta)]
▸ is there an indoor pool? tem piscina coberta? [teng peesseena kobeh-ta]

infection a infecção [eenfessowng]
▸ I have an eye infection estou com uma infecção nos olhos [eeshto kong ooma eenfessowng nooz ol-yoosh]

information *(facts)* a informação [eenfoh-massowng]; *(service, department)* as informações [eenfoh-massoyngsh]
▸ a piece of information uma informação [ooma eenfoh-massowng]
▸ may I ask you for some information? posso lhe pedir mais informações? [possool-yee pedjeeh myz eenfoh-massoyngsh]
▸ where can I find information on...? onde posso encontrar informações sobre...? [ondjee possoo enkontrar eenfoh-massoyngsh sobree]

injection *(medicine)* a injeção [eenjessowng]
▸ am I going to need an injection? vou ter que tomar injeção? [vo teh kee tomar eenjessowng]

injure ferir [fereeh]
▸ to injure oneself ferir-se [fereeh-see]
▸ I injured myself me machuquei [mee mashookay]

inside dentro (de) [dentroo (djee)]
▸ are you allowed inside the castle? dá para entrar no castelo? [da para entrah noo kashteloo]
▸ we'd prefer a table inside preferimos uma mesa dentro [prefereemooz ooma meza dentroo]

insurance o seguro [segooroo]
▸ what does the insurance cover? o que o seguro cobre? [oo ke oo segooroo kobree]

insure *(house, car)* segurar [segoorah]
▸ yes, I'm insured sim, tenho seguro [seeng tenyoo segooroo]

interesting interessante [eenteressantchee]
▸ it's not a very interesting place não é um lugar muito interessante [nowng eh oom loogah mweentoo eenteressantchee]

international call a chamada internacional [shamada eenteh-nassyonow]
▸ I'd like to make an international call queria fazer uma chamada internacional [keree-a fazer ooma shamada eenteh-nassyonow]

Internet a Internet [eenteh-netchee]
▸ where can I connect to the Internet? onde eu posso me conectar à Internet? [ondjee ew possoo mee konectar a eenteh-netchee]

introduce *(present)* apresentar [aprezentah]
▸ to introduce oneself apresentar-se [aprezentah-see]
▸ allow me to introduce myself: I'm Michael permita-me que eu me apresente: meu nome é Michael [peh-meeta-mee kee ew mee aprezentchee mew nomee eh Michael]

invite convidar [konveedah]

▸ I'd like to invite you to dinner next weekend eu queria convidá-lo para jantar no próximo final de semana [ew keree-a konveeda-loo para jantah noo prosseemeoo feenow djee semana]

iron *(for ironing)* o ferro (de passar roupa) [fehoo (djee passah hopa)] ◆ passar [passah]

▸ I need an iron preciso de um ferro (de passar roupa) [presseezoo djee oom fehoo (djee passah hopa)]

itch a coceira [kossayra]

▸ I've got an itch on my left leg estou com uma coceira na perna esquerda [eeshto kong ooma kossayra na peh-na eeshkeh-da]

itinerary o itinerário [eetcheenerar-yoo]

▸ is it possible to modify the planned itinerary? dá para modificar o itinerário planejado? [da para modjeefeekar oo eetcheenerar-yoo planejadoo]

j

January janeiro [janayroo]

▸ January 4th quatro de janeiro [kwatroo djee janayroo]

Jet Ski® o Jet Ski® [jetchee eeshkee]

▸ I'd like to rent a Jet Ski® eu queria alugar um Jet Ski® [ew keree-a alooogar oom jetchee eeshkee]

job *(employment)* o trabalho [trabalyoo]

▸ I'm looking for a summer job in the area estou procurando um trabalho de verão na região [eeshto prokoorandoo oom trabalyoo djee verowng na hej-yowng]

joke a piada [pee-ada] ◆ brincar [breenkah]

▸ it's beyond a joke! isto já não tem graça [eeshtoo ja nowng teng grassa]

▸ I was just joking eu estava só brincando [ew eeshtava so breenkandoo]

journey a viagem [vee-ajeng]

▸ how long does the journey take? quanto tempo dura a viagem? [kwantoo tempoo doora a vee-ajeng]

juice *(from fruit)* o suco [sookoo]

▸ what types of juice do you have? que tipo de suco você tem? [ke tcheepoo djee sookoo vosse teng]

July julho [joolyoo]

▸ July 4th quatro de julho [kwatroo djee joolyoo]

June o junho [joonyoo]

▸ June 2nd dia dois de junho [djee-a doysh djee joonyoo]

just *(recently)* recém [hesseng]; *(at that moment)* justamente [jooshta-mentchee]; *(only, simply)* simplesmente [seempleesh-mentchee]

▸ he just left ele acabou de sair [elee akabo djee sa-eeh]
▸ I'll just have one só quero um [so keroo oom]

k

kayak o caiaque [kayakee]

▸ can we rent kayaks? dá para alugar caiaques? [da para aloogah kayakeesh]

keep *(retain)* ficar com [feekah kong]; *(promise)* manter [manteh]; *(appointment)* ir [eeh]

▸ I'm sorry, I won't be able to keep the appointment desculpe, não vou poder ir ao encontro [djeeshkoowpee nowng vo poder eer ow enkontroo]
▸ keep the change fique com o troco [feekee kong oo trokoo]

key *(for a door, a container)* a chave [shavee]; *(on a keyboard, phone)* a tecla [tekla]

▸ which is the key to the front door? qual é a chave da porta da frente? [kwal eh a shavee da poh-ta da frentchee]

kilometer o quilômetro [keelometroo]

▸ how much is it per kilometer? quanto faz por quilômetro? [kwantoo fash poh keelometroo]

kind *(nice)* gentil [jentcheew] ♦ *(sort, type)* o tipo [tcheepoo]

▸ that's very kind of you é muita gentileza sua [eh mweenta jentcheeleza soo-a]
▸ what's your favorite kind of music? qual é o seu tipo favorito de música? [kwal eh oo sew tcheepoo favoreetoo djee moozeeka]

kitchen a cozinha [kozeenya]

▸ is the kitchen shared? a cozinha é compartilhada? [a kozeenya eh kompah-tcheel-yada]

Kleenex® o lenço (de papel) [lensoo (djee papew)]

▸ do you have any Kleenex®? tem um lenço? [teng oom lensoo]

knife a faca [faka]

▸ could I have a knife? tem como conseguir uma faca? [teng komoo konsegeer ooma faka]

know conhecer [konyesseh]

▸ I don't know this town very well não conheço esta cidade muito bem [nowng konyessoo eshta seedadjee mweentoo beng]
▸ I know the basics but no more than that conheço o básico, mas não mais do que isso [konyessoo oo bazeekoo myj nowng mysh doo kee eessoo]

▸ do you know each other? vocês se conhecem? [vossesh see konyesseng]

knowledge o conhecimento [konyessee-mentoo]

▸ she has a good knowledge of French ela tem um bom conhecimento de francês [ella teng oom bong konyessee-mentoo djee fransesh]

▸ without my knowledge sem o meu conhecimento [seng oo mew konyessee-mentoo]

ladies' room o banheiro feminino [banyayroo femeeneenoo]

▸ where's the ladies' room? onde fica o banheiro feminino? [ondjee feeka oo banyayroo femeeneenoo]

lake o lago [lagoo]

▸ can you go swimming in the lake? dá para nadar no lago? [dá para nadah noo lagoo]

lamp a lâmpada [lampada]

▸ the lamp doesn't work a lâmpada não funciona [a lampada nowng foonss-yona]

land *(plane)* aterrissar [atehee-sah]

▸ what time is the plane scheduled to land? a que horas o avião deve aterrissar? [a kee oraz oo avee-owng devee atehee-sah]

landmark o ponto de referência [pontoo djee heferenss-ya]

▸ do you recognize any landmarks? reconhece algum ponto de referência? [hekon-yessee owgoom pontoo djee heferenss-ya]

lane *(on a highway)* a pista [peeshta]; *(for a bus)* o corredor [kohedoh]

▸ a four-lane highway uma auto-estrada de quatro pistas [ooma owto-eeshtrada djee kwatroo peeshtash]

laptop o laptop [laptop]

▸ my laptop's been stolen roubaram meu laptop [hobarowng mew laptop]

last último(ma) [oowtcheemoo(ma)] ♦ durar [doorah]

▸ when does the last bus go? quando sai o último ônibus? [kwandoo sy oo oowtcheemoo oneeboosh]

▸ when is the last subway train? a que horas sai o último trem do metrô? [a kee orash sy oo oowtcheemoo treng doo metro]

last name o sobrenome [sobreenomee]

▸ could I have your last name? você poderia me dizer seu sobrenome? [vosse poderee-a mee djeezeh sew sobreenomee]

late atrasado(da) [atrazadoo(da)] ♦ tarde [tah-djee]

▸ the plane is two hours late o avião está duas horas atrasado [oo avee-owng eeshta doo-az oraz atrazadoo]

‣ could you tell me if the 1:17 to Rio is running late? você poderia me informar se o vôo da uma e dezessete para o Rio está atrasado? [vosse poderee-a mee eenfohmah see oo vo-oo da ooma ee dezassetchee para oo hee-oo eeshta atrazadoo]

later mais tarde [mysh tah-djee]

‣ is there a later bus? tem um ônibus mais tarde? [teng oom oneeboosh maysh tahdjee]

‣ see you later! vejo você depois! [vejoo vosse depoysh], até depois! [a-te depoysh]

latest último(ma) [oowtcheemoo(ma)]

‣ what's the latest time we can check out? a que horas temos que sair do hotel? [a kee orash temoosh kee sa-eeh doo otew]

laugh a risada [heezada] ✦ rir [heeh]

‣ I just did it for a laugh só fiz para me divertir [so feesh para mee djeeveh-tcheeh]

Laundromat® a lavanderia [lavanderee-a]

‣ is there a Laundromat® nearby? tem uma lavanderia por aqui? [teng ooma lavanderee-a por akee]

laundry *(clothes)* as roupas [hopash]; *(business, room)* a lavanderia [lavanderee-a]

‣ where can we do our laundry? onde a gente pode lavar as roupas? [ondjee a jentchee podjee lavar ash hopash]

‣ where's the nearest laundry? onde fica a lavanderia mais próxima? [ondjee feeka a lavanderee-a mysh prosseema]

lawyer o advogado [advogadoo], a advogada [advogada]

‣ I'm a lawyer sou advogado/advogada [so advogadoo/advogada]

‣ I need a lawyer preciso de um advogado [presseezoo djee oom advogadoo]

leaflet o folheto [folyetoo]

‣ do you have any leaflets in English? tem alguns folhetos em inglês? [teng owgoonsh folyetoosh eng eenglesh]

learn aprender [aprendeh]

‣ I've just learned a few words from a book acabei de aprender algumas palavras num livro [akabay djee aprender owgoomash palavrash noom leevroo]

least menor [menoh] ✦ menos [menoosh] ✦ **at least** pelo menos [peloo menoosh]

‣ it's the least I can do é o mínimo que eu posso fazer [eh oo meeneemoo kee ew possoo fazeh]

‣ not in the least de forma alguma [djee foh-ma owgooma]

‣ to say the least para não dizer outra coisa [para nowng djeezer otra koyza]

‣ it's at least a three-hour drive é uma viagem de pelo menos três horas [eh ooma vee-ajeng djee peloo menoosh trez orash]

leave *(go away from)* partir [pah-tcheeh]; *(let stay, forget to take)* deixar [dayshah] ✦ *(go away)* ir embora [eer embora]

‣ can I leave my backpack at the reception desk? posso deixar minha mochila na recepção? [possoo dayshah meenya mosheela na hessep-sowng]

▶ can I leave the car at the airport? posso deixar o carro no aeroporto? [possoo dayshar oo kahoo noo a-eropoh-too]

▶ leave us alone! nos deixe em paz! [nosh dayshee eng paj]

▶ I've left something on the plane deixei alguma coisa no avião [dayshay owgooma koyza noo avee-owng]

▶ I'll be leaving at nine o'clock tomorrow morning saio amanhã às nove horas da manhã [sy-oo amanyang ash novee orash da manyang]

left *(not right)* esquerdo(da) [eeshkeh-doo(da)] ◆ a esquerda [eeshkeh-da]

▶ to be left ficar [feekah]

▶ are there any tickets left for...? ainda tem alguma entrada para...? [a-eenda teng owgooma entrada para]

▶ to the left (of) à esquerda (de) [a eeshkeh-da (djee)]

left-hand da esquerda [da eeshkeh-da]

▶ on your left-hand side do seu lado esquerdo [doo sew ladoo eeshkeh-doo]

leg a perna [peh-na]

▶ I have a pain in my left leg está me doendo a perna esquerda [eeshta mee dwendoo a peh-na eeshkeh-da]

▶ I can't move my leg não consigo mexer a perna [nowng konseegoo mesher a peh-na]

lemon o limão [leemowng]

▶ can I have some lemons? eu queria alguns limões, por favor [ew keree-a owgoonsh leemoyngsh poh favoh]

lend emprestar [empreshtah]

▶ could you lend us your car? você poderia nos emprestar o carro? [vosse poderee-a noz empreshtar oo kahoo]

lens a lente [lentchee]

▶ there's something on the lens tem alguma coisa na lente [teng owgooma koyza na lentchee]

▶ I have hard lenses uso lentes duras [oozoo lentcheesh doorash]

▶ I have soft lenses uso lentes gelatinosas [oozoo lentcheesh jelatcheenozash]

less menos [menoosh]

▶ less and less cada vez menos [kada vesh menoosh]

▶ a little less um pouco menos [oom pokoo menoosh]

lesson a aula [owla]

▶ how much do lessons cost? quanto custam as aulas? [kwantoo kooshtowng az owlash]

▶ can we take lessons? podemos ter aulas? [podemoosh ter owlash]

let off *(allow to disembark)* deixar [dayshah]

▶ could you let me off here, please? você poderia me deixar aqui? [vosse poderee-a mee dayshar akee]

letter a carta [kah-ta]

▶ I would like to send this letter to the States queria enviar esta carta para os Estados Unidos [keree-a envee-ar eshta kah-ta para ooz eeshtadooz ooneedoosh]

▶ I confirmed my reservation by letter confirmei a reserva por carta [konfeeh-may a hezeh-va poh kah-ta]

level *(amount)* o nível [neevev]; *(of a building)* o andar [andah]; *(of a ship)* o convés [konvesh]

▶ do you know if cabin 27 is on this level? você sabe se a cabine vinte e sete fica neste convés? [vosse sabee see a kabeenee veentchee ee setchee feeka nesh-tchee konvesh]

license a licença [leessensa]; *(for driving)* a carteira de motorista [kah-tayra djee motoreeshta]

▶ do you need a license to hunt here? precisa de licença para caçar aqui? [presseeza djee leessensa para kassar akee]

▶ I left my driver's license in my hotel room deixei minha carteira de motorista no quarto do hotel [dayshay meenya kah-tayra djee motoreeshta noo kwah-too doo otew]

license number o número da placa [noomeroo da plaka]

▶ I got the license number tenho o número da placa [tenyoo oo noomeroo da plaka]

license plate a placa [plaka]

▶ the license plate is broken a placa está quebrada [a plaka eeshta kebrada]

lifebelt a bóia salva-vidas [boya sowva veedash]

▶ throw me a lifebelt! me joga uma bóia salva-vidas! [mee joga ooma boya sowva veedash]

lifeboat o bote salva-vidas [botchee sowva-veedash]

▶ how many lifeboats are there? quantos botes salva-vidas tem? [kwantoosh botcheesh sowva-veedash teng]

lifejacket o colete salva-vidas [koletchee sowva-veedash]

▶ are there any lifejackets? tem algum colete salva-vidas? [teng owgoom koletchee sowva-veedash]

light *(brightness, in a lamp)* a luz [looj]; *(on a car)* o farol [farow]; *(regulating traffic)* o semáforo [semaforoo]; *(for a cigarette)* o fogo [fogoo]

▶ the light doesn't work a luz não funciona [a looj nowng foonss-yona]

▶ could you check the lights? você poderia verificar os faróis? [vosse poderee-a vereefeekar oosh faroysh]

▶ stop at the next light pare no próximo semáforo [paree noo prosseemoo semaforoo]

▶ do you have a light? tem fogo? [teng fogoo]

lighter o isqueiro [eeshkayroo]

▶ can I borrow your lighter? me empresta o teu isqueiro? [mee empreshta oo tew eeshkayroo]

likes

▶ I really love that painting **eu adoro esse quadro** [ew adoroo essee kwadroo]

▶ I like your brother **gosto do teu irmão** [goshtoo doo tew eeh-mowng]

▶ I've got a soft spot for her **tenho uma queda por ela** [tenyoo ooma keda por ella]

▶ I think she's very nice **acho ela muito legal** [ashoo ella mweentoo legow]

lighthouse o farol [farow]

▶ are there boat trips to the lighthouse? **tem passeios de barco para o farol?** [teng passayoosh djee bah-koo para oo farow]

like como [komoo] ♦ gostar [goshtah]

▶ it's quite like English **se parece bastante com inglês** [see paressee bashtantchee kong eenglesh]

▶ I like it **eu gosto disso** [ew goshtoo djeessoo]

▶ I don't like it **não gosto disso** [nowng goshtoo djeessoo]

▶ do you like it here? **gosta do lugar?** [goshta doo loogah]

▶ I like Chinese food very much **adoro comida chinesa** [adoroo komeeda sheeneza]

▶ do you like the movies? **gosta de cinema?** [goshta djee seenema]

▶ would you like a drink? – yes, I'd love one **quer um drinque? – sim, adoraria** [ker oom dreenkee seeng adoraree-a]

▶ I'd like to speak to the manager **gostaria de falar com o gerente** [goshtaree-a djee falah kong oo jerentchee]

lime a lima [leema]

▶ can I have some limes? **eu queria algumas limas, por favor** [ew keree-a owgoomash leemash poh favoh]

limit o limite [leemeetchee] ♦ limitar [leemeetah]

▶ is that area off limits? **é proibido entrar nessa área?** [eh pro-eebeedoo entrah nessa aree-a]

dislikes

▶ I hate football **detesto futebol** [deteshtoo footcheebow]

▶ I can't stand him **eu não o suporto** [ew nowng oo soopoh-too]

▶ I don't really like him/her **eu realmente não gosto dele/dela** [ew hee-owmentchee nowng goshtoo delee/della]

▶ I'm not really into walking **não gosto muito de caminhar** [nowng goshtoo mweentoo djee kameenyah]

line *(gen)* a linha [leenya]; *(of people waiting)* a fila [feela]
- the line was busy a linha estava ocupada [a leenya eeshtava okoopada]
- we had to stand in line for 15 minutes tivemos que ficar na fila por quinze minutos [tcheevemoosh ke feekah na feela poh keenzee meenootoosh]
- which line do I take to get to ...? que linha eu pego para ir para...? [ke leenya ew pegoo para eeh para]

lipstick o batom [batong]
- I need to buy some lipstick preciso comprar um batom [presseezoo komprar oom batong]

listen ouvir [oveeh], escutar [eeshkootah]
- listen, I really need to see a doctor escuta, eu realmente preciso ver um médico [eeshkoota ew hee-owmentchee presseezoo ver oom medjeekoo]
- listen to me carefully me escuta com atenção [mee eeshkoota kong atenssowng]

liter o litro [leetroo]
- a two-liter bottle of soda uma garrafa de dois litros de refrigerante [ooma gahafa djee doysh leetroosh djee hefree-jerantchee]

little pequeno(na) [pekenoo(na)] ✦ pouco [pokoo] ✦ **a little** um pouco [oom pokoo]
- it's for a little girl é para uma menininha [eh para ooma meneeneenya]
- as little as possible o mínimo possível [oo meeneemoo posseevew]
- I speak a little Portuguese falo um pouco de português [faloo oom pokoo djee poh-toogesh]
- we've only got a little money left sobrou só um pouco de dinheiro [sobro so oom pokoo djee djeenyayroo]
- a little bit um pouquinho [oom pokeenyoo]
- a little less um pouco menos [oom pokoo menoosh]
- a little more um pouco mais [oom pokoo mysh]

live morar [morah]
- do you live around here? você mora por aqui? [vosse mora por akee]
- I live in Porto Alegre moro em Porto Alegre [moroo eng poh-too alegree]

live music a música ao vivo [moozeeka ow veevoo]
- I'd like to go to a bar with live music eu queria ir a um bar que tenha música ao vivo [ew keree-a eer a oom bar kee tenya moozeeka ow veevoo]

living room a sala de estar [sala djee eeshtah]
- I can sleep in the living room posso dormir na sala de estar [possoo doh-meeh na sala djee eeshtah]

loaf (of bread) o pão [powng]
- I'd like one of those large loaves queria um desses pães grandes [keree-a oom desseesh pyngsh grandjeesh]

local local [lokow]
- what's the local specialty? qual é a especialidade local? [kwal eh a eeshpess-yaleedadjee lokow]

lock a fechadura [feshadoora] ◆ fechar (com chave) [feshah (kong shavee)]
> the lock's broken a fechadura está quebrada [a feshadoora eeshta kebrada]
> I locked the door fechei a porta [feshay a poh-ta]

lock out
> to lock oneself out chavear-se pelo lado de fora [shavee-ah-see peloo ladoo djee fora]
> I've locked myself out fechei a porta e deixei a chave dentro de casa [feshay a poh-ta ee dayshay a shavee dentroo djee kaza]

long *(in space)* comprido(da) [kompreedoo(da)]; *(in time)* longo(ga) [longoo(ga)] ◆ ao longo [ow longoo]
> it's 2 meters long mede dois metros de comprimento [medjee doysh metroosh djee kompreementoo]
> I waited for a long time esperei muito tempo [eeshperay mweentoo tempoo]
> how long? quanto? [kwantoo]
> how long will it take? quanto tempo vai levar? [kwantoo tempoo vy levah]
> we're not sure how long we're going to stay não temos certeza de quanto tempo vamos ficar [nowng temoosh seh-teza djee kwantoo tempoo vamoosh feekah]

look *(with eyes)* a olhada [olyada]; *(appearance)* o aspecto [ashpektoo] ◆ *(with eyes)* olhar [olyah]; *(seem)* parecer [paresseh]
> could you have a look at my car? poderia dar uma olhada no meu carro? [poderee-a dar ooma olyada noo mew kahoo]
> no, thanks, I'm just looking não, obrigado, estou só olhando [nowng obreegadoo eeshto so olyandoo]
> what does she look like? como ela é? [komoo ella eh]
> you look like your brother você parece o seu irmão [vosse paressee oo sew eeh-mowng]
> it looks like it's going to rain parece que vai chover [paressee kee vy shoveh]

look after cuidar [kweedah]
> can someone look after the children for us? alguém poderia cuidar das crianças para nós? [owgeng poderee-a kweedah dash kree-ansah para nosh]
> can you look after my things for a minute? poderia cuidar das minhas coisas um minuto? [poderee-a kweedah dash meenyash koyzash oom meenootoo]

look for procurar [prokoorah]
> I'm looking for a good restaurant that serves regional cuisine estou procurando um bom restaurante que sirva a culinária local [eeshto prokoorandoo oom bong heshtow-rantchee ke seeh-va a kooleenarya lokow]

lose *(be unable to find)* perder [peh-deh]
> I've lost the key to my room perdi a chave do quarto [peh-djee a shavee doo kwah-too]
> I've lost my way me perdi [mee peh-djee]

lost perdido(da) [peh-djeedoo(da)]
> who do you have to see about lost luggage? onde a gente tem que ir para

informar perda de bagagem? [ondjee a jentchee teng kee eeh para eenfoh-mah peh-da djee bagajeng]

▸ could you help me? I seem to be lost você poderia me ajudar? acho que estou perdido [vosse poderee-a mee ajoodah ashoo kee eeshto peh-djeedoo]

▸ to get lost perder-se [peh-deh-see]

▸ get lost! desaparece! [djeeza-paressee]

lost-and-found os achados e perdidos [ashadooz ee peh-djeedoosh]

▸ where's the lost-and-found? onde ficam os achados e perdidos? [ondjee feekowng ooz ashadooz ee peh-djeedoosh]

lot ◆ a lot muito [mweentoo]

▸ a lot of ... muito... [mweentoo]

▸ are there a lot of things to see around here? tem muita coisa para ver por aqui? [teng mweenta koyza para veh por akee]

▸ will there be a lot of other people there? será que vai ter muita gente lá? [sera kee vy teh mweenta jentchee la]

▸ thanks a lot muito obrigado [mweentoo obreegadoo]

loud (noise, voice) forte [foh-tchee]; (music) alto(ta) [owtoo(ta)]

▸ the television is too loud a televisão está muito alta [a televeezowng eeshta mweentoo owta]

loudly (speak) alto [owtoo]

▸ can you speak a little more loudly? você pode falar um pouco mais alto? [vosse podjee falar oom pokoo myz owtoo]

love amar [amah]

▸ I love you eu te amo [ew tchee amoo]

▸ I love the movies eu amo cinema [ew amoo seenema]

▸ I love cooking eu adoro cozinhar [ew adoroo kozeenyah]

lovely maravilhoso(sa) [maraveel-yozoo(za)]

▸ what a lovely room! que quarto adorável! [ke kwah-too adoravew]

▸ it's lovely today hoje está fazendo um dia maravilhoso [ojee eeshta fazendo oom djee-a maravel-yozoo]

low baixo(xa) [by-shoo(sha)]

▸ temperatures are in the low twenties a temperatura passa um pouco dos vinte graus [a temperatoora passa oom pokoo doosh veentchee growsh]

low beam a luz baixa [loosh by-sha]

▸ keep your lights on low beam mantenha as luzes baixas [mantenya ash loozeesh by-shash]

lower baixar [by-shah] ◆ inferior [eenferee-oh]

▸ is it OK if I lower the blind a little? te importa se eu baixar um pouco a persiana? [tchee eempoh-ta see ew by-shar oom pokoo a peh-see-ana]

▸ how do we get to the lower level? como a gente vai até o andar de baixo? [komoo a jentchee vy a-te oo andah djee by-shoo]

lunch

Lunch is the main meal of the day for Brazilians. It takes place between midday and 1 p.m. and lasts from 30 minutes to an hour. Brazilians do not usually have a *sesta* (afternoon nap), but some people might have a rest for 15 minutes or so. The most popular everyday dish is *feijão com arroz* (rice with black beans). On Sundays, lunch is later and traditionally takes the form of a *churrasco* (barbecue), at which family and friends all gather.

low-fat *(yogurt)* de baixa caloria [djee by-sha kaloree-a]
▸ do you have any low-fat yogurt? tem algum iogurte de baixa caloria? [teng owgoom yoguh-tchee djee by-sha kaloree-a]

low season baixa estação [by-sha eeshtassowng]
▸ what are prices like in the low season? como são os preços na baixa estação? [komoo sowng oosh pressoosh na by-sha eeshtassowng]

low tide a maré baixa [ma-re by-sha]
▸ what time is low tide today? a que hora a maré baixa hoje? [a kee ora a ma-re by-sha ojee]

luck a sorte [soh-tchee]
▸ good luck! boa sorte! [boa soh-tchee]

luggage a bagagem [bagajeng]
▸ my luggage hasn't arrived a minha bagagem não chegou [a meenya bagajeng nowng shego]
▸ I'd like to report the loss of my luggage eu queria informar a perda da minha bagagem [ew keree-a eenfoh-mar a peh-da da meenya bagajeng]

luggage cart o carrinho para bagagem [kaheenyoo para bagajeng]
▸ I'm looking for a luggage cart estou procurando um carrinho para bagagem [eeshto prokoorandoo oom kaheenyoo para bagajeng]

lunch o almoço [owmossoo]
▸ to have lunch almoçar [owmossah]
▸ what time is lunch served? a que horas servem o almoço? [a kee orash seh-veng oo owmossoo]

m

machine-washable lavável à máquina [lavavew a makeena]
  ▸ is it machine-washable? dá para lavar na máquina? [da para lavah na makeena]

maid a camareira [kamarayra]
  ▸ what time does the maid come? a que horas passa a camareira? [a kee orash passa a kamarayra]

maid service o serviço de quarto [seh-veessoo djee kwah-too]
  ▸ is there maid service? tem serviço de quarto? [teng seh-veessoo djee kwah-too]

mailbox a caixa de correio [ky-sha djee kohayoo]
  ▸ where's the nearest mailbox? onde fica a caixa de correio mais próxima? [ondjee feeka a ky-sha djee kohayoo mysh prosseema]

main course o prato principal [pratoo preenseepow]
  ▸ what are you having for your main course? o que você vai pedir como prato principal? [oo ke vosse vy pedjeeh komoo pratoo preenseepow]

mainline da linha principal [da leenya peenseepow]
  ▸ where are the mainline trains? onde estão os trens da linha principal? [ondjee eeshtowng oosh trensh da leenya preenseepow]

make fazer [fazeh]
  ▸ how is this dish made? como se faz esse prato? [komoo see faz essee pratoo]
  ▸ I hope to make new friends here espero fazer novos amigos aqui [eehsperoo fazeh novooz ameegooz akee]

make up *(compensate for)* recuperar [hekooperah]; *(invent)* inventar [eenventah]
  ▸ will we be able to make up the time we've lost? será que vamos conseguir recuperar o tempo perdido? [sera ke vamoosh konsegeeh hekooperar oo tempoo pehdjeedoo]

man o homem [omeng]
  ▸ that man is bothering me esse homem está me irritando [essee omeng eeshta mee eeheetandoo]

man-made artificial [ah-tcheefeess-yow]
  ▸ it's man-made é artificial [eh ah-tcheefeess-yow]

many muito(ta) [mweentoo(ta)]
  ▸ there are many good restaurants here há muitos bons restaurantes aqui [a mweentoosh bonsh heshtow-rantcheez akee]
  ▸ how many? quantos? [kwantoosh]
  ▸ how many days will you be staying? quantos dias vocês vão ficar? [kwantoosh djee-ash vossesh vowng feekah]

meat

Meat figures prominently on Brazilian menus, both in *churrascarias* (restaurants selling barbecued meat) and in restaurants in general. Among the treats on offer are *picanha*, *matambre* and *contrafilé* (different cuts of beef), *presunto* (ham), *salsichão* (salami), and *coração de galinha* (chicken heart), served with *farofa* (fried cassava flour with flavoring).

---

map o mapa [mapa]
- where can I buy a map of the area? onde eu posso comprar um mapa da região? [ondjee ew possoo komprar oom mapa da hej-yowng]
- can you show me where we are on the map? você pode me mostrar onde nós estamos no mapa? [vosse podjee mee moshtrah ondjee noz eeshtamoosh noo mapa]
- can I have a map of the subway? eu gostaria de um mapa do metrô, por favor [ew goshtaree-a djee oom mapa doo metro poh favoh]

March o março [mah-soo]
- March 1st primeiro de março [preemayroo djee mah-soo]

market a feira [fayra]
- is there a market in the square every day? tem feira na praça todos os dias? [teng fayra na prassa todooz oosh djee-ash]

married casado(da) [kazadoo(da)]
- are you married? você é casado? [vosse eh kazadoo]

mass *(religion)* a missa [meessa]
- what time is mass? a que horas é a missa? [a kee oraz eh a meessa]

match *(for lighting)* o fósforo [foshforoo]
- do you have any matches? tem fósforo? [teng foshforoo]

matter importar [eempoh-tah]
- it doesn't matter não importa [nowng eempoh-ta]

mattress o colchão [kowshowng]
- the mattresses are saggy os colchões estão afundados [oosh kowshoyngz eeshtowng afoondadoosh]

May maio [my-oo]
- May 9th nove de maio [novee djee my-oo]

maybe talvez [towvesh]
- maybe the weather will be better tomorrow talvez o tempo melhore amanhã [towvez oo tempoo melyoree amanyang]

meal a refeição [hefay-sowng]
- are meals included? estão incluídas as refeições? [eeshtowng eenklweedaz ash hefay-soyngsh]

mean *(signify)* significar [seegneefeekah]; *(matter)* importar [eempoh-tah]; *(intend)* dizer a sério [djeezer a seryoo]

▶ what does that word mean? o que significa essa palavra? [oo ke seegneefeeka essa palavra]

▶ I mean it é sério [eh seryoo]

▶ I didn't mean it não disse isso a sério [nowng djeessee eessoo a seryoo]

meat a carne [kah-nee]

▶ I don't eat meat não como carne [nowng komoo kah-nee]

mechanic o mecânico [mekaneekoo]

▶ what did the mechanic say was wrong with the car? o que o mecânico disse que tinha o carro? [o kee oo mekaneekoo djeessee kee tcheenya oo kahoo]

medication a medicação [medjeekassowng]

▶ I'm not taking any other medication at the moment não estou tomando nenhuma outra medicação no momento [nowng eeshto tomandoo nen-yooma otra medjeekassowng noo momentoo]

medicine o remédio [hemed-yoo]

▶ how many times a day do I have to take the medicine? quantas vezes por dia eu tenho que tomar o remédio? [kwantash vezeesh poh djee-a ew tenyoo kee tomar oo hemed-yoo]

medium *(size)* médio(dia) [medyoo(dya)]; *(steak)* mal passado(da) [mow passadoo (da)] ◆ *(in size)* o tamanho médio [tamanyoo medyoo]

▶ I'd like my steak medium, please eu queria o meu filé mal passado, por favor [ew keree-a oo mew fee-le mow passadoo poh favoh]

▶ do you have this shirt in a medium? tem essa camisa em tamanho médio? [teng essa kameeza eng tamanyoo medyoo]

meet *(by chance, arrangement)* encontrar-se com [enkontrah-see kong]; *(make the acquaintance of)* conhecer [konyesseh]

▶ meet you at 9 o'clock in front of the town hall me encontre às nove na frente da prefeitura [mee encontree ash novee na frentchee da prefaytoora]

▶ I have to meet my friend at 9 o'clock tenho que encontrar meu amigo às nove [tenyoo kee enkontrah mew ameegoo ash novee]

▶ pleased to meet you prazer em conhecê-lo [prazer eng konyesse-loo]

▶ goodbye! it was nice meeting you tchau! prazer em conhecê-lo [tchow prazer eng konyesse-loo]

▶ Carlos, I'd like you to meet Mr. Veloso Carlos, quero que conheça o Sr. Veloso [kah-loosh keroo kee konyessa oo senyoh velozoo]

▶ where shall we meet? onde nos encontramos? [ondjee noz enkontramoosh]

▶ what time are we meeting tomorrow? a que horas nos encontramos amanhã? [a kee orash noz enkontramooz amanyang]

member *(of a club)* o sócio [sossyoo], a sócia [sossya]

▶ do you have to be a member? tem que ser sócio? [teng kee seh sossyoo]

men's room o banheiro masculino [banyayroo mashkooleenoo]
▶ where's the men's room? onde fica o banheiro masculino? [ondjee feeka oo banyayroo mashkooleenoo]

menu o menu [menoo]
▶ can we see the menu? podemos ver o menu? [podemoosh ver oo menoo]
▶ do you have a menu in English? tem um menu em inglês? [teng oom menoo eng eenglesh]
▶ do you have a children's menu? tem um menu para crianças? [teng oom menoo para kree-ansash]

message a mensagem [mensajeng]
▶ can you take/can I leave a message? posso deixar recado? [possoo dayshah hekadoo]
▶ did you get my message? você recebeu meu recado? [vosse hessebew mew hekadoo]

meter *(measurement)* o metro [metroo]; *(device)* o medidor [medjeedoh]
▶ it's about five meters long tem cerca de cinco metros de comprimento [teng seh-ka djee seenkoo metroosh djee kompreementoo]

midday o meio-dia [mayoo-djee-a]
▶ we have to be there by midday temos que estar lá ao meio-dia [temoosh kee eeshtah la ow mayoo-djee-a]

midnight a meia-noite [maya-noytchee]
▶ it's midnight é meia-noite [eh maya-noytchee]

mileage *(distance)* a quilometragem [keelometrajeng]
▶ is there unlimited mileage? a quilometragem é livre? [a keelometrajeng eh leevree]

milk o leite [laytchee]
▶ a liter of milk um litro de leite [oom leetroo djee laytchee]
▶ tea with milk chá com leite [sha kong laytchee]

milk chocolate o chocolate com leite [shokolatchee kong laytchee]
▶ I prefer milk chocolate prefiro chocolate com leite [prefeeroo shokolatchee kong laytchee]

mind *(object)* importar-se [eempoh-tah-see]
▶ I don't mind não me importo [nowng mee eempoh-too]
▶ do you mind if I smoke? você se importa se eu fumar? [vosse see eempoh-ta see ew foomah]
▶ do you mind if I open the window? você se importa se eu abrir a janela? [vosse see eempoh-ta see ew abreer a janela]
▶ never mind deixa para lá [daysha para la]

mineral water a água mineral [agwa meenerow]
▶ could I have a bottle of mineral water, please? uma garrafa de água mineral, por favor [ooma gahafa djee agwa meenerow poh favoh]

minus menos [menoosh]
- it's minus two degrees outside! está fazendo menos dois graus lá fora! [eeshta fazendoo menoosh doysh growsh la fora]

minute o minuto [meenootoo]
- we'll go in a minute vamos num minuto [vamoosh noom meenootoo]

mirror o espelho [eeshpelyoo]
- the mirror's cracked o espelho está rachado [oo eeshpelyoo eeshta hashadoo]

miss *(be too late for)* perder [peh-deh]; *(regret the absence of)* sentir saudades de [sentcheeh sowdadjeesh djee]
- I've missed my connection perdi minha conexão [peh-djee meenya koneksowng]
- we're going to miss the bus vamos perder o ônibus [vamoosh peh-deh oo oneeboosh]
- I missed you senti saudades suas [sentchee sowdadjeesh soo-ash]

missing perdido(da) [peh-djeedoo(da)]
- one of my suitcases is missing não sei onde foi parar uma das minhas malas [nowng say ondjee foy parar ooma dash meenyash malash]

mistake o erro [ehoo]
- I think there's a mistake with the bill acho que tem algum erro com a conta [ashoo kee teng owgoom ehoo kong a konta]
- you've made a mistake with my change você me deu o troco errado [vosse mee dew oo trokoo ehadoo]

moment o momento [momentoo]
- for the moment, we prefer staying in Salvador no momento preferimos ficar em Salvador [noo momentoo prefereemoosh feekar eng sow-vadoh]

Monday a segunda-feira [segoonda-fayra], a segunda [segoonda]
- we're arriving/leaving on Monday estamos chegando/saindo na segunda [eeshtamoosh shegandoo/sa-eendoo na segoonda]

money o dinheiro [djeenyayroo]
- I don't have much money não tenho muito dinheiro [nowng tenyoo mweentoo djeenyayroo]
- where can I change money? onde eu posso trocar dinheiro? [ondjee ew possoo trokah djeenyayroo]
- I want my money back quero meu dinheiro de volta [keroo mew djeenyayroo djee vowta]

money order a ordem de pagamento [oh-deng djee pagamentoo]
- I'm waiting for a money order estou esperando a ordem de pagamento [eeshto eeshperandoo a oh-deng djee pagamentoo]

month o mês [mesh]
- I'm leaving in a month vou embora dentro de um mês [vo embora dentroo djee oom mesh]

monument o monumento [monoomentoo]
- what does this monument commemorate? o que este monumento está comemorando? [oo ke esh-tchee monoomentoo eeshta komemorandoo]

more mais [mysh]
- can we have some more bread? poderia trazer mais pão? [poderee-a trazeh mysh powng]
- a little more um pouco mais [oom pokoo mysh]
- could I have a little more wine? poderia trazer um pouco mais de vinho? [poderee-a trazer oom pokoo mysh djee veenyoo]
- I don't want any more, thank you não quero mais, obrigado [nowng keroo mysh obreegadoo]
- I don't want to spend any more não quero gastar mais [nowng keroo gashtah mysh]

morning a manhã [manyang]
- the museum is open in the morning o museu abre de manhã [oo moozew abree djee manyang]

morning-after pill a pílula do dia seguinte [peeloola doo djee-a segeentchee]
- I need the morning-after pill preciso da pílula do dia seguinte [presseezoo da peeloola doo djee-a segeentchee]

mosque a mesquita [meshkeeta]
- where's the nearest mosque? onde fica a mesquita mais próxima? [ondjee feeka a meshkeeta mysh prosseema]

most a maioria de [a myoree-a djee] ◆ a maioria [myoree-a] ◆ (to the greatest extent) o mais [oo mysh], a mais [a mysh]; (very) muito [mweentoo]
- are you here most days? você fica aqui boa parte do tempo? [vosse feeka akee boa pah-tchee doo tempoo]
- that's the most I can offer isso é o máximo que eu posso oferecer [eessoo eh oo masseemoo kee ew possoo oferesseh]

mother a mãe [myng]
- this is my mother esta é a minha mãe [eshta eh a meenya myng]

motorboat a lancha com motor [lansha kong motoh]
- can we rent a motorboat? podemos alugar uma lancha com motor? [podemooz aloogar ooma lansha kong motoh]

motorcycle a moto [motoo]
- I'd like to rent a motorcycle eu queria alugar uma moto [ew keree-a aloogar ooma motoo]

mountain a montanha [montanya]
- in the mountains nas montanhas [nash montanyash]

mountain hut o chalé nas montanhas [sha-le nash montanyash]
- we slept in a mountain hut dormimos num chalé nas montanhas [dohmeemoosh noom sha-le nash montanyash]

mouth a boca [boka]
- I've got a strange taste in my mouth estou com um gosto estranho na boca [eeshto kong oom goshtoo eeshtranyoo na boka]

move *(movement)* o movimento [moveementoo]; *(step, measure)* a medida [medjeeda] ◆ mover(-se) [moveh(-see)], movimentar(-se) [movementah(-see)]
- I can't move my leg não consigo mexer a perna [nowng konseegoo mesher a pehna]
- don't move him não mexe nele [nowng meshee nelee]

movie o filme [feewmee]
- have you seen ...'s latest movie? você viu o último filme do ...? [vosse veew oo oowtcheemoo feewmee doo]
- it's a subtitled movie é um filme com legenda [eh oom feewmee kong lejenda]

movie theater o cinema [seenema]
- where is there a movie theater? onde tem um cinema? [ondjee teng oom seenema]
- what's on at the movie theater? o que está passando no cinema? [oo kee eeshta passandoo noo seenema]

much muito(ta) [mweentoo(ta)]
- I don't have much money não tenho muito dinheiro [nowng tenyoo mweentoo djeenyayroo]
- how much is it? quanto custa? [kwantoo kooshta]
- how much is it for one night? quanto custa uma noite? [kwantoo kooshta ooma noytchee]
- how much is it per day and per person? quanto custa por dia e por pessoa? [kwantoo kooshta poh djee-a ee poh pesso-a]
- how much does it cost per hour? quanto custa por hora? [kwantoo kooshta por ora]
- how much is a ticket to Curitiba? quanto custa uma passagem para Curitiba? [kwantoo kooshta ooma passajeng para kooreetcheeba]

museum o museu [moozew]
- what time does the museum open? a que horas abre o museu? [a kee oraz abree oo moozew]

music a música [moozeeka]
- what kind of music do they play in that club? que tipo de música eles tocam naquele bar? [ke tcheepoo djee moozeeka eleesh tokowng nakelee bah]

must dever [deveh]
- that must cost a lot isso deve custar um monte [eesoo devee kooshtar oom montchee]

mustard a mostarda [moshtah-da]
- is it strong mustard? essa mostarda é forte? [essa moshtah-da eh foh-tchee]

n

nail *(on a finger, a toe)* a unha [oonee]
- I need to cut my nails preciso cortar as unhas [presseezoo koh-tah az oonyash]

nail polish o esmalte (de unhas) [eejmowtchee (djee oonyash)]
- I'd like to find nail polish in a dark shade of red tenho que encontrar um esmalte de uma cor vermelho-escura [tenyoo kee enkontrar oom eejmowtchee djee ooma koh veh-melyoo-eeshkoora]

name o nome [nomee]
- what is your name? qual é o seu nome? [kwal eh oo sew nomee]
- my name is Patrick meu nome é Patrick [mew nomee eh Patrick]
- hello, my name's John oi, meu nome é John [oy mew nomee eh John]
- I have a reservation in the name of Jackson tenho uma reserva no nome de Jackson [tenyoo ooma hesseh-va noo nomee djee Jackson]

napkin o guardanapo [gwah-danapoo]
- could I have a clean napkin, please? poderia trazer um guardanapo limpo, por favor? [poderee-a trazer oom gwah-danapoo leempoo poh favoh]

national holiday o feriado nacional [feree-adoo nass-yonow]
- tomorrow is a national holiday amanhã é feriado nacional [amanyang eh feree-adoo nass-yonow]

nationality a nacionalidade [nass-yonalee-dadjee]
- what nationality are you? de que nacionalidade você é? [djee ke nass-yonalee-dadjee vosse eh]

nature a natureza [natooreza]
- I like to take long walks outdoors and enjoy nature eu quero caminhar ao ar livre e desfrutar a natureza [ew keroo kameenyar ow ah leevree ee djeeshfrootar a natooreza]

nausea a náusea [nowzee-a]
- I've had nausea all day tive náusea o dia todo [tcheevee nowzee-a oo djee-a todoo]

near próximo(ma) [prosseemoo(ma)] ◆ perto [peh-too] ◆ perto de [peh-too djee]
- where's the nearest subway station? qual é a estação de metrô mais perto? [kwal eh a eeshtassowng djee metro mysh peh-too]
- it's near the station é perto da estação [eh peh-too da eeshtassowng]
- very near ... muito perto de... [mweentoo peh-too djee]

nearby perto [peh-too]
- is there a supermarket nearby? tem um supermercado perto? [teng oom soopeh-meh-kadoo peh-too]

need a necessidade [nessessee-dadjee] ◆ precisar [presseezah]
- I need something for a cough preciso de alguma coisa para tosse [presseezoo djee owgooma koyza para tossee]
- I need to be at the airport by six (o'clock) preciso estar no aeroporto às seis (horas) [presseezoo eeshtah noo a-eropoh-too ash saysh (orash)]
- we need to go temos que ir [temoosh kee eeh]

neither nenhum(ma) [nenyoom(ma)] ◆ também não [tambeng nowng] ◆ nem [neng]
- neither of us nenhum de nós [nenyoom djee nosh]
- me neither nem eu [neng ew]

neutral o ponto morto [pontoo moh-too]
- make sure the car's in neutral certifique-se de que o carro está em ponto morto [seh-tcheefeekee-see djee kee oo kahoo eeshta eng pontoo moh-too]

never nunca [noonka]
- I've never been to Fortaleza before nunca tinha ido para Fortaleza [noonka tcheenya eedoo para foh-taleza]

new novo(va) [novoo(va)]
- could we have a new tablecloth, please? poderiam colocar uma toalha nova, por favor? [poderee-owng kolokar ooma twalya nova poh favoh]

news as notícias [noteess-yash]
- a piece of news uma notícia [ooma noteess-ya]
- that's great news! que ótima notícia! [ke otcheema noteess-ya]
- I heard it on the news ouvi nas notícias [ovee nash noteess-yash]

newspaper o jornal [joh-now]
- do you have any English-language newspapers? tem algum jornal em inglês? [teng owgoom joh-now eng eenglesh]

New Year o Ano Novo [anoo novoo]
- Happy New Year! feliz Ano Novo! [feleez anoo novoo]

New Year's Day o Primeiro do Ano [preemayroo doo anoo]
- are stores open on New Year's Day? as lojas abrem em Primeiro do Ano? [ash lojaz abreng eng preemayroo doo anoo]

next próximo(ma) [prosseemoo(ma)]
- when is the next guided tour? quando é a próxima visita guiada? [kwandoo eh a prosseema veezeeta ghee-ada]
- when is the next bus to Curitiba? quando é o próximo ônibus para Curitiba? [kwandoo eh oo prosseemoo oneeboosh para kooreetcheeba]
- what time is the next flight to Dallas? a que horas sai o próximo vôo para Dallas? [a kee orash sy oo prosseemoo vo-oo para Dallas]
- can we park next to the tent? podemos estacionar do lado da barraca? [podemooz eeshtass-yoonah doo lado da bahaka]

nice (vacation, food) bom(boa) [bong(boa)]; (kind) agradável [argradavew]; (likable) simpático(ca) [seempatcheekoo(ka)]

▸ have a nice holiday! tenha boas férias! [tenya boash feree-ash]

▸ we found a really nice little hotel achamos um hotelzinho muito agradável [ashamooz oom otewzeenyoo mweentoo agradavew]

▸ goodbye! it was nice meeting you até logo! foi um prazer conhecê-lo [a-te logoo foy oom prazeh konyesse-loo]

night a noite [noytchee]

▸ how much is it per night? quanto custa por noite? [kwantoo kooshta poh noytchee]

▸ I'd like to stay an extra night eu gostaria de ficar mais uma noite [ew goshtaree-a djee feekah myz ooma noytchee]

nightclub a casa noturna [kaza notooh-na]

▸ are there any good nightclubs in this town? tem alguma casa noturna boa nesta cidade? [teng owgooma kaza notooh-na boa neshta seedadjee]

nine nove [novee]

▸ there are nine of us somos nove [somoosh novee]

▸ we have a reservation for nine (o'clock) temos uma reserva para as nove (horas) [temooz ooma hezeh-va para ash novee (orash)]

no não [nowng]

▸ no thanks! não, obrigado [nowng obreegadoo]

▸ a cup of tea with no milk or sugar, please uma xícara de chá sem leite nem açúcar, por favor [ooma sheekara djee sha seng laytchee neng assookah poh favoh]

nobody ninguém [neengeng]

▸ there's nobody at the reception desk não tem ninguém na recepção [nowng teng neengeng na hessepsowng]

noise o barulho [baroolyoo]

▸ to make a noise fazer barulho [fazeh baroolyoo]

▸ I heard a funny noise ouvi um barulho engraçado [ovee oom baroolyoo engrassadoo]

noisy barulhento(ta) [barool-yentoo]

▸ I'd like another room: mine is too noisy eu queria outro quarto, o meu é muito barulhento [ew keree-a otroo kwah-too oo mew eh mweentoo barool-yentoo]

nonsmoker o(a) não-fumante [nowng-foomantchee]

▸ we're nonsmokers não fumamos [nowng foomamoosh]

nonsmoking para não-fumantes [para nowng-foomantcheesh]

▸ is this restaurant nonsmoking? esse restaurante é para não-fumantes? [essee heshtow-rantshee eh para nowng-foomantcheesh]

nonsmoking compartment/section a ala dos não-fumantes [ala doosh nowng-foomantcheesh]

▸ I'd like a seat in a nonsmoking compartment/section eu queria um lugar na ala dos não-fumantes [ew keree-a oom loogah na ala doosh nowng-foomantcheesh]

numbers

In numbers Brazilians use a comma where we use a decimal point, and vice-versa. So, *123,25* is 123.25, and *25.260,12* is 25,260.12. Sometimes, people say *meia* instead of *seis* for the number 6, especially when saying a telephone number.

nonstop direto(ta) [djeeretoo(ta)] ◆ sem parar [seng parah]
▸ I'd like a nonstop flight from Rio to Chicago eu queria um vôo direto do Rio para Chicago [ew keree-a oom vo-oo djeeretoo doo hee-oo para Chicago]

noon o meio-dia [mayoo-djee-a]
▸ we leave at noon nós vamos ao meio-dia [nosh vamooz ow mayoo-djee-a]

no one ninguém [neengeng]
▸ there's no one there não tem ninguém aqui [nowng teng neengeng akee]

normal normal [noh-mow]
▸ is it normal for it to rain as much as this? é normal chover tanto assim? [eh noh-mow shoveh tantoo asseeng]

not não [nowng]
▸ I don't like spinach não gosto de espinafre [nowng goshtoo djee eeshpeenafree]
▸ I don't think so acho que não [ashoo kee nowng]
▸ not at all de forma alguma [djee foh-ma owgooma]

note o bilhete [beelyetchee]
▸ could I leave a note for him? eu poderia deixar um bilhete para ele? [ew poderee-a dayshar oom beelyetchee para elee]

nothing nada [nada]
▸ there's nothing to do here in the evening não tem nada para fazer aqui de noite [nowng teng nada para fazer akee djee noytchee]
▸ there's nothing I can do about it não tem nada que eu possa fazer [nowng teng nada kee ew possa fazeh]

November novembro [novembroo]
▸ November 7th sete de novembro [setchee djee novembroo]

now agora [agora]
▸ what should we do now? o que devemos fazer agora? [oo ke devemoosh fazer agora]

number o número [noomeroo]
▸ my name is... and my number is... meu nome é... e meu número é... [mew nomee eh ee mew noomeroo eh]

occupied *(bathroom)* ocupado(da) [okoopadoo(da)]
▸ the restroom's occupied o banheiro está ocupado [oo banyayroo eeshta okoopadoo]

ocean o oceano [oss-yanoo]
▸ we'd like to see the ocean while we're here a gente queria ver o oceano enquanto estamos aqui [a jentchee keree-a ver oo oss-yanoo enkwantoo eeshtamooz akee]

o'clock
▸ it's eight o'clock são oito horas [sowng oytoo orash]

October outubro [otoobroo]
▸ October 12th doze de outubro [dozee djee otoobroo]

of de [djee]
▸ one of us um de nós [oom djee nosh]

off
▸ an island off the coast of Brazil uma ilha perto da costa do Brasil [ooma eelya peh-too da koshta doo brazeew]
▸ this sweater is 50 percent off! este casaco está com cinqüenta por cento de desconto! [esh-tchee kazakoo eeshta kong seenkwenta poh sentoo djee djeeshkontoo]

offer oferecer [oferesseh]
▸ can I offer you a cigarette? posso lhe oferecer um cigarro? [possool-yee oferesseh oom seegahoo]

office o escritório [eeshkree-toryoo]
▸ where is the hotel office? onde fica o escritório do hotel? [ondjee feeka oo eeshkree-toryoo doo otew]

often com freqüência [kong frekwenss-ya]
▸ how often does the ferry sail? com que freqüência a balsa sai? [kong ke frekwenss-ya a bowsa sy]

oil o óleo [olee-oo]
▸ could you check the oil, please? você poderia verificar o óleo, por favor? [vosse poderee-a vereefeekar oo olee-oo poh favoh]

OK bem [beng] ◆ certo [seh-too]
▸ that's OK está bem [eeshta beng]
▸ do you think it's still OK? você acha que ainda está bem? [vosse asha kee a-eenda eeshta beng]

old velho(lha) [velyoo(ya)]
- how old are you? quantos anos você tem? [kwantooz anoosh vosse teng]
- I'm 18 years old tenho dezoito anos [tenyoo dezoytoo anoosh]
- have you visited the old town? você visitou a cidade antiga? [vosse veezeeto a seedadjee antcheega]

on ligado(da) [leegadoo(da)]
- how long is it on for? quanto tempo vai ficar? [kwantoo tempoo vy feekah]

once *(on one occasion)* uma vez [ooma vesh]; *(previously)* antes [antcheesh]
- I've been here once before eu já estive aqui uma vez [ew ja eesh-tcheevee akee ooma vesh]
- please do it at once por favor, faz isso de uma vez [poh favoh faz eessoo djee ooma vesh]

one um [oom]
- a table for one, please uma mesa para um, por favor [ooma meza para oom poh favoh]

one-way (ticket) a passagem de ida [passajeng djee eeda]
- how much is a one-way ticket downtown? quanto custa uma passagem de ida para o centro? [kwantoo kooshta ooma passajeng djee eeda para oo sentroo]
- a second-class one-way ticket to São Paulo uma passagem de ida de segunda classe para São Paulo [ooma passajeng djee eeda djee segoonda klassee para sowng powloo]

only só [so], somente [somentchee]
- that's the only one left foi o único que sobrou [foy oo ooneekoo kee sobro]

open aberto(ta) [abeh-too(ta)] ◆ abrir [abreeh]
- is the bank open at lunchtime? o banco fica aberto no horário do almoço? [oo bankoo feeka abeh-too noo oraryoo doo owmossoo]
- is the museum open all day? o museu abre todo dia? [oo moozew abree todoo djee-a]
- at what time is ... open? a que horas abre...? [a kee oraz abree]

---

opinions

- personally, I don't think it's fair pessoalmente não acho que isso seja justo [pesswow-mentchee nowng ashoo kee eessoo seja jooshtoo]
- I think he's right acho que ele está certo [ashoo kee elee eeshta seh-too]
- I don't want to say não vou dizer [nowng vo djeezeh]
- I'm not sure não tenho certeza [nowng tenyoo seh-teza]
- no idea! nem idéia! [neng eedaya]
- it depends depende [dependjee]

▶ can I open the window? posso abrir a janela? [possoo abreer a janela]

▶ what time do you open? a que horas abre? [a kee oraz abree]

open-air ao ar livre [ow ah leevree]

▶ is there an open-air swimming pool? tem piscina ao ar livre? [teng peesseena ow ah leevree]

operating room o centro cirúrgico [sentroo seerooh-jeekoo]

▶ is she still in the operating room? ela ainda está no centro cirúrgico? [ella a-eenda eeshta noo sentroo seerooh-jeekoo]

opinion a opinião [opeenyowng]

▶ in my opinion, ... na minha opinião, ... [na meenya opeenyowng]

orange laranja [laranja] ◆ *(fruit)* a laranja [laranja]; *(color)* o laranja [laranja]

▶ I'd like a kilo of oranges eu queria um quilo de laranja [ew keree-a oom keeloo djee laranja]

orange juice o suco de laranja [sookoo djee laranja]

▶ I'll have a glass of orange juice eu quero um copo de suco de laranja [ew keroo oom kopoo djee sookoo djee laranja]

▶ I'd like a freshly squeezed orange juice eu queria um suco de laranja feito na hora [ew keree-a oom sookoo djee laranja faytoo na ora]

order *(in a restaurant, a café)* o pedido [pedjeedoo]; *(by mail)* a encomenda [enkomenda] ◆ *(in a restaurant, a café)* pedir [pedjeeh]; *(by mail)* encomendar [enkomendah]

▶ this isn't what I ordered: I asked for... não foi o que eu pedi: eu pedi ... [nowng foy oo kee ew pedjee ew pedjee]

▶ I ordered a coffee eu pedi um café [ew pedjee oom kaffe]

▶ we'd like to order now queríamos fazer o pedido [keree-amoosh fazer oo pedjeedoo]

organize organizar [oh-ganeezah]

▶ can you organize the whole trip for us? você pode organizar toda a excursão para nós? [vosse podjee oh-ganeezah toda a eeshkooh-sowng para nosh]

other outro(tra) [otroo(tra)]

▶ I'll have the other one eu fico com o outro [ew feekoo kong oo otroo]

▶ on the other side of the street no outro lado da rua [noo otroo ladoo da hoo-a]

▶ go ahead; I'm going to wait for the others pode ir, eu vou esperar pelos outros [podjee eeh ew vo eeshperah pelooz otroosh]

out-of-date vencido(da) [venseedoo(da)]

▶ I think my passport is out-of-date acho que meu passaporte está vencido [ashoo kee mew passapoh-tchee eeshta venseedoo]

outside call a chamada externa [shamada eeshter-na]

▶ I'd like to make an outside call eu queria fazer uma chamada externa [ew keree-a fazer ooma shamada eeshter-na]

outside line a linha para fora [leenya para fora]
 ▸ how do you get an outside line? como consigo linha para fora? [komoo konseegoo leenya para fora]

overheat sobreaquecer [sobree-akesseh]
 ▸ the engine is overheating o motor está sobreaquecendo [oo motoh eeshta sobree-akessendoo]

owner o dono [donoo], a dona [donna]
 ▸ do you know who the owner is? você sabe quem é o dono? [vosse sabee keng eh oo donoo]

pack *(of cigarettes)* o maço [massoo]; *(of chewing gum)* o pacote [pakotchee]
 ◆ *(for a trip)* fazer a mala [fazer a mala]
 ▸ how much is a pack of cigarettes? quanto custa um maço de cigarros? [kwantoo kooshta oom massoo djee seegahoosh]
 ▸ I need to pack preciso fazer as malas [presseezoo fazer ash malash]

package *(wrapped object, vacation deal)* o pacote [pakotchee]; *(of butter)* o pote [potchee]
 ▸ I'd like to send this package to New York by airmail eu gostaria de enviar este pacote para Nova York por correio aéreo [ew goshtaree-a djee envee-ar esh-tchee pakotchee para nova york poh kohayoo a-eree-oo]
 ▸ do you have weekend packages? vocês têm pacotes para finais de semana? [vossesh tayeng pakotcheesh para feenysh djee semana]

package tour o pacote turístico [pakotchee tooreesh-tcheekoo]
 ▸ it's my first time on a package tour é a primeira vez que faço um pacote turístico [eh a preemayra vesh kee fassoo oom pakotchee tooreesh-tcheekoo]

padlock o cadeado [kadjee-adoo]
 ▸ I'd like to buy a padlock for my bike eu queria comprar um cadeado para a minha bicicleta [ew keree-a komprar oom kadjee-adoo para a meenya beesseekleta]

pain *(physical)* a dor [doh]
 ▸ I'd like something for pain eu queria alguma coisa para dor [ew keree-a owgooma koyza para doh]
 ▸ I have a pain here me dói aqui [mee doy akee]

painkiller o analgésico [anow-jezeekoo]
 ▸ I have a really bad toothache: can you give me a painkiller, please? estou com uma dor de dente horrível: você poderia me dar um analgésico, por favor? [eeshto kong ooma doh djee dentchee oheevew vosse poderee-a mee dar oom anow-jezeekoo poh favoh]

pair *(of gloves, socks)* o par [pah]
- a pair of shoes um par de sapatos [oom pah djee sapatoosh]
- a pair of pants um par de luvas [oom pah djee loovash]
- do you have a pair of scissors? tem uma tesoura? [teng ooma tezora]

pants as calças [kowsash]
- a pair of pants umas calças [oomash kowsash]
- there is a hole in these pants tem um furo nessas calças [teng oom fooroo nessash kowsash]

pantyhose a meia-calça [maya-kowsa]
- I got a run in my pantyhose minha meia-calça puxou um fio [meenya maya-kowsa poosho oom fee-oo]

paper *(for writing on)* o papel [papew]; *(newspaper)* o jornal [joh-now] ◆ **papers** *(official documents)* a documentação [dokoomentassowng]
- a piece of paper um papel [oom papew]
- here are my papers aqui está minha documentação [akee eeshta meenya dokoomentassowng]

parasol o guarda-sol [gwah-da-sow]
- can you rent parasols? dá para alugar guarda-sóis? [da para aloogah gwah-da-soysh]

pardon *(forgiveness)* o perdão [peh-downg] ◆ *(forgive)* perdoar [peh-dwah]
- I beg your pardon? *(asking for repetition)* como? [komoo]
- I beg your pardon! *(to apologize)* me desculpe! [mee djeeshkoowpee]; *(showing disagreement)* como é? [komoo eh]
- pardon me? *(asking for repetition)* como? [komoo]
- pardon me! *(to get past)* com licença! [kong leessensa]; *(to apologize)* desculpe! [djeeshkoowpee]; *(showing disagreement)* como é? [komoo eh]

park estacionar [eeshtass-yonah]
- can we park our trailer here? podemos estacionar nosso trailer aqui? [podemooz eeshtass-yonah nossoo trayler akee]
- am I allowed to park here? posso estacionar aqui? [possoo eeshtass-yonar akee]

parking o estacionamento [eeshtass-yonamentoo]
- is there any parking near the hostel? tem algum estacionamento perto do albergue? [teng owgoom eeshtass-yonamentoo peh-too doo owbeh-ghee]

parking lot o estacionamento [eeshtass-yonamentoo]
- is there a parking lot nearby? tem um estacionamento por aqui? [teng oom eeshtass-yonamentoo por akee]

parking space o espaço para estacionar [eeshpassoo para eeshtass-yonah]
- is it easy to find a parking space in town? é fácil achar espaço para estacionar na cidade? [eh fasseew ashar eeshpassoo para eeshtass-yonah na seedadjee]

part a parte [pah-tchee]
- what part of Brazil are you from? de que parte do Brasil você é? [djee ke pah-tchee doo brazeew vosse eh]
- I've never been to this part of Brazil before nunca fui para esta região do Brasil antes [noonka fwee para essa hej-yowng do brazeew antcheesh]

party a festa [feshta] ♦ festejar [feshtejah]
- I'm planning a little party tomorrow estou planejando uma festinha amanhã [eeshto planejandoo ooma fesh-tcheenya amanyang]

pass (hand) passar [passah]; (in a car) ultrapassar [oowtrapassah]
- can you pass me the salt? pode me passar o sal? [podjee mee passar oo sow]
- can you pass on this road? dá para ultrapassar nessa estrada? [da para oowtrapassah nessa eeshtrada]

passage (corridor) o corredor [kohedoh]
- I heard someone outside in the passage ouvi alguém no corredor [ovee owgeng noo kohedoh]

passenger o passageiro [passajayroo], a passageira [passajayra]
- is this where the passengers from the Sao Paulo flight arrive? é aqui que chegam os passageiros do vôo de São Paulo? [eh akee kee shegowng oosh passajayroosh doo vo-oo djee sowng powloo]

passport o passaporte [passapoh-tchee]
- I've lost my passport perdi meu passaporte [peh-djee mew passapoh-tchee]
- I forgot my passport esqueci meu passaporte [eeshkessee mew passapoh-tchee]
- my passport has been stolen roubaram meu passaporte [hobarowng mew passapoh-tchee]

past e [ee]
- twenty past twelve doze e vinte [dozee ee veentchee]

path (track) o caminho [kameenyoo]
- is the path well-marked? o caminho está bem sinalizado? [oo kameenyoo eeshta beng seenaleezadoo]

pay pagar [pagah]
- do I have to pay a deposit? tenho que pagar entrada? [tenyoo kee pagar entrada]
- do you have to pay to get in? tem que pagar para entrar? [teng kee pagah para entrah]
- can you pay by credit card? dá para pagar com cartão de crédito? [da para pagah kong kah-towng djee kredjeetoo]
- we're going to pay separately vamos pagar separado [vamoosh pagah separadoo]

pay-per-view TV o pay-per-view [pay-per-view]
- is there pay-per-view TV in the room? tem pay-per-view no quarto? [teng pay-per-view noo kwah-too]

pay-per-view channel o canal pay-per-view [kanow pay-per-view]
- are there any pay-per-view channels? tem algum canal pay-per-view? [teng owgoom kanow pay-per-view]

pedestrian o(a) pedestre [pedeshtree] ✦ para pedestres [para pedeshtreesh]
  ▸ is this just a pedestrian street? essa rua é só para pedestres? [essa hoo-a eh so para pedeshtreesh]

pedestrian mall a rua para pedestres [hoo-a para pedeshtreesh]
  ▸ can you direct me to the pedestrian mall? pode me levar diretamente para a rua para pedestres? [podjee mee levah djeereta-mentchee para a hoo-a para pedeshtreesh]

pen a caneta [kaneta]
  ▸ can you lend me a pen? pode me emprestar uma caneta? [podjee mee empreshtar ooma kaneta]

pencil o lápis [lapeesh]
  ▸ can you lend me a pencil? pode me emprestar um lápis? [podjee mee empreshtar oom lapeesh]

penicillin a penicilina [penee-seeleena]
  ▸ I'm allergic to penicillin sou alérgico à penicilina [so aleh-jeekoo a penee-seeleena]

pepper a pimenta [peementa]
  ▸ pass the pepper, please me alcança a pimenta? [mee owkansa a peementa]

percent a porcentagem [poh-sentajeng]
  ▸ could you knock 10 percent off the price? você poderia me dar um desconto de dez por cento no preço? [vosse poderee-a mee dar oom djeeshkontoo djee desh poh sentoo noo pressoo]

performance (show) a apresentação [aprezentassowng]; (in a movie theater) a sessão [sessowng]
  ▸ what time does the performance begin? a que horas começa a apresentação? [a kee orash komessa a aprezentassowng]

perfume o perfume [peh-foomee]
  ▸ how much is this perfume? quanto custa este perfume? [kwantoo kooshta esh-tchee peh-foomee]

perhaps talvez [tow-vesh]
  ▸ perhaps you can help me? talvez você pudesse me ajudar? [tow-vesh vosse poodessee mee ajoodah]

person a pessoa [pesso-a]
  ▸ how much is it per hour and per person? quanto custa por hora e por pessoa? [kwantoo kooshta por ora ee poh pesso-a]

pet o animal de estimação [aneemow djee eesh-tcheemassowng]
  ▸ are pets allowed? são permitidos animais de estimação? [sowng peh-meet-cheedooz aneemysh djee eesh-tcheemassowng]

phone o telefone [telefonee] ✦ telefonar [telefonah]
  ▸ can I use the phone? posso usar o telefone? [possoo oozar oo telefonee]

phone booth o orelhão [orelyowng], a cabine telefônica [kabeenee telefoneeka]

▸ is there a phone booth near here? **tem um orelhão por aqui?** [teng oom orelyowng por akee]

phone call a ligação [leegassowng]

▸ I'd like to make a phone call **eu queria fazer uma ligação** [ew keree-a fazer ooma leegassowng]

phonecard o cartão telefônico [kah-towng telefoneekoo]

▸ where can I buy a phonecard? **onde eu posso comprar um cartão telefônico?** [ondjee ew possoo komprar oom kah-towng telefoneekoo]

photo a foto [fotoo]

▸ can I take photos in here? **posso bater fotos aqui?** [possoo bateh fotooz akee]
▸ could you take a photo of us? **você poderia tirar uma foto de nós?** [vosse poderee-a tcheerar ooma fotoo djee nosh]
▸ I'd like copies of some photos **eu queria cópia de algumas fotos** [ew keree-a kopya djee owgoomash fotoosh]

photography a fotografia [fotografee-a]

▸ is photography allowed in the museum? **se pode bater fotografias no museu?** [see podjee bateh fotografee-ash noo moozew]

picnic o piquenique [peekeeneekee]

▸ could we go for a picnic by the river? **será que a gente poderia fazer um piquenique no rio?** [sera kee a jentchee poderee-a fazer oom peekeeneekee noo hee-oo]

piece o pedaço [pedasoo]

▸ a piece of cake, please **um pedaço de bolo, por favor** [oom pedasoo djee boloo poh favoh]
▸ a piece of advice **um conselho** [oom konselyoo]
▸ a piece of news **uma notícia** [ooma noteess-ya]

---

on the phone

▸ hello? **alô?** [allo]
▸ Jane Stewart speaking **é Jane Stewart** [eh Jane Stewart]
▸ I'd like to speak to Jack Adams **eu queria falar com Jack Adams** [ew keree-a falah kong Jack Adams]
▸ hold the line **aguarde um instante na linha, por favor** [agwah-djee oom eenshtantchee na leenya poh favoh]
▸ can you call back in ten minutes? **posso lhe ligar de volta em dez minutos?** [possool-yee leegah djee vowta eng dej meenootoosh]
▸ would you like to leave a message? **gostaria de deixar recado?** [goshtaree-a djee dayshah hekadoo]
▸ you have the wrong number **é engano** [eh enganoo]

---

pill o comprimido [kompreemeedoo]
- a bottle of pills um vidro de comprimidos [oom veedroo djee kompreemeedoosh]
- the Pill *(contraceptive)* a Pílula [a peeloola]

pillow o travesseiro [travessayroo]
- could I have another pillow? teria como conseguir outro travesseiro? [teree-a komoo konsegeer otroo travessayroo]

pizza a pizza [peetsa]
- I'd like a large mushroom pizza eu queria uma pizza grande de cogumelo [ew keree-a ooma peetsa grandjee djee kogoomeloo]

place *(area, seat)* o lugar [loogah]; *(house)* a casa [kaza]; *(place setting)* o jogo de talheres [jogoo djee tal-yereesh]
- can you recommend a nice place to eat? você me recomenda um bom lugar para comer? [vosse mee hekomenda oom loogah para komeh]
- do you want to change places with me? quer trocar de lugar comigo? [keh trokah djee loogah komeegoo]

plain claro(ra) [klaroo(ra)]
- do you have any plain yogurt? tem iogurte natural? [teng yogooh-tchee natoorow]

plan o plano [planoo] ♦ planejar [planejah]
- do you have plans for tonight? tem planos para hoje à noite? [teng planoosh para ojee a noytchee]
- I'm planning to stay for just one night estou pensando em ficar por só mais uma noite [eeshto pensando eng feekah poh so myz ooma noytchee]

plane o avião [avee-owng]
- which gate does the plane depart from? de que portão sai o avião? [djee ke poh-towng sy oo avee-owng]
- when's the next plane to Curitiba? quando é o próximo vôo para Curitiba? [kwandoo eh oo prosseemoo vo-oo para kooreetcheeba]

plate o prato [pratoo]
- this plate's got a crack in it este prato está rachado [esh-tchee pratoo eeshta hashadoo]

platform *(at a station)* a plataforma [platafoh-ma]
- which platform does the subway train leave from? de que plataforma sai o trem? [djee ke platafoh-ma sy oo treng]

play *(at a theater)* a peça [pessa] ♦ *(sport, game)* jogar [jogah]; *(instrument, music)* tocar [tokah]
- do you play tennis? você joga tênis? [vosse joga teneesh]
- I play the cello eu toco violoncelo [ew tokoo vee-olonselloo]

playroom a sala de jogos [sala djee jogoosh]
- is there a children's playroom here? tem uma sala de jogos para crianças aqui? [teng ooma sala djee jogoosh para kree-ansaz akee]

police

Officers of the *polícia militar*, which has nothing to do with the army, are the people to go to if you have had something stolen. The color of their uniform will depend on the Brazilian state you are in. You can also go to a *delegacia* to report a theft. Don't confuse them with the *polícia civil* or *polícia federal*, who wear black jackets and deal with major crime such as drug trafficking and corruption. There is no local police force in Brazil.

please por favor [poh favoh]
  ▶ please sit down sente-se, por favor [sentchee-see poh favoh]
  ▶ can I come in? – please do posso entrar – por favor [possoo entrah poh favoh]

pleased feliz [feleej]
  ▶ pleased to meet you que bom te ver [ke bong tchee veh]

pleasure o prazer [prazeh]
  ▶ with pleasure! com prazer! [kong prazeh]
  ▶ it's a pleasure foi um prazer [foy oom prazeh]

plug *(on electrical equipment)* a tomada [tomada]
  ▶ where can I find an adaptor for the plug on my hairdryer? onde eu posso achar um adaptador para a tomada do meu secador de cabelo? [ondjee ew possoo ashar oom adaptadoh para a tomada doo mew sekadoh djee kabeloo]

plug in ligar na tomada [leegah na tomada]
  ▶ can I plug my cellphone in here to recharge it? posso ligar meu celular nessa tomada para recarregar? [possoo leegah mew seloolah nessa tomada para hekahegah]

point *(moment)* o momento [momentoo]; *(spot, location)* o ponto [pontoo]
  ◆ *(direct)* apontar [apontah]
  ▶ points of the compass pontos cardeais [pontoosh kah-djee-ysh]
  ▶ can you point me in the direction of the freeway? você pode me indicar a direção da auto-estrada? [vosse podjee mee eendjeekah a djeeressowng da owto-eeshtrada]

police a polícia [poleess-ya]
  ▶ call the police! chame a polícia! [shamee a poleess-ya]
  ▶ what's the number for the police? qual é o número da polícia? [kwal eh oo noomeroo da poleess-ya]

police station a delegacia [delegassee-a]
  ▶ where is the nearest police station? onde fica a delegacia mais perto? [ondjee feeka a delegassee-a mysh peh-too]

at the post office

To send a letter, you have to go to an *agência dos Correios* (post office). If it is a *carta simples* (ordinary letter), you only have to buy a stamp to send it. If the letter already has a stamp, you can put it straight into a *caixa de correio* (mailbox), without going to the *agência*. If it is a package or a valuable item, you can send it by *encomenda simples* (parcel post), *carta registrada* (registered letter) or *Sedex* (Brazilian equivalent of FedEx®). The *Correios* do not accept credit cards.

pool *(for swimming)* a piscina [peesseena]
- main pool piscina principal [peesseena preenseepow]
- children's pool piscina das crianças [peesseena dash kree-ansash]
- is the pool heated? é uma piscina térmica? [eh ooma peesseena teh-meeka]
- is there an indoor pool? tem piscina coberta? [teng peesseena kobeh-ta]

pork o porco [poh-koo]
- I don't eat pork não como porco [nowng komoo poh-koo]

portable portátil [poh-tatcheew]
- do you have a portable heater we could borrow? tem algum aquecedor portátil para nos emprestar? [teng owgoom akessedoh poh-tatcheew para noz empreshtah]

portion a porção [poh-sowng]
- the portions at that restaurant are just right as porções daquele restaurante são boas [ash poh-soyngsh dakelee heshtow-rantchee sowng boash]

possible possível [posseevew]
- without sauce, if possible sem molho, se possível [seng molyoo see posseevew]

postcard o cartão-postal [kah-towng-poshtow]
- where can I buy postcards? onde eu posso comprar cartões-postais? [ondjee ew possoo komprah kah-toyngsh-poshtysh]
- how much are stamps for postcards to the States? quanto custam os selos para os Estados Unidos? [kwantoo kooshtowng oosh seloosh para ooz eeshtadooz ooneedoosh]

post office a agência dos Correios [ajenss-ya doosh kohayoosh]
- where is the nearest post office? onde fica a agência dos Correios mais próxima? [ondjee feeka a ajenss-ya doosh kohayoosh mysh prosseema]

power *(electricity)* a luz [looj]
- there's no power não tem luz [nowng teng looj]

power failure a falta de luz [fowta djee looj]
- there's a power failure houve uma falta de luz [ovee ooma fowta djee looj]

▶ how long is the power failure expected to last? **quanto tempo se espera que dure a falta de luz?** [kwantoo tempoo see eshpera kee dooree a fowta djee looj]

prawn o camarão [kamarowng]

▶ I'd like to try a dish with prawns **eu queria um prato com camarão** [ew keree-a oom pratoo kong kamarowng]

prefer preferir [prefereeh]

▶ I'd prefer black tea **eu preferiria chá preto** [ew prefereeree-a sha pretoo]

▶ I'd prefer you not smoke **eu preferiria que você não fumasse** [ew prefereeree-a kee vosse nowng foomassee]**prescription** *(medicine)* a receita [hessayta]

▶ is it only available by prescription? **só dá para comprar com receita?** [so da para komprah kong hessayta]

present o presente [prezentchee]

▶ where can we buy presents around here? **onde podemos comprar presentes por aqui?** [ondjee podemoosh komprah prezentcheesh por akee]

pretty bonito(ta) [boneetoo(ta)]

▶ she's a very pretty girl **é uma garota muito bonita** [eh ooma garota mweentoo boneeta]

price *(cost)* o preço [pressoo]

▶ what's the price of gas today? **qual é o preço da gasolina hoje?** [kwal eh oo pressoo da gazoleena ojee]

▶ if the price is right **se o preço estiver certo** [see oo pressoo eesh-tcheeveh seh-too]

price list a lista de preços [leeeshta djee pressoosh]

▶ do you have a price list? **tem uma lista de preços?** [teng ooma leeshta djee pressoosh]

print *(photograph)* a cópia [kopya]

▶ could I have another set of prints? **eu queria outro jogo de cópias** [ew keree-a otroo jogoo djee kopyash]

private *(not public)* particular [pah-tcheekoolah]; *(personal)* pessoal [pesswow]

▶ is it a private beach? **é uma praia particular?** [eh ooma pry-a pah-tcheekoolah]

problem o problema [problema]

expressing a preference

▶ I prefer red wine to white wine **prefiro vinho tinto a vinho branco** [prefeeroo veenyoo tcheentoo a veenyoo brankoo]

▶ I'd rather fly than go by bus **é melhor ir de avião do que de ônibus** [eh melyor eeh djee avee-owng doo kee djee oneeboosh]

▶ Saturday would suit me better **para mim sábado fica melhor** [para meeng sabadoo feeka melyoh]

public transportation

In Brazil, the main method of public transportation is the bus. When using the bus, you pay cash to the *cobrador* (in São Paulo) or *trocador* (in Rio). In bigger cities such as São Paulo and Rio de Janeiro, you can also use the *metrô* (subway), but there is a limited number of lines. You buy *metrô* tickets at the *guichê* (ticket office). The names of the lines can be either a number or a name (or both) depending on the city. And be warned: *metrô* trains don't run all night.

> there's a problem with the central heating tem um problema com o aquecimento central [teng oom problema kong oo akesseementoo sentrow]
> no problem não tem problema [nowng teng problema]

program *(for an event)* o programa [programa]
> could I see a program? eu poderia ver o programa? [ew poderee-a ver oo programa]

pronounce *(word)* pronunciar [pronoonss-yah]
> how is that pronounced? como se pronuncia? [komoo see pronoonsee-a]

public público(ca) [poobleekoo(ka)] ◆ o público [poobleekoo]
> let's go somewhere less public vamos para um lugar mais reservado [vamoosh para oom loogah mysh hezeh-vadoo]
> is the castle open to the public? o castelo está aberto ao público? [oo kashteloo eeshta abeh-too ow poobleekoo]

public holiday o feriado [feree-adoo]
> is tomorrow a public holiday? amanhã é feriado? [amanyang eh feree-adoo]

public transportation o transporte público [tranjpoh-tche poobleekoo]
> can you get there by public transportation? dá para chegar lá usando transporte público? [da para shegah la oozandoo tranjpoh-tche poobleekoo]

pull *(muscle)* estirar [eesh-tcheerah]; *(tooth)* arrancar [ahankah]
> I've pulled a muscle estirei um músculo [eesh-tcheeray oom mooshkooloo]

puncture furar [foorah]
> the tire's been punctured furou o pneu [fooro oo pnew]

purpose *(reason)* a razão [hazowng]; *(aim)* o objetivo [objetcheevoo] ◆ **on purpose** de propósito [djee propozeetoo]
> sorry, I didn't do it on purpose desculpe, não fiz de propósito [djeeshkoowpee nowng feesh djee propozeetoo]

purse *(handbag)* a bolsa [bowsa]; *(change purse)* a niqueleira [neekelayra]
> my purse was stolen roubaram minha bolsa [hobarowng meenya bowsa]

push empurrar [empoohah]

▸ can you help us push the car? você pode nos ajudar a empurrar o carro? [vosse podjee noz ajoodar a empoohar oo kahoo]

put *(into place, position)* pôr [poh], colocar [kolokah]

▸ is there somewhere I can put my bags? tem algum lugar onde eu possa colocar as malas? [teng owgoom loogar ondjee ew possa kolokar ash malash]

put down *(set down)* deixar [dayshah]

▸ can we put our things down in the corner? podemos deixar nossas coisas no canto? [podemoosh dayshah nossash koyzash noo cantoo]

put on *(clothes)* colocar [kolokah]; *(TV, radio, heating)* ligar [leegah]; *(on telephone)* colocar com [kolokah kong]

▸ can you put the heat on? você pode ligar o aquecedor? [vosse podjee leegar oo akessedoh]

▸ can you put Miss Martin on, please? você poderia me colocar com a senhorita Martin, por favor? [vosse poderee-a mee kolokah kong a senyoreeta Martin poh favoh]

put out *(cigarette, fire)* apagar [apagah]

▸ can you please put your cigarette out? você poderia apagar o cigarro, por favor? [vosse poderee-a apagar oo seegahoo poh favoh]

put up *(erect)* montar [montah]; *(provide accommodations for)* alojar [alojah]

▸ can we put up our tent here? podemos montar a barraca aqui? [podemoosh montar a bahaka akee]

q

quarter *(fourth)* o quarto [kwah-too]

▸ I'll be back in a quarter of an hour volto em quinze minutos [vowtoo eng keenzee meenootoosh]

▸ a quarter past/after one uma e quinze [ooma ee keenzee]

▸ a quarter to/of one quinze para as duas [keenzee para ash doo-ash]

quay o cais [kysh]

▸ is the boat at the quay? o barco está no cais? [oo bah-koo eeshta noo kysh]

question a pergunta [peh-goonta]

▸ can I ask you a question? posso lhe fazer uma pergunta? [possool-yee fazer ooma peh-goonta]

quickly rápido [hapeedoo]

▸ everyone speaks so quickly todo mundo fala tão rápido [todoo moondoo fala towng hapeedoo]

quiet calmo(ma) [kowmoo(ma)]

▶ is it a quiet beach? é uma praia calma? [eh ooma pry-a kowma]
▶ do you have anything quieter? tem algo mais tranqüilo? [teng owgoo mysh trankweeloo]

quite *(rather)* bem [beng]
▶ it's quite expensive around here as coisas estão bem caras por aqui [ash koyzaz eeshtowng beng karash por akee]

r

racket *(for tennis)* a raquete [haketchee]
▶ can you rent rackets? dá para alugar raquete? [da para aloogah haketchee]

radiator o radiador [hadjee-adoh]
▶ the radiator's leaking tem um vazamento no radiador [teng oom vazamentoo noo hadjee-adoh]

radio *(set)* o rádio [hadjoo]
▶ the radio doesn't work o rádio não funciona [oo hadjoo nowng foonss-yona]

radio station a estação de rádio [eeshtassowng djee hadjoo]
▶ can you get any English-language radio stations here? dá para pegar alguma estação de rádio em inglês aqui? [da para pegar owgooma eeshtassowng djee hadjoo eng eenglez akee]

railroad *(system, organization)* a ferrovia [fehovee-a]; *(track)* a estrada de ferro [eeshtrada djee fehoo]
▶ what region does this railroad cover? até que região essa estrada de ferro vai? [a-te ke hej-yowng essa eeshtrada djee fehoo vy]

rain chover [shoveh]
▶ it's raining está chovendo [eeshta shovendoo]

random
▶ at random aleatoriamente [alyatoree-amentchee]

rare *(meat)* bem mal passado(da) [beng mow passadoo(da)]
▶ rare, please bem mal passsado, por favor [beng mow passadoo poh favoh]

rate *(price)* a tarifa [tareefa]
▶ what's your daily rate? qual é a sua tarifa diária? [kwal eh a soo-a tareefa djee-arya]

rate of exchange a taxa de câmbio [tasha djee kambyoo]
▶ they offer a good rate of exchange eles oferecem uma boa taxa de câmbio [eleez oferesseng ooma boa tasha djee kambyoo]

razor *(for wet shaving)* o barbeador [bah-bee-adoh]; *(electric)* o barbeador elétrico [bah-bee-ador eletreekoo]
▶ where can I buy a new razor? onde eu posso comprar um barbeador novo?

[ondjee possoo komprar oom bah-bee-adoh novoo]

razor blade a lâmina de barbear [lameena djee bah-bee-ah]
  ▸ I need to buy some razor blades preciso comprar algumas lâminas de barbear [presseezoo komprar owgoomash lameenash djee bah-bee-ah]

ready (prepared) pronto(ta) [prontoo(ta)]; (willing) disposto(ta) [djeesh-poshtoo (ta)]
  ▸ when will it be ready? quando vai ficar pronto? [kwandoo vy feekah prontoo]

really (actually) realmente [hee-owmentchee]; (very) muito [mweentoo]
  ▸ really? mesmo? [mejmoo]

receipt (for a purchase, bill, meal) a nota [nota]; (for rent, for a taxi) o recibo [hesseeboo]
  ▸ can I have a receipt, please? poderia me dar uma nota, por favor? [poderee-a mee dar ooma nota poh favoh]

receive (package, letter) receber [hessebeh]
  ▸ I should have received the package this morning eu deveria ter recebido o pacote hoje de manhã [ew deveree-a teh hessebeedoo oo pakotchee ojee djee manyang]

reception (welcome, party, for TV ou radio) a recepção [hessepsowng]; (for a cellphone) a cobertura [kobeh-toora]
  ▸ there's no reception não tem sinal [nowng teng seenow]
  ▸ I'm looking for the Mackenzie wedding reception estou procurando a recepção do casamento dos Mackenzie [eeshto prokoorandoo a hessepsowng doo kazamentoo doosh Mackenzie]

reception desk (at hotel) a recepção [hessepsowng]
  ▸ can I leave my backpack at the reception desk? posso deixar minha mochila na recepção? [possoo dayshah meenya mosheela na hessepsowng]

recline reclinar [hekleenah]
  ▸ do you mind if I recline my seat? você se importa se eu reclinar minha cadeira? [vosse see eempoh-ta see ew hekleenah meenya kadayra]

recommend recomendar [hekomendah]
  ▸ could you recommend another hotel? você poderia me recomendar outro hotel? [vosse poderee-a mee hekomendar otroo otew]
  ▸ could you recommend a restaurant? você poderia recomendar um restaurante? [vosse poderee-a hekomendar oom heshtow-rantchee]
  ▸ what do you recommend? o que você recomenda? [oo kee vosse hekomenda]

record store a loja de discos [loja djee djeeshkoosh]
  ▸ I'm looking for a record store estou procurando uma loja de discos [eeshto prokoorandoo ooma loja djee djeeshkoosh]

rec center, recreation center o centro de recreação [sentroo djee hekree-assowng]
  ▸ what kinds of activities does the recreation center offer? que tipo de atividades

são oferecidas no centro de recreação? [ke tcheepoo djee atcheevee-dadjeesh sowng oferesseedash noo sentroo djee hekree-assowng]

red *(dress)* vermelho(lha) [veh-melyoo(ya)]; *(hair)* ruivo(va) [hweevoo(va)] ◆ *(color)* o vermelho [veh-melyoo]; *(wine)* o tinto [tcheentoo]
  ▸ dressed in red vestida de vermelho [vesh-tcheeda djee veh-melyoo]
  ▸ what kinds of red wine do you have? que tipo de vinho tinto você tem? [ke tcheepoo djee veenyoo tcheentoo vosse teng]

redhead o ruivo [hweevoo], a ruiva [hweeva]
  ▸ a tall redhead wearing glasses uma ruiva alta usando óculos [ooma hweeva owta oozandoo okooloosh]

red light o sinal vermelho [seenow veh-melyoo]
  ▸ you failed to stop at a red light você não parou no sinal vermelho [vosse nowng paro noo seenow veh-melyoo]

reduced *(price, rate)* reduzido(da) [hedoozeedoo(da)]
  ▸ is there a reduced rate for students? tem um preço reduzido para estudantes? [teng oom pressoo hedoozeeedoo para eeshtoo-dantcheesh]

reduced-price *(ticket)* com preço reduzido [kong pressoo hedoozeedoo]
  ▸ two reduced-price tickets and one full-price duas meias entradas e uma inteira [doo-ash mayaz entradaz ee ooma eentayra]

reduction a redução [hedoossowng]
  ▸ do you have reductions for groups? tem redução no preço para grupos? [teng hedoossowng noo pressoo para groopoosh]

red wine o vinho tinto [veenyoo tcheentoo]
  ▸ a bottle of red wine uma garrafa de vinho tinto [ooma gahafa djee veenyoo tcheentoo]

refresher course o curso de atualização [kooh-soo djee atwaleezassowng]
  ▸ I need a refresher course preciso de um curso de atualização [presseezoo djee oom kooh-soo djee atwaleezassowng]

refuge *(for animals)* o refúgio [hefooj-yoo]
  ▸ we'd like to visit the wildlife refuge gostaríamos de visitar o refúgio de vida selvagem [goshtaree-amoosh djee veezeetar oo hefooj-yoo djee veeda sew-vajeng]

refundable reembolsável [hee-embowsavew]
  ▸ are the tickets refundable? as entradas são reembolsáveis? [az entradash sowng hee-embowsavaysh]

regards as lembranças [lembransash] ◆ **with regard to** em relação a [eng helassowng a]
  ▸ give my regards to your parents! dê minhas lembranças aos seus pais! [de meenyash lembransaz owsh sewsh pysh]
  ▸ I'm calling you with regard to ... estou lhe telefonando em relação a... [eeshtol-yee telefonandoo eng helassowng a]

region a região [hej-yowng]
- in the north region of Bahia na região norte da Bahia [na hej-yowng noh-tchee da ba-ee-a]

registered letter, registered mail a carta registrada [kah-ta hejeesh-trada]
- I'd like to send a registered letter/a letter by registered mail eu queria enviar uma carta registrada [ew keree-a envee-ar ooma kah-ta hejeesh-trada]

registration *(of car)* o licenciamento [leessensee-amentoo]
- here's the car's registration aqui está o licenciamento do carro [akee eeshta oo leessensee-amentoo doo kahoo]

relative o(a) parente [parentchee]
- I have relatives in Rio tenho parentes no Rio [tenyoo parentcheez noo hee-oo]

remember lembrar [lembrah], lembrar-se de [lembrah-see djee]
- do you remember me? se lembra de mim? [see lembra djee meeng]
- I can't remember his name não consigo me lembrar do nome dele [nowng konseegoo mee lembrah doo nomee delee]

remote (control) o controle (remoto) [kontrolee (hemotoo)]
- I can't find the remote for the TV não consigo achar o controle (remoto) da TV [nowng konseegoo ashar oo kontrolee (hemotoo) da te-ve]

rent o aluguel [aloogew] ◆ alugar [aloogah]
- how much is the rent per week? quanto custa o aluguel por semana? [kwantoo kooshta oo aloogew poh semana]
- I'd like to rent a car for a week eu queria alugar um carro por uma semana [ew keree-a aloogar oom kahoo por ooma semana]
- I'd like to rent a boat eu queria alugar um barco [ew keree-a aloogar oom bah-koo]
- does it work out cheaper to rent the equipment by the week? vale a pena alugar o equipamento por semana? [valee a pena aloogar oo ekeepamentoo poh semana]

rental *(renting)* o aluguel [aloogew]; *(apartment)* o apartamento alugado [apah-tamentoo aloogadoo]; *(house)* a casa alugada [kaza aloogada]; *(car)* o carro alugado [kahoo aloogadoo]
- we have the rental for two weeks temos o aluguel de duas semanas [temooz oom aloogew djee doo-ash semanash]

repair o conserto [konseh-too] ◆ consertar [konseh-tah]
- will you be able to make the repairs today? você vai conseguir fazer os consertos hoje? [vosse vy konsegeeh fazer oosh konseh-tooz ojee]
- how long will it take to repair? quanto tempo vai levar para consertar? [kwantoo tempoo vy levah para konseh-tah]

repeat repetir [hepetcheeh]
- can you repeat that, please? pode repetir, por favor? [podjee hepetcheeh poh favoh]

report *(theft)* informar [eenfoh-mah]
- I'd like to report something stolen eu queria informar um roubo [ew keree-a eenfoh-mar oom hoboo]

restaurants

You can either go to a *restaurante à la carte*, where you order a complete meal, or you can go to a *bufê* (buffet), where all the food is laid and you go up and serve yourself. In this case, you can either pay *por quilo* (according to the weight of what you've eaten) or choose a *bufê livre*, where you pay a fixed price and eat as much as you want. Drinks and desserts are not usually included, you have to pay for them separately. In some *restaurantes à la carte*, you can ask for the traditional *à la minuta*, which includes white rice, a steak, French fries, fried egg and salad.

▸ I'd like to report the loss of my credit cards eu queria informar que perdi meus cartões de crédito [ew keree-a eenfoh-mah kee peh-djee mewsh kah-toyngsh djee kredjeetoo]

reservation a reserva [hezeh-va]
  ▸ do you have to make a reservation? tem que fazer reserva? [teng kee fazeh hezeh-va]
  ▸ I have a reservation in the name of Kennedy tenho uma reserva no nome de Kennedy [tenyoo ooma hezeh-va noo nomee djee Kennedy]

reserve *(ticket, room)* a reserva [hezeh-va]
  ▸ hello, I'd like to reserve a table for two for tomorrow night at 8 oi, eu queria reservar uma mesa para duas pessoas para amanhã às oito horas [oy ew keree-a hezeh-var ooma meza para doo-ash pesso-ash para amanyang az oytoo orash]

reserved *(booked)* reservado(da) [hezeh-vadoo(da)]
  ▸ is this table reserved? esta mesa está reservada? [eshta meza eeshta hezeh-vada]

rest *(relaxation)* o descanso [djeesh-kansoo] ◆ *(relax)* descansar [djeesh-kansah]
  ▸ I've come here to get some rest eu vim aqui para descansar [ew veeng akee para djeesh-kansah]

restaurant o restaurante [heshtow-rantchee]
  ▸ are there any good restaurants around here? tem algum restaurante bom por aqui? [teng owgoom heshtow-rantchee bong por akee]

restriction a restrição [heshtreessowng]
  ▸ are there restrictions on how much luggage you can take? tem restrição na quantidade de bagagem que dá para levar? [teng heshtreessowng na kwantchee-dadjee djee bagajeng kee da para levah]

restroom o banheiro [banyayroo]
  ▸ is there a restroom on the bus? tem banheiro no ônibus? [teng banyayroo noo oneeboosh]

retired aposentado(da) [apozentadoo(da)]
  ▸ I'm retired now agora estou aposentado [agora eeshto apozentadoo]

return *(arrival back)* a volta [vowta] ♦ devolver [devowveh]
> when do we have to return the car? quando que nós temos que devolver o carro? [kwandoo kee nosh temoosh kee devowver oo kahoo]

return trip a viagem de volta [vee-ajeng djee vowta]
> the return trip is scheduled for 6 o'clock a viagem de volta está marcada para as seis horas [a vee-ajeng djee vowta eeshta mah-kada para ash sayz orash]

rice o arroz [ahosh]
> I'd like some rice please eu queria arroz, por favor [ew keree-a ahosh poh favoh]

ride *(trip in a car, on a bike and motorcycle)* o passeio [passayoo]; *(lift)* a carona [karona]
> do you want a ride? quer uma carona? [ker ooma karona]
> where can we go for a ride around here? onde a gente pode passear por aqui? [ondjee a jentchee podjee passee-ah por akee]

riding *(on horseback)* a equitação [ekeetassowng]
> to go riding montar [montah]

right direito(ta) [djeeraytoo(ta)] ♦ a direita [djeerayta]
> to the right (of) à direita (de) [a djeerayta (djee)]
> that's right é isso aí [eh eessoo a-ee]
> I don't think the check's right acho que a conta está errada [ashoo kee a konta eeshta ehada]
> is this the right bus for Rio? é este o ônibus para o Rio? [eh esh-tchee oo oneeboosh para oo hee-oo]
> is this the right number? é este o número certo? [eh esh-tchee oo noomeroo seh-too]
> take the next right na próxima vire à direita [na prosseema veeree a djeerayta]
> you have to turn right tem que dobrar à direita [teng kee dobrar a djeerayta]

---

at a restaurant

> I'd like to reserve a table for tonight eu queria reservar uma mesa para hoje à noite [ew keree-a hezeh-var ooma meza para ojee a noytchee]
> can we see the menu? podemos ver o cardápio? [podemoosh ver oo kah-dapyoo]
> do you have a set menu? vocês têm o menu do dia? [vossesh tayeng oo menoo do djee-a]
> rare/medium/well done, please bem mal passado/mal passado/bem passado, por favor [beng mow passadoo/mow passadoo/beng passadoo poh favoh]
> can I have the check, please? você pode trazer a conta, por favor? [vosse podjee trazer a konta poh favoh]

right-hand à direita [a djeerayta]
> it's on the right-hand side of the steering column fica à direita da direção [feeka a djeerayta da djeeressowng]

right of way a prioridade [pree-oree-dadjee]
> who has the right of way here? quem tem prioridade aqui? [keng teng pree-oree-dadjee akee]

road a estrada [eeshtrada]
> which road do I take for Brasília? que estrada eu pego para Brasília? [ke eeshtrada ew pegoo para brazeelya]
> what is the speed limit on this road? qual é o limite de velocidade nesta estrada? [kwal eh oo leemeetchee djee velossee-dadjee neshta eeshtrada]

rob (person) roubar [hobah]
> I've been robbed me roubaram [mee hobarowng]

rock climbing o alpinismo [owpeeneejmoo]
> can you go rock climbing here? dá para praticar alpinismo aqui? [da para pratcheekar owpeeneejmoo akee]

roller skate os patins [patcheengsh]
> where can we rent roller skates? onde a gente pode alugar patins? [ondjee a jentchee podjee aloogah patcheengsh]

room (bedroom, in a house, building) o quarto [kwah-too]; (space) o espaço [eeshpassoo]
> do you have any rooms available? tem quartos vagos? [teng kwah-toosh vagoosh]
> how much is a room with a bathroom? quanto custa um quarto com banheiro? [kwantoo kooshta oom kwah-too kong banyayroo]
> I've reserved a room for tonight under the name Pearson reservei um quarto para hoje à noite em nome de Pearson [hezeh-vay oom kwah-too para ojee a noytchee eng nomee djee Pearson]
> can I see the room? dá para ver o quarto? [da para ver oo kwah-too]

rosé (wine) rosé [ho-ze] ◆ o vinho rosé [veenyoo ho-ze]
> could you recommend a good rosé? você poderia recomendar um bom vinho rosé? [vosse poderee-a hekomendar oom bong veenyoo ho-ze]

round trip a viagem de ida e volta [vee-ajeng djee eeda ee vowta]
> how long will the round trip take? quanto tempo leva a viagem de ida e volta? [kwantoo tempoo leva a vee-ajeng djee eeda ee vowta]

round-trip ticket a passagem de ida e volta [passajeng djee eeda ee vowta]
> two round-trip tickets to Fortaleza, please duas passagens de ida e volta para Fortaleza, por favor [doo-ash passajengsh djee eeda ee vowta para foh-taleza poh favoh]
> I'd like a round-trip ticket to Natal, leaving on the 3rd and coming back on the 9th eu queria uma passagem de ida e volta para Natal, indo no dia três e voltando no dia nove [ew keree-a ooma passajeng djee eeda ee vowta para natow eendoo noo djee-a tresh ee vowtandoo noo djee-a novee]

route a rota [hota]

▸ is there an alternative route we could take? tem uma rota alternativa que a gente poderia pegar? [teng ooma hota owteh-natcheeva kee a jentchee poderee-a pegah]

row *(of seats)* a fila [feela]

▸ can we have seats in the front row? você pode nos dar lugares na primeira fila? [vosse podjee nosh dah loogareesh na preemayra feela]

rowboat o bote a remo [botchee a hemoo]

▸ can we rent a rowboat? dá para alugar botes a remo? [da para aloogah botcheez a hemoo]

rubber ring a bóia [boya]

▸ where can I buy a rubber ring? onde eu posso comprar uma bóia? [ondjee ew possoo komprar ooma boya]

run *(on foot)* a corrida [koheeda]; *(in a car)* o passeio [passayoo]; *(for skiing)* a pista [peeshta] ✦ *(on foot)* correr [koheh]; *(bus)* passar [passah]; *(engine)* funcionar [foonss-yonah] ✦ *(traffic light)* passar [passah]

▸ I'm going for a run vou dar uma corrida [vo dar ooma koheeda]

▸ the bus runs every half hour o ônibus passa a cada meia hora [oo oneeboosh passa a kada maya ora]

running a corrida [koheeda]

▸ where can you go running here? onde a gente pode ir dar uma corrida aqui? [ondjee a jentchee podjee eeh dar ooma koheeda akee]

run out of ficar sem [feekah seng]

▸ I've run out of gas fiquei sem gasolina [feekay seng gazoleena]

S

safe seguro(ra) [segooroo(ra)] ✦ *(for valuables)* o cofre [kofree]

▸ is it safe to swim here? é seguro nadar aqui? [eh segooroo nadar akee]

▸ is it safe to camp here? é seguro acampar aqui? [eh segooroo akampar akee]

▸ is there a safe in the room? tem cofre no quarto? [teng kofree noo kwah-too]

sail *(of a boat)* a vela [vela]

▸ we need to adjust that sail precisamos ajustar aquela vela [presseezamooz ajooshtar akela vela]

sailboat o veleiro [velayroo]

▸ can we rent a sailboat? dá para alugar um veleiro? [da para aloogar oom velayroo]

sailing a vela [vela]

▸ to go sailing ir velejar [eeh velejah]

▸ I'd like to take beginners' sailing classes eu queria fazer uma aulas de vela para iniciantes [ew keree-a fazer oomaz owlash djee vela para eeneess-yantcheesh]

salad a salada [salada]

▸ can I just have a salad? pode me trazer só uma salada, por favor? [podjee mee trazeh so ooma salada poh favoh]

sale *(selling)* a venda [venda]; *(at reduced prices)* a liquidação [leekeedassowng]

▸ is it for sale? está à venda? [eeshta a venda]

▸ can you get your money back on sale items? devolvem o dinheiro nos produtos em liquidação? [devovveng oo djeenyayroo noosh prodootooz eng leekeedassowng]

sales tax o IVA [eeva]

▸ is sales tax included? o IVA está incluído? [oo eeva eeshta eenklweedoo]

▸ can you deduct the sales tax? dá para deduzir o IVA? [da para dedoozeer oo eeva]

salt o sal [sow]

▸ can you pass me the salt? pode me passar o sal? [podjee mee passar oo sow]

▸ it doesn't have enough salt tem pouco sal [teng pokoo sow]

salty salgado(da) [sowgadoo(da)]

▸ it's too salty tem muito sal [teng mweentoo sow]

same mesmo(ma) [mejmoo(ma)]

▸ I'll have the same quero o mesmo [keroo oo mejmoo]

▸ the same (as) o mesmo (que) [oo mejmoo (kee)]

▸ it's the same as yours é o mesmo que tu [eh oo mejmoo kee too]

sandwich o sanduíche [sandweeshe]

▸ a chicken sandwich, please um sanduíche de frango, por favor [oom sandweeshe djee frangoo poh favoh]

Saturday o sábado [sabadoo]

▸ Saturday, September 13th sábado, treze de setembro [sabadoo trezee djee setembroo]

▸ it's closed on Saturdays fecha aos sábados [fesha owsh sabadoosh]

sauce o molho [molyoo]

▸ do you have a sauce that isn't too strong? tem um molho que não seja tão forte? [teng oom molyoo kee nowng seja towng foh-tchee]

sauna a sauna [sowna]

▸ is there a sauna? tem sauna? [teng sowna]

sausage a salsicha [sowseesha]

▸ I'd like to try some of the hot sausage eu queria provar uma dessas salsichas picantes [ew keree-a provar ooma dessash sowseeshash peekantcheesh]

say dizer [djeezeh]

▸ how do you say 'good luck' in Portuguese? como se diz 'good luck' em português? [komoo see djeesh good luck eng poh-toogesh]

scared

▸ to be scared estar assustado(da) [eeshtar assooshtadoo(da)]

▸ I'm scared of spiders tenho medo de aranha [tenyoo medoo djee aranya]

scheduled flight o vôo regular [vo-oo hegoolah]

▸ when is the next scheduled flight to Dallas? qual é o próximo vôo regular para Dallas? [kwal eh oo prosseemoo vo-oo hegoolah para Dallas]

school *(for children)* o colégio [kolej-yoo], a escola [eeshkola]; *(college, university)* a universidade [ooneeveh-seedadjee]

▸ are you still in school? você ainda está na escola? [vosse a-eenda eeshta na eeshkola]

scoop *(of ice cream)* a bola [bolla]

▸ I'd like a cone with two scoops eu queria duas bolas de sorvete [ew keree-a doo-ash bollash djee soh-vetchee]

scooter a motocicleta [motoseekleta]

▸ I'd like to rent a scooter eu queria alugar uma motocicleta [ew keree-a aloogar ooma motoseekleta]

Scotch *(whiskey)* o Scotch [scotch]

▸ a Scotch on the rocks, please um Scotch com gelo, por favor [oom scotch kong jeloo poh favoh]

Scotch tape® Durex® [dooreks]

▸ do you have any Scotch tape®? tem Durex®? [teng dooreks]

scrambled eggs os ovos mexidos [ovoosh mesheedoosh]

▸ I'd like scrambled eggs for breakfast eu queria ovos mexidos no café da manhã [ew keree-a ovoosh mesheedoosh noo kaffe da manyang]

screen *(room in a movie theater)* a sala [sala]

▸ how many screens does the movie theater have? quantas salas tem esse cinema? [kwantash salash teng essee seenema]

scuba diving o mergulho [meh-goolyoo]

▸ can we go scuba diving? podemos ir mergulhar? [podemooz eeh meh-goolyah]

sea o mar [mah]

▸ the sea is rough o mar está agitado [oo mar eeshta ajeetadoo]

▸ how long does it take to walk to the sea? quanto tempo a gente leva para chegar ao mar caminhando? [kwantoo tempoo a jentchee leva para shegar ow mah kameenyandoo]

seasick enjoado(da) [enjwadoo(da)]

▸ I feel seasick estou enjoado [eeshto enjwadoo]

seasickness o enjôo [enjo-oo]

▸ can you give me something for seasickness, please? você pode me dar alguma coisa para enjôo, por favor? [vosse podjee mee dar owgooma koyza para enjo-oo poh favoh]

seaside resort o balneário [bownee-aryoo]
- what's the nearest seaside resort? qual é o balneário mais perto? [kwal eh oo bownee-aryoo mysh peh-too]

season *(of the year)* a estação [eeshtassowng]
- what is the best season to come here? qual é a melhor estação para vir aqui? [kwal eh a melyor eeshtassowng para veer akee]

season ticket a entrada para toda a temporada [entrada para toda a temporada]
- how much is a season ticket? quanto custa a entrada para toda a temporada? [kwantoo kooshta a entrada para toda a temporada]

seat *(chair)* a cadeira [kadayra]; *(in a bus, car)* o banco [bankoo]; *(in a theater, a movie theater)* a poltrona [powtrona]
- is this seat taken? este lugar está ocupado? [esh-tchee loogar eeshta okoopadoo]
- excuse me, I think you're (sitting) in my seat desculpe, mas acho que você está no meu lugar [djeeshkoowpee myz ashoo kee vosse eeshta noo mew loogah]

second *(unit of time)* o segundo [segoondoo]; *(gear)* a segunda [segoonda]
◆ segundo(da) [segoondoo(da)]
- wait a second! espera um segundo! [eeshpera oom segoondoo]
- is it in second? está em segunda? [eeshta eng segoonda]
- it's the second street on your right é a segunda rua à direita [eh a segoonda hoo-a a djeerayta]

second class a segunda classe [segoonda klassee] ◆ de segunda classe [djee segoonda klassee]
- your seat's in second class sua poltrona é na segunda classe [soo-a powtrona eh na segoonda klassee]
- to travel second class viajar de segunda classe [vee-ajah djee segoonda klassee]

see ver [veh]
- I'm here to see Dr. Brown estou aqui para ver o Dr. Brown [eeshto akee para ver oo dotoh Brown]
- can I see the room? posso ver o quarto? [possoo ver oo kwah-too]
- I'd like to see the dress in the window eu gostaria de ver o vestido da vitrine [ew goshtaree-a djee ver oo vesh-tcheedoo da veetreenee]
- see you soon! até logo mais! [a-te logoo mysh]
- see you later até mais tarde! [a-te mysh tah-djee]
- see you (on) Thursday! até quinta! [a-te keenta]

self-service *(restaurant)* self-service [self-service]; *(gas station)* de auto-serviço [djee owto-seh-veessoo] ◆ *(restaurant)* o restaurante com bufê [heshtow-rantchee kong boofe]; *(gas station)* o posto de auto-serviço [poshtoo djee owto-seh-veessoo]; *(system)* o sistema de self-service [seeshtema djee self-service]
- is it self-service? é self-service? [eh self-service]

sell vender [vendeh]
- do you sell stamps? você vende selos? [vosse vendjee seloosh]

▸ the radio I was sold is defective o rádio que me venderem está com defeito [oo hadyoo ke mee venderowng eeshta kong defaytoo]

send enviar [envee-ah]
▸ I'd like to send this package to Los Angeles by airmail eu queria enviar este pacote para Los Angeles por correio aéreo [ew keree-a envee-ar esh-tchee pakotchee para Los Angeles poh kohayoo a-eree-oo]
▸ could you send a tow truck? você poderia mandar um reboque? [vosse poderee-a mandar oom hebokee]

separately *(individually)* separadamente [separadamentchee]
▸ is it sold separately? é vendido separadamente? [eh vendjeedoo separadamentch-ee]

September setembro [setembroo]
▸ September 9th nove de setembro [novee djee setembroo]

serve *(meal, drink, customer)* servir [seh-veeh]; *(town, station)* ir [eeh]
▸ when is breakfast served? a que horas é servido o café da manhã? [a kee oraz eh seh-veedoo oo kaffe da manyang]
▸ are you still serving lunch? vocês ainda estão servindo almoço? [vossez a-eenda eeshtowng seh-veendoo owmossoo]

service *(in a restaurant)* o atendimento [atendjee-mentoo] ◆ *(car)* fazer uma revisão em [fazer ooma heveezowng eng]
▸ the service was terrible o atendimento era horroroso [oo atendjeementoo era ohorozoo]
▸ we have to have the car serviced temos que fazer uma revisão no carro [temoosh kee fazer ooma heveezowng noo kahoo]

service charge a taxa de serviço [tasha djee seh-veessoo]
▸ is the service charge included? a taxa de serviço já está incluída? [a tasha djee seh-veessoo ja eeshta eenklweeda]

set *(of cookware)* o conjunto [konjoontoo]; *(of keys)* o jogo [jogoo] ◆ *(sun)* pôr-se [poh-see]
▸ do you have a spare set of keys? você tem um jogo extra de chaves? [vosse teng oom jogoo eshtra djee shaveesh]
▸ what time does the sun set? a que horas o sol se põe? [a kee oraz oo sow see poyng]

seven sete [setchee]
▸ there are seven of us somos sete [somoosh setchee]

several vários(rias) [varyoosh(yash)]
▸ I've been before, several years ago já estive lá, faz vários anos [ja eesh-tcheevee la faj varyooz anoosh]

shade *(shadow)* a sombra [sombra]
▸ can we have a table in the shade? poderíamos sentar numa mesa na sombra? [poderee-amoosh sentar nooma meza na sombra]

shake *(bottle)* agitar [ajeetah] ◆ *(in agreement)* fechar acordo [feshar akoh-doo]
  ▸ to shake hands apertar as mãos [apeh-tar ash mowngsh]
  ▸ let's shake aperta aqui [apeh-ta akee]

shame *(remorse, humiliation)* a vergonha [veh-gonya]; *(pity)* a pena [pena]
  ▸ (what a) shame! que pena! [ke pena]

shampoo o xampu [shampoo]
  ▸ do you have any shampoo? tem xampu? [teng shampoo]

share compartilhar [kompah-tcheelyah]
  ▸ we're going to share it: can you bring us two plates? vamos compartilhar: pode nos trazer dois pratos? [vamoosh kompah-tcheelyah podjee nosh trazeh doysh pratoosh]

shared *(bathroom, kitchen)* compartilhado(da) [kompah-tcheelyadoo(da)]
  ▸ is the bathroom shared? o banheiro é compartilhado? [oo banyayroo eh kompah-tcheelyadoo]

shaver o barbeador [bah-bee-adoh]
  ▸ where can I buy a new shaver? onde eu posso comprar um novo barbeador? [ondjee ew possoo komprar oom novoo bah-bee-adoh]

sheet *(for a bed)* o lençol [lensow]; *(of paper)* a folha [folya]
  ▸ could you change the sheets? você poderia trocar os lençóis? [vosse poderee-a trokar oosh lensoysh]

ship o navio [navee-oo]
  ▸ when does the ship dock? quando o navio atraca? [kwandoo oo navee-oo atraka]

shoe o sapato [sapatoo]
  ▸ what sort of shoes should you wear? que tipo de sapato você deve usar? [ke tchepoo djee sapatoo vosse devee oozah]

shoe size o número (do sapato) [noomeroo (doo sapatoo)]
  ▸ what's your shoe size? que número você calça? [ke noomeroo vosse kowsa]

shop *(store)* a loja [loja]
  ▸ what time do the shops downtown close? a que horas as lojas fecham no centro? [a kee oraz ash lojash feshowng noo sentroo]

shopping as compras [komprash]
  ▸ where can you go shopping around here? onde a gente pode ir para fazer compras por aqui? [ondjee a jentchee podjee eeh para fazeh komprash por akee]

shopping bag o saco plástico [sakoo plash-tcheekoo]
  ▸ can I have a plastic shopping bag, please? pode me dar um saco plástico, por favor? [podjee mee dar oom sakoo plash-tcheekoo poh favoh]

shopping center o shopping center [shopping center]
  ▸ I'm looking for a shopping center estou procurando um shopping center [eeshto prokoorandoo oom shopping center]

shop window a vitrine [veetreenee]

▸ we've just been peeking in the shop windows estivemos olhando as vitrines [eesh-tcheevemooz olyandoo ash veetreeneesh]

short *(in time, length)* curto(ta) [kooh-too(ta)]; *(in height)* baixo(xa) [by-shoo(sha)]

▸ we're only here for a short time vamos ficar aqui só um pouco [vamoosh feekar akee so oom pooko]

▸ we'd like to do a shorter trip queríamos fazer uma viagem mais curta [kereeamoosh fazer ooma vee-ajeng mysh kooh-ta]

▸ I'm two dollars short estão me faltando dois dólares [eeshtowng mee fowtandoo doysh dolareesh]

shortcut o atalho [atalyoo]

▸ is there a shortcut? tem um atalho? [teng oom atalyoo]

short wave a onda curta [onda kooh-ta]

▸ can you get any English stations on short wave? dá para pegar alguma estação em inglês em ondas curtas? [da para pegar owgooma eeshtassowng eng eenglesh eng ondash kooh-tash]

should dever [deveh]

▸ what should I do? o que eu deveria fazer? [oo kee ew deveree-a fazeh]

show *(at the theater)* a apresentação [aprezentassowng]; *(at the movies)* a exibição [ezeebeessowng] ◆ *(let see)* mostrar [moshtrah]

▸ what time does the show begin? a que horas começa o espetáculo? [a kee orash komessa oo eeshpetakooloo]

▸ could you show me where that is on the map? você poderia me mostrar no mapa onde fica isso? [vosse poderee-a mee moshtrah noo mapa ondjee feeka eessoo]

▸ could you show me the room? poderia me mostrar o quarto? [poderee-a mee moshtrar oo kwah-too]

shower *(device)* o chuveiro [shoovayroo]; *(act)* a ducha [doosha]; *(of rain)* o aguaceiro [agwassayroo]

▸ I'd like a room with a shower, please eu queria um quarto com chuveiro, por favor [ew keree-a oom kwah-too kong shoovayroo poh favoh]

▸ how does the shower work? como funciona o chuveiro? [komoo foonss-yona oo shoovayroo]

▸ the shower is leaking o chuveiro fica pingando [oo shoovayroo feeka peengandoo]

shower head o espalhador do chuveiro [eeshpal-yadoh doo shoovayroo]

▸ the shower head is broken o espalhador do chuveiro está quebrado [oo eeshpal-yadoh doo shoovayroo eeshta kebradoo]

shrimp o camarão [kamarowng]

▸ I'm allergic to shrimp sou alérgico a camarão [so aleh-jeekoo a kamarowng]

shut *(door, window)* fechar [feshah]

▸ the window won't shut a janela não fecha [a janela nowng fesha]

shutter *(on a window)* a veneziana [venezee-ana]; *(on a camera)* o obturador [obtooradoh]

▶ are there shutters on the windows? tem veneziana nas janelas? [teng venezee-ana nash janelash]

shuttle *(vehicle)* o serviço de conexão [seh-veessoo djee koneksowng]

▶ is there a shuttle to the airport? tem um serviço de conexão para o aeroporto? [teng oom seh-veessoo djee koneksowng para oo a-eropoh-too]

sick *(unwell)* doente [dwentchee]

▶ I feel sick estou enjoado [eeshto enjwadoo]

▶ to be sick *(be unwell)* estar doente [eeshtah dwentchee]; *(vomit)* vomitar [vomeetah]

side *(of the body, an object, opposing part)* o lado [ladoo]; *(edge)* a borda [bohda]

▶ I have a pain in my right side me dói o lado direito do corpo [mee doy oo ladoo djeeraytoo doo koh-poo]

▶ could we have a table on the other side of the room? poderia colocar uma mesa do outro lado do quarto? [poderee-a kolokar ooma meza doo otroo ladoo doo kwah-too]

▶ which side of the road do we drive on here? em que lado da estrada a gente tem que dirigir aqui? [eng ke ladoo da eeshtrada a jentchee teng kee djeereejeer akee]

sidewalk a calçada [kowsada]

▶ the sidewalks are very clean here as calçadas estão muito limpas aqui [ash kowsadaz eeshtowng mweentoo leempaz akee]

sight *(seeing)* a visão [veezowng] ◆ **sights** *(of a place)* os pontos de interesse [pontoosh djee eenteressee]

▶ I'm having problems with my sight estou tendo problemas de visão [eeshto tendoo problemash djee veezowng]

▶ what are the sights that are most worth seeing? quais são os pontos de interesse que valem mais a pena ver? [kwysh sowng oosh pontoosh djee eenteressee kee valeng myz a pena veh]

sign assinar [asseenah]

▶ do I sign here? assino aqui? [asseenoo akee]

signpost a sinalização [senaleezassowng]

▶ does the route have good signposts? a estrada tem uma boa sinalização? [a eeshtrada teng ooma boa seenaleezassowng]

silver *(metal)* a prata [prata]

▶ is it made of silver? é feito de prata? [eh faytoo djee prata]

since desde [dej-djee] ◆ *(in time)* desde que [dej-djee kee]; *(because)* já que [ja kee], como [komoo]

▶ I've been here since Tuesday estou aqui desde terça-feira [eeshto akee dej-djee teh-sa-fayra]

▶ it hasn't rained once since we've been here não choveu nem uma vez desde que estamos aqui [nowng shovew neng ooma vesh dej-djee kee eeshtamooz akee]

single *(only one)* só [so]; *(unmarried)* solteiro(ra) [sowtayroo(ra)] ◆ *(CD)* o CD com só uma música [se-de kong so ooma moozeeka]

▶ not a single one nem um [neng oom]

▶ I'm single sou solteiro/solteira [so sowtayroo/sowtayra]

▶ she's a single woman in her thirties é uma mulher solteira de trinta e poucos anos [eh ooma moolyeh sowtayra djee treenta ee pokooz anoosh]

single bed a cama de solteiro [kama djee sowtayroo]

▶ we'd prefer two single beds preferimos duas camas de solteiro [prefereemoosh doo-ash kamash djee sowtayroo]

single room o quarto de solteiro [kwah-too djee sowtayroo]

▶ I'd like to book a single room for 5 nights, please eu queria reservar um quarto de solteiro por cinco noites, por favor [ew keree-a hezeh-var oom kwah-too djee sowtayroo poh seenkoo noytcheesh poh favoh]

sister a irmã [eeh-mang]

▶ I have two sisters tenho duas irmãs [tenyoo doo-az eeh-mangsh]

sit sentar [sentah]

▶ may I sit at your table? posso sentar na sua mesa? [possoo sentah na soo-a meza]

▶ is anyone sitting here? tem alguém sentado aqui? [teng owgeng sentadoo akee]

site *(of a town, a building)* a localização [lokaleezassowng]; *(archeological)* o sítio [seetyoo]

▶ can we visit the site? podemos visitar o sítio? [podemoosh veezeetar oo seetyoo]

sitting *(for a meal)* o turno [tooh-noo]

▶ is there more than one sitting for lunch? tem mais de um turno para o almoço? [teng mysh djee oom tooh-noo para oo owmossoo]

six seis [saysh]

▶ there are six of us somos seis [somoosh saysh]

sixth sexto(ta) [seshtoo(ta)]

▶ our room is on the sixth floor nosso quarto fica no sexto andar [nossoo kwah-too feeka noo seshtoo andah]

size *(of a person, clothes)* o tamanho [tamanyoo]; *(of shoes)* o número [noomeroo]

▶ do you have another size? tem outro tamanho? [teng otroo tamanyoo]

▶ do you have it in a smaller size? tem em um tamanho menor? [teng noom tamanyoo menoh]

▶ I take or I'm a size 38 *(shoes)* calço trinta e oito [kalsoo treenta ee oytoo]; *(clothes)* meu tamanho é trinta e oito [mew tamanyoo eh treenta ee oytoo]

sleep dormir [doh-meeh]

▶ I slept well dormi bem [doh-mee beng]

▶ I can't sleep não consigo dormir [nowng konseegoo doh-meeh]

sleeping bag o saco de dormir [sakoo djee doh-meeh]
- where can I buy a new sleeping bag? onde eu posso comprar um saco de dormir novo? [ondjee ew possoo komprar oom sakoo djee doh-meeh novoo]

sleeping pill o comprimido para dormir [kompreemeedoo para doh-meeh]
- I'd like some sleeping pills eu queria alguns comprimidos para dormir [ew keree-a owgoonsh kompreemeedoosh para doh-meeh]

slice *(of bread, ham)* a fatia [fatchee-a] ♦ fatiar [fatchee-ah]
- a thin slice of ham uma fatia fina de presunto [ooma fatchee-a feena djee prezoontoo]

slim *(person)* magro(gra) [magroo(gra)]
- she's slim ela é magra [ella eh magra]

slow *(gen)* devagar [djeevagah]; *(clock, watch)* atrasado(da) [atrazadoo(da)]
- the fog was slow to clear demorou para sumir o nevoeiro [demoro para soomeer oo nevwayroo]
- is that clock slow? aquele relógio está atrasado? [akelee heloj-yoo eeshta atrazadoo]

slowly devagar [djeevagah]
- could you speak more slowly, please? você pode falar um pouco mais devagar, por favor? [vosse podjee falar oom pokoo mysh djeevagah poh favoh]

small pequeno(na) [pekenoo(na)]
- do you have anything smaller? tem alguma coisa menor? [teng owgooma koyza menoh]

smell *(notice a smell of)* sentir cheiro de [sentcheeh shayroo djee] ♦ *(have a smell)* cheirar [shayrah]; *(have a bad smell)* cheirar mal [shayrah mow]
- can you smell something burning? você sente cheiro de coisa queimada? [vosse sentchee shayroo djee koyza kaymada]
- it smells in here tem cheiro ruim aqui [teng shayroo hoo-eeng akee]

smoke a fumaça [foomassa] ♦ *(person)* fumar [foomah]
- is the smoke bothering you? a fumaça está incomodando você? [a foomassa eeshta eenkomodandoo vosse]
- do you mind if I smoke? você se importa se eu fumar? [vosse see eempoh-ta see ew foomah]
- no thanks, I don't smoke não, obrigado, não fumo [nowng obreegadoo nowng foomoo]

smoker o(a) fumante [foomantchee]
- are you smokers or nonsmokers? para fumantes ou não? [para foomantcheez o nowng]

smoking
- is smoking allowed here? se pode fumar aqui? [see podjee foomar akee]
- I can't stand smoking eu não agüento o cigarro [ew nowng agwentoo oo seegahoo]

smoking compartment, smoking section a ala para fumantes [ala para foomantcheesh]

▸ is there a smoking compartment? **tem ala para fumantes?** [teng ooma ala para foomantcheesh]

▸ I'd like a table in the smoking section **eu queria uma mesa na ala para fumantes** [ew keree-a ooma meza na ala para foomantcheesh]

sneaker o tênis [teneesh]

▸ your sneakers are really trendy! **seus tênis estão bem na moda!** [sewsh teneesh eeshtowng beng na moda]

snorkel o tubo de oxigênio [tooboo djee oksee-jenyoo]

▸ I'd like to rent a snorkel and mask, please **eu queria alugar um tubo de oxigênio e uma máscara, por favor** [ew keree-a aloogar oom tooboo djee oksee-jenyoo ee ooma mashkara poh favoh]

so *(to such a degree)* tão [towng]; *(also)* também [tambeng]; *(consequently)* por isso [por eessoo]

▸ it's so big! **é tão grande!** [eh towng grandjee]

▸ there's so many choices I don't know what to have **tem tantas opções que eu não sei o que escolher** [teng tantaz opsoyngsh kee ew nowng say oo kee eeshkolyeh]

▸ I'm hungry – so am I! **estou com fome – eu também!** [eeshto kong fomee ew tambeng]

soap o sabão [sabowng]

▸ there's no soap **não tem sabão** [nowng teng sabowng]

socket *(in a wall)* a tomada [tomada]

▸ is there a socket I can use to recharge my cell? **tem uma tomada onde eu possa recarregar o meu celular?** [teng ooma tomada ondjee ew possa heka-hegar oo mew seloolah]

solution a solução [soloossowng]

▸ that seems to be the best solution **essa parece ser a melhor solução** [essa paressee ser a melyoh soloossowng]

▸ I'd like some rinsing solution for soft lenses **eu queria uma solução de limpeza para lentes gelatinosas** [ew keree-a ooma soloossowng djee leempeza para lentcheesh jelatchee-nozash]

some *(an amount of)* um pouco de [oom pokoo djee]; *(a number of)* algum(ma) [owgoom(ma)]

▸ I'd like some coffee **eu queria um pouco de café** [ew keree-a oom pokoo djee kaffe]

▸ some friends recommended this place **alguns amigos recomendaram este lugar** [owgoonz ameegoosh hekomendarowng esh-tchee loogah]

▸ can I have some? **pode colocar um pouco?** [podjee kolokar oom pokoo]

saying sorry

The word *desculpe* is the normal way of apologizing to anybody, from friends and family to complete strangers. If you want to be more formal and emphatic, say *perdão*.

somebody, someone alguém [owgeng]
  ▸ somebody left this for you alguém deixou isso para ti [owgeng daysho eessoo para tchee]

something algo [owgoo], alguma coisa [owgooma koyza]
  ▸ is something wrong? tem alguma coisa errada? [teng owgooma koyza ehada]

somewhere algum lugar [owgoom loogah]
  ▸ I'm looking for somewhere to stay estou procurando um lugar para ficar [eeshto prokoorandoo oom loogah para feekah]
  ▸ somewhere near here algum lugar perto daqui [owgoom loogah peh-too dakee]
  ▸ somewhere else algum outro lugar [owgoom otroo loogah]

son o filho [feelyoo]
  ▸ this is my son este é o meu filho [esh-tchee eh oo mew feelyoo]

soon logo [logoo]
  ▸ see you soon! até logo! [a-te logoo]
  ▸ as soon as possible o quanto antes [oo kwantoo antcheesh]

sore throat a dor de garganta [doh djee gah-ganta]
  ▸ I have a sore throat estou com dor de garganta [eeshto kong doh djee gah-ganta]

sorry
  ▸ I'm sorry desculpe [djeeshkoowpee], sinto muito [seentoo mweentoo]
  ▸ sorry I'm late desculpe, estou atrasado [djeeshkoowpee eeshto atrazadoo]
  ▸ I'm sorry, but this seat is taken desculpe, mas este lugar está ocupado [djeeshkoowpee myz esh-tchee loogar eeshta okoopadoo]
  ▸ sorry to bother you lamento incomodá-lo [lamentoo eenkomoda-loo]
  ▸ sorry? *(asking for repetition)* como? [komoo]
  ▸ no, sorry não, sinto muito [nowng seentoo mweentoo]

sound *(of footsteps, conversation, voice)* o som [song]; *(of a TV, radio)* o volume [voloomee]
  ▸ can you turn the sound down? pode abaixar o volume? [podjee a-by-shar oo voloomee]

souvenir a lembrancinha [lembran-seenyash]
  ▸ where can I buy souvenirs? onde eu posso comprar lembrancinhas? [ondjee ew possoo komprah lembran-seenyash]

souvenir shop a loja de lembranças [loja djee lembranssash]

▸ I'm looking for a souvenir shop estou procurando uma loja de lembrancinhas [eeshto prokoorandoo ooma loja djee lembran-seenyash]

spa *(town)* a estação de águas minerais [eeshtassowng djee agwash meenerysh]; *(health club)* o spa [spa]; *(bathtub)* a banheira de hidromassagem [banyayra djee eedro-massajeng]

▸ the spa's not working a banheira de hidromassagem não está funcionando [a banyayra djee eedro-massajeng nowng eeshta foonss-yonando]

space o espaço [eeshpassoo]

▸ is there space for another bed in the room? tem espaço para outra cama no quarto? [teng eeshpassoo para otra kama noo kwah-too]

▸ I'd like a space for one tent for two days eu queria espaço para uma barraca por dois dias [ew keree-a eeshpassoo para ooma bahaka por doysh djee-ash]

▸ do you have any spaces farther from the road? vocês têm lugares mais longes da estrada? [vossesh tayng loogareesh mysh lonjeesh da eeshtrada]

spade *(child's toy)* a pazinha [pazeenya]

▸ my son's left his spade at the beach o meu filho deixou a pazinha na praia [oo mew feelyoo daysho a pazeenya na pry-a]

spare *(clothes, battery)* extra [eshtra] ◆ *(tire)* o estepe [eeshtepee]; *(part)* a peça de reposição [pessa djee hepozeessowng]

▸ should I take some spare clothes? eu deveria levar algumas roupas extras? [ew deveree-a levar owgoomash hopaz eshtrash]

▸ I don't have any spare cash não tenho nenhum dinheiro extra [nowng tenyoo nenyoom djeen-yayroo eshtra]

▸ I've got a spare ticket for the game eu tenho uma entrada sobrando para o jogo [ew tenyoo ooma entrada sobrandoo para oo jogoo]

spare part a peça de reposição [pessa djee hepozeessowng]

▸ where can I get spare parts? onde eu consigo peças de reposição? [ondjee ew konseegoo pessash djee hepozeessowng]

spare tire o estepe [eeshtepee]

▸ the spare tire's flat too o estepe também está furado [oo eeshtepee tambeng eeshta fooradoo]

spare wheel o estepe [eeshtepee]

▸ there's no spare wheel não tem estepe [nowng teng eeshtepee]

sparkling *(water)* com gás [kong gash]; *(wine)* espumante [eeshpoomantchee]

▸ could I have a bottle of sparkling water, please? poderia me trazer uma garrafa de água com gás, por favor? [poderee-a mee trazer ooma gahafa djee agwa kong gash poh favoh]

speak falar [falah]

▸ I speak hardly any Portuguese eu falo português mal e porcamente [ew faloo poh-toogesh mow ee poh-kamentchee]

- is there anyone here who speaks English? **tem alguém aqui que fale inglês?** [teng owgeng akee kee falee eenglesh]
- could you speak more slowly? **você poderia falar mais devagar?** [vosse poderee-a falah mysh djeevagah]
- hello, I'd like to speak to Mr...; this is... **oi, eu gostaria de falar com o Sr....; aqui é...** [oy ew goshtaree-a djee falah kong oo senyoh akee eh]
- who's speaking please? **quem está falando?** [keng eeshta falandoo]
- hello, Gary speaking **olá, é o Gary** [o-la eh oo Gary]

special o prato do dia [pratoo doo djee-a]

- what's today's special? **qual é o prato do dia?** [kwal eh oo pratoo doo djee-a]

specialist o(a) especialista [eeshpess-yaleeshta]

- could you refer me to a specialist? **você poderia me recomendar um especialista?** [vosse poderee-a mee hekomendar oom eeshpess-yaleeshta]

specialty a especialidade [eeshpess-yaleedadjee]

- what are the local specialties? **quais são as especialidades locais?** [kwysh sowng az eeshpess-yaleedadjeesh lokysh]

speed limit o limite de velocidade [leemeetchee djee velossee-dadjee]

- what's the speed limit on this road? **qual é o limite de velocidade nessa estrada?** [kwal eh oo leemeetchee djee velossee-dadjee nessa eeshtrada]

speedometer o velocímetro [velosseemetroo]

- the speedometer's broken **o velocímetro está quebrado** [oo velosseemetroo eeshta kebradoo]

speed trap o radar [hadah]

- are there lots of speed traps in the area? **tem muitos radares na região?** [teng mweentoosh hadareesh na hej-yowng]

spell escrever [eeshkreveh]

- how do you spell your name? **como se escreve o seu nome?** [komoo see eeshkrevee oo sew nomee]

spend *(money)* gastar [gashtah]; *(time, vacation)* passar [passah]

- we are prepared to spend up to 2000 reais **estamos dispostos a gastar até dois mil reais** [eeshtamoosh djeesh-poshtooz a gashtar a-te doysh meew hee-ysh]
- I spent a month in Bahia a few years ago **passei um mês na Bahia há alguns anos** [passay oom mesh na ba-ee-a a owgoonz anoosh]

spicy picante [peekantchee]

- is this dish spicy? **este prato é picante?** [esh-tchee pratoo eh peekantchee]

spoon a colher [kol-yeh]

- could I have a spoon? **poderia me alcançar uma colher?** [poderee-a mee owkansar ooma kol-yeh]

sport o esporte [eeshpoh-tchee]

- do you play any sports? **você pratica algum esporte?** [vosse pratcheeka owgoom eeshpoh-tchee]

▸ I play a lot of sports pratico muitos esportes [pratcheekoo mweentooz eeshpoh-tcheesh]

sporty *(person)* esportista [eeshpoh-tcheeshta]

▸ I'm not very sporty não sou muito esportista [nowng so mweentoo eeshpoh-tcheeshta]

sprain torcer [toh-seh]

▸ I think I've sprained my ankle acho que torci o tornozelo [ashoo kee toh-see oo toh-nozeloo]

▸ my wrist is sprained torci o pulso [toh-see oo poow-soo]

square *(in a town)* a praça [prassa]

▸ where is the main square? onde fica a praça principal? [ondjee feeka a prassa preenseepow]

stain a mancha [mansha]

▸ can you remove this stain? você consegue remover esta mancha? [vosse konsegee hemover eshta mansha]

stairs as escadas [eeshkadash]

▸ where are the stairs? onde ficam as escadas? [ondjee feekowng az eeshkadash]

stall *(car, engine)* enguiçar [engeessah]

▸ the engine keeps stalling o motor vive enguiçando [oo motoh veevee engeessandoo]

stamp *(for letter, postcard)* o selo [seloo]

▸ do you sell stamps? você vende selos? [vosse vendjee seloosh]

stand *(stall, booth)* a banca [banka], a barraca [bahaka]; *(in a stadium)* a arquibancada [ah-keebankada] ◆ *(tolerate)* agüentar [agwentah] ◆ *(be upright)* estar de pé [eeshtah djee pe]; *(get up)* ficar de pé [feekah djee pe]

▸ where's stand number five? onde fica a arquibancada número cinco? [ondjee feeka a ah-keebankada noomeroo seenkoo]

start *(begin)* começar [komessah]; *(function)* arrancar [ahankah]

▸ when does the concert start? quando começa o concerto? [kwandoo komessa oo konseh-too]

▸ the car won't start o carro não arranca [oo kahoo nowng ahanka]

starving faminto(ta) [fameentoo(ta)]

▸ I'm absolutely starving estou morrendo de fome [eeshto mohendoo djee fomee]

States

▸ the States os Estados Unidos [ooz eeshtadooz ooneedoosh]

▸ I'm from the States sou dos Estados Unidos [so dooz eeshtadooz ooneedoosh]

▸ have you ever been to the States? você já foi para os Estados Unidos? [vosse ja foy para ooz eeshtadooz ooneedoosh]

station a estação [eeshtassowng]; *(police)* a delegacia [delegassee-a]

▸ to the bus station, please! para a rodoviária, por favor! [para a hodovee-aree-a poh favoh]

▸ where is the nearest subway station? onde fica a estação de metrô mais próxima? [ondjee feeka a eeshtassowng djee metro mysh prosseema]

stay *(in a place)* ficar [feekah] ♦ *(visit)* a estadia [eeshtadjee-a]

▸ we're planning to stay for two nights estamos pensando em ficar por duas noites [eeshtamoosh pensandoo eng feekah poh doo-ash noytcheesh]

▸ a two-week stay uma estadia de dois dias [ooma eeshtadjee-a djee doysh djee-ash]

steak o bife [beefee]

▸ I'd like a steak and fries eu queria um bife com fritas [ew keree-a oom beefee kong freetash]

steal *(money, wallet, necklace)* roubar [hobah]

▸ my passport was stolen roubaram meu passaporte [hobarowng mew passapoh-tchee]

▸ our car has been stolen nosso carro foi roubado [nossoo kahoo foy hobadoo]

steering a direção [djeeressowng]

▸ there's a problem with the steering tem um problema com a direção [teng oom problema kong a djeeressowng]

steering wheel o volante [volantchee], a direção [djeeressowng]

▸ the steering wheel is very stiff a direção está muito dura [a djeeressowng eeshta mweentoo doora]

stick shift *(lever)* a alavanca de câmbio manual [alavanka djee kambyoo manwow]; *(car)* o carro com câmbio manual [kahoo kong kambyoo manwow]

▸ is it a stick shift or an automatic? é um carro com câmbio manual ou automático? [eh oom kahoo kong kambyoo manwow o owtomatcheekoo]

still ainda [a-eenda]

▸ how many kilometers are there still to go? quantos quilômetros ainda faltam? [kwantoosh keelometrooz a-eenda fowtowng]

▸ we're still waiting to be served ainda estamos esperando para sermos servidos [a-eenda eeshtamooz eeshperandoo para seh-moosh seh-veedoosh]

sting *(wasp, nettle)* picar [peekah]

▸ I've been stung by a wasp fui picado por uma vespa [fwee peekadoo por ooma veshpa]

stomach o estômago [eeshtomagoo]

▸ my stomach hurts meu estômago está doendo [mew eeshtomagoo eeshta dwendoo]

stomachache a dor de estômago [doh djee eeshtomagoo]

▸ I have a really bad stomachache estou com uma dor de estômago horrorosa [eeshto kong ooma doh djee eeshtomagoo ohoroza]

stop a parada [parada] ♦ parar [parah]

▸ is this the right stop for ...? esta é a parada certa para...? [eshta eh a parada seh-ta para]

▸ stop it! pare com isso! [paree kong eessoo]

▸ where in town does the shuttle stop? em que parte da cidade fica a conexão? [eng ke pah-tchee da seedadjee feeka a koneksowng]

▸ please stop here pare aqui, por favor [paree akee poh favoh]

▸ do we stop at Rio? a gente pára no Rio? [a jentchee para noo hee-oo]

store *(place selling goods)* a loja [loja]

▸ are there any bigger stores in the area? tem lojas maiores por aqui? [teng lojash my-oreesh por akee]

store window a vitrine [veetreenee]

▸ the store windows are beautifully decorated at Christmas as vitrines são maravilhosamente decoradas no Natal [ash veetreeneesh sowng maraveel-yozamentchee dekoradash noo natow]

storm o temporal [temporow]

▸ is there going to be a storm? vai ter um temporal? [vy ter oom temporow]

straight *(line, road)* reto(ta) [hetoo(ta)]; *(hair)* liso(sa) [leezoo(za)] ◆ *(in a straight line)* reto [hetoo]

▸ you have to keep going straight você tem que continuar reto [vosse teng kee konteenwah hetoo]

street a rua [hoo-a]

▸ will this street take me to the station? essa rua me leva até a estação? [essa hoo-a mee leva a-te a eeshtassowng]

streetcar o bonde [bondjee]

▸ can you buy tickets on the streetcar? dá para comprar bilhetes no bonde? [da para komprah beel-yetcheesh noo bondjee]

▸ which streetcar line do we have to take? que linha de bonde nós temos que pegar? [ke leenya djee bondjeesh nosh temoosh kee pegah]

▸ where is the nearest streetcar stop? onde fica a parada mais próxima de bonde? [ondjee feeka a parada mysh prosseema djee bondjee]

---

in a store

▸ no, thanks, I'm just looking não, obrigado, estou só olhando [nowng obreegadoo eeshto so olyandoo]

▸ how much is this? quanto custa? [kwantoo kooshta]

▸ I take a size 38/I'm a size 38 meu tamanho é trinta e oito [mew tamanyoo eh treenta ee oytoo]

▸ can I try this coat on? posso experimentar este casaco? [possoo eeshper-eementar esh-tchee kazakoo]

▸ can it be exchanged? dá para trocar? [da para trokah]

street map o mapa de ruas [mapa djee hoo-ash]
> where can I buy a street map? onde eu posso comprar um mapa de ruas? [ondjee ew possoo komprar oom mapa djee hoo-ash]

strong forte [foh-tchee]
> is the current very strong here? a corrente é muito forte aqui? [a kohentchee eh mweentoo foh-tchee akee]

stuck
> to be stuck *(jammed)* estar entupido(da) [eeshtar entoopeedoo(da)]; *(trapped)* estar preso(sa) [eeshtah prezoo(za)]
> someone is stuck in the elevator tem alguém preso no elevador [teng owgeng prezoo noo elevadoh]

student o(a) estudante [eeshtoo-dantchee]
> I'm a student sou estudante [so eeshtoo-dantchee]

student discount o desconto para estudantes [djeeshkontoo para eeshtoo-dantcheesh]
> do you have student discounts? vocês dão desconto para estudantes? [vossesh downg djeeshkontoo para eeshtoo-dantcheesh]

studio (apartment) o JK [jota ka]
> I'm renting a studio apartment estou alugando um JK [eeshto aloogandoo oom jota ka]

style o estilo [eesh-tcheeloo]
> she has a lot of style ela tem muito estilo [ella teng mweentoo eesh-tcheeloo]

subway o metrô [metro]
> can I have a map of the subway? poderia me conseguir um mapa do metrô? [poderee-a mee konsegeer oom mapa doo metro]

subway train o trem [treng]
> when's the last subway train from this station? a que horas sai o último trem desta estação? [a kee orash sy oo oowtcheemoo treng deshta eeshtassowng]

sudden repentino(na) [hepen-tcheenoo(na)]
> all of a sudden de repente [djee hepentchee]

sugar o açúcar [assookah]
> can you pass me the sugar? você pode me passar o açúcar? [vosse podjee mee passar oo assookah]

suggest *(propose)* sugerir [soojereeh]
> do you have anything else you can suggest? você tem alguma outra coisa para sugerir? [vosse teng owgooma otra koyza para soojereeh]

suit *(be convenient for)* cair [ka-eeh]
> that suits me perfectly isso me cai perfeitamente [eessoo mee ky peh-faytamentchee]
> it doesn't suit me isso não é para mim [eessoo nowng eh para meeng]

suitcase a mala [mala]
- one of my suitcases is missing sumiu uma das minhas malas [soomyoo ooma dash meenyash malash]
- my suitcase was damaged in transit estragaram minha mala no transporte [eeshtragarowng meenya mala noo tranjpoh-tchee]

summer o verão [verowng]
- in (the) summer no verão [noo verowng]

summer vacation as férias de verão [feree-ash djee verowng]
- we've come here for our summer vacation estamos aqui de férias de verão [eestamooz akee djee feree-ash djee verowng]

sun o sol [sow]
- the sun's very strong at this time of day o sol está muito forte nesta hora do dia [oo sow eeshta mweentoo foh-tchee neshta ora doo djee-a]

sunburn a queimadura (do sol) [kaymadoora (doo sow)]
- I've got a bad sunburn me queimei bastante [mee kaymay bashtantchee]
- do you have cream for a sunburn? tem algum creme para queimaduras (de sol)? [teng owgoom kremee para kaymadoorash (djee sow)]

Sunday o domingo [domeengoo]
- where can I find a doctor on a Sunday? onde eu consigo achar um médico no domingo? [ondjee ew konseegoo ashah oom medjeekoo noo domeengoo]
- are the stores open on Sunday? as lojas abrem no domingo? [ash lojaz abreng noo domeengoo]

sun deck a capota [kapota]
- how do I get onto the sun deck? como eu faço para subir à capota? [komoo ew fassoo para soobeer a kapota]

sunglasses os óculos de sol [okooloosh djee sow]
- I've lost my sunglasses perdi meus óculos de sol [peh-djee mewz okooloosh djee sow]

sunny (day, weather) ensolarado(da) [ensolaradoo(da)]
- it's sunny está fazendo sol [eeshta fazendoo sow]

sunrise o amanhecer [amanyesseh]
- what time is sunrise? a que horas nasce o sol? [a kee orash nassee oo sow]

sunset o pôr-do-sol [poh-doo-sow]
- isn't the sunset beautiful? o pôr-do-sol não é lindo? [oo poh-doo-sow nowng eh leendoo]

suntan lotion o bronzeador [bronzee-adoh]
- I'd like SPF 30 suntan lotion eu queria um bronzeador com fator trinta [ew keree-a oom bronzee-adoh kong fatoh treenta]

supermarket o supermercado [soopeh-meh-kadoo]
- is there a supermarket nearby? tem um supermercado por aqui? [teng oom soopeh-meh-kadoo por akee]

surcharge o acréscimo [akresseemoo]
- do I have to pay a surcharge? tenho que pagar acréscimo? [tenyoo kee pagar akresseemoo]

sure
- are you sure that's how you say it? tem certeza de que se diz assim? [teng sehteza djee kee see djeez asseeng]

surfboard a prancha de surfe [pransha djee sooh-fee]
- is there somewhere we can rent surfboards? tem algum lugar onde a gente possa alugar pranchas de surfe? [teng owgoom loogar ondjee a jentchee possa aloogah pranshash djee sooh-fee]

surfing o surfe [sooh-fee]
- can we go surfing around here? dá para surfar por aqui? [da para sooh-fah por akee]

surprise a surpresa [sooh-preza]
- what a nice surprise! que surpresa agradável! [ke sooh-preza agradavew]

surrounding area as redondezas [hedondezash]
- Rio and the surrounding area o Rio e as redondezas [oo hee-oo ee ash hedondezash]

swallow engolir [engoleeh]
- the ATM outside has swallowed my credit card o caixa automático lá fora engoliu meu cartão de crédito [oo ky-sha owto-matcheekoo la fora engolyoo mew kahtowng djee kredjeetoo]
- it hurts when I swallow dói quando eu engulo [doy kwandoo ew engooloo]

swim nadar [nadah] ♦ o nado [nadoo]
- is it safe to swim here? é seguro nadar aqui? [eh segooroo nadar akee]
- to go for a swim dar uma nadada [dar ooma nadada]

swimming pool a piscina [peesseena]
- is there an open-air swimming pool? tem uma piscina ao ar livre? [teng ooma peesseena ow ah leevree]

switch (for a light) o interruptor [eente-hooptoh]; (on a TV, radio) o botão [botowng]
- the switch doesn't work o interruptor não funciona [oo eente-hooptoh nowng foonss-yona]

switch off (light, appliance, electricity) desligar [djeej-leegah]; (radio) apagar [apagah]
- where do you switch the light off? como se apaga a luz? [komoo see apaga a loosh]
- my cell was switched off meu celular estava desligado [mew seloolar eeshtava djeej-leegadoo]

switch on ligar [leegah]
- where do I switch this light on? onde eu ligo esta luz? [ondjee ew leegoo eshta looj]

synagogue a sinagoga [seenagoga]

▸ where's the nearest synagogue? onde fica a sinagoga mais próxima? [ondjee feeka a seenagoga mysh prosseema]

table a mesa [meza]

▸ I've reserved a table in the name of... reservei uma mesa em nome de... [hezehvay ooma meza eng nomee djee]

▸ a table for four, please! uma mesa para quatro, por favor! [ooma meza para kwatroo poh favoh]

table tennis o pingue-pongue [peengee-pongee]

▸ are there tables for table tennis? tem mesa de pingue-pongue? [teng meza djee peengee-pongee]

table wine o vinho de mesa [veenyoo djee meza]

▸ a bottle of red table wine uma garrafa de vinho tinto de mesa [ooma gahafa djee veenyoo tcheentoo djee meza]

take *(get hold of, steal)* pegar [pegah]; *(time)* tomar [tomah]; *(carry, lead, accompany, transport)* levar [levah]; *(require)* exigir [ezeejeeh]; *(wear)* usar [oozah]

▸ someone's taken my bag alguém pegou a minha bolsa [owgeng pego a meenya bowsa]

▸ can you take me to this address? você pode me levar até este endereço? [vosse podjee mee levar a-te esh-tchee enderessoo]

▸ are you taking the plane or the bus to Rio? você vai pegar o avião ou o ônibus para o Rio? [vosse vy pegar oo avee-owng o oo oneeboosh para oo hee-oo]

▸ which road should I take? que estrada eu devo tomar? [ke eeshtrada ew devoo tomah]

▸ I take a size 40 meu tamanho é quarenta [mew tamanyoo eh kwarenta]

▸ how long does the trip take? quanto tempo leva a viagem? [kwantoo tempoo leva a vee-ajeng]

▸ how long does it take to get to Santos? quanto tempo leva para chegar a Santos? [kwantoo tempoo leva para shegar a santoosh]

▸ could you take a photo of us? você poderia tirar uma foto nossa? [vosse poderee-a tcheerar ooma fotoo nossa]

take back *(to a store)* devolver [devowv-veh]; *(to one's home)* levar (de volta) [levah djee vowta]

▸ I'm looking for a present to take back to my son estou procurando um presente para levar para o meu filho [eeshto prokoorandoo oom prezentchee para levah para oo mew feelyoo]

take down *(bags, luggage)* baixar [by-shah]
- could you take these bags down, please? você poderia baixar essas malas, por favor? [vosse poderee-a by-shar essash malash poh favoh]

take in *(bags, luggage)* guardar [gwah-dah]
- can you have someone take in my bags, please? será que teria alguém para guardar minhas malas, por favor? [sera ke teree-a owgeng para gwah-dah meenyash malash poh favoh]

taken *(seat)* ocupado(da) [okoopadoo(da)]
- sorry, this seat is taken desculpe, este lugar está ocupado [djeesh-koowpee esh-tchee loogar eeshta okoopadoo]

take up *(bags, luggage)* subir [soobeeh]
- can someone take our bags up to our room? alguém pode subir as malas para o nosso quarto? [owgeng podjee soobeer ash malash para oo nosso kwah-too]

talk conversar [konveh-sah]
- could I talk with you for a moment? posso conversar com você um instante? [possoo konveh-sah kong vosse oom eenshtantchee]
- you have no right to talk to me like that você não tem direito de falar comigo assim [vosse nowng teng djeeraytoo djee falah komeegoo asseeng]

tall *(person, tree, building)* alto(ta) [owtoo(ta)]
- what's that tall building over there? que edifício alto é aquele ali? [ke edjeefeess-yoo owtoo eh akelee alee]

tank *(for gas)* o tanque [tankee]
- is the tank full? o tanque está cheio? [oo tankee eeshta shayoo]

tap water a água da torneira [agwa da toh-nayra]
- just some tap water, please um pouco de água da torneira, por favor [oom pooko djee agwa da toh-nayra poh favoh]

taste o gosto [goshtoo] ♦ *(sense)* sentir gosto de [sentcheeh goshtoo djee]; *(try)* experimentar [eeshpereeementah] ♦ saborear [saboree-ah]
- I can't taste anything não sinto gosto de nada [nowng seentoo goshtoo djee nada]
- would you like to taste the wine? gostaria de experimentar o vinho? [goshtaree-a djee eeshperee-mentar oo veenyoo]
- it tastes funny tem um gosto engraçado [teng oom goshtoo engrassadoo]

tax o imposto [eemposhtoo]
- does this price include tax? este preço inclui impostos? [esh-tchee pressoo eenklooy eemposhtoosh]

taxi o táxi [taksee]
- how much does a taxi cost from here to the station? quanto custa um táxi daqui até a estação? [kwantoo kooshta oom taksee dakee a-te a eeshtassowng]
- I'd like to reserve a taxi to take me to the airport, please eu queria reservar um táxi para me levar até o aeroporto, por favor [ew keree-a hezeh-var oom taksee para mee levar a-te oo a-eropoh-too poh favoh]

taxi cabs

When getting into a taxi cab in Brazil, say to the driver *por favor, me leve até...* (please take me to...) and the address you want to go to. If it is during the day, it is wise to check that the driver has set the meter to *bandeira 1*, because at night taxi cabs usually use *bandeira 2*, which is more expensive. You can also ask the driver how much the trip will cost: *quanto custa a corrida até...?* And when you reach your destination, if you're satisfied with the service, you can say *fique com o troco* (keep the change).

taxi driver o(a) taxista [takseeshta]
  ▸ can you ask the taxi driver to wait? pode pedir para o taxista esperar? [podjee pedjeeh para oo takseeshta eeshperah]

taxi stand o ponto de táxi [pontoo djee taksee]
  ▸ where can I find a taxi stand? onde eu posso achar um ponto de táxi? [ondjee ew possoo ashar oom pontoo djee taksee]

tea *(drink)* o chá [sha]
  ▸ tea with milk chá com leite [sha kong laytchee]
  ▸ tea without milk chá sem leite [sha seng laytchee]

teach ensinar [enseenah]
  ▸ so, you teach Portuguese? maybe you could help me! então você ensina português? talvez você pudesse me ajudar! [entowng vosse enseena poh-toogesh tow-vesh vosse poodessee mee ajoodah]

teacher o professor [professoh], a professora [professora]
  ▸ I'm a teacher sou professor/professora [so professoh/professora]

taking a taxi

  ▸ could you call me a taxi, please? poderia chamar um táxi, por favor? [poderee-a shamar oom taksee poh favoh]
  ▸ to the station/airport, please para a estação/o aeroporto, por favor [para a eeshtassowng/oo a-eropoh-too poh favoh]
  ▸ stop here/at the lights/at the corner, please pare aqui/no semáforo/na esquina, por favor [paree akee/noo semaforoo/na eeshkeena poh favoh]
  ▸ can you wait for me? você pode ficar esperando? [vosse podjee feekar eeshperandoo]
  ▸ how much is it? quanto deu? [kwantoo de-oo]
  ▸ keep the change fique com o troco [feekee kong oo trokoo]

telephone o telefone [telefonee] ♦ telefonar [telefonah]
  ▸ can I use the telephone? posso usar o telefone? [possoo oozar oo telefonee]

telephone booth a cabine telefônica [kabeenee telefoneeka]
  ▸ is there a telephone booth near here? tem uma cabine telefônica por aqui? [teng ooma kabeenee telefoneeka por akee]

telephone call a ligação [leegassowng]
  ▸ I'd like to make a telephone call eu queria fazer uma ligação [ew keree-a fazer ooma leegassowng]

television a televisão [televeezowng]
  ▸ what's on television tonight? o que vai dar na televisão hoje de noite? [oo kee vy dah na televeezowng ojee djee noytchee]

tell dizer [djeezeh]
  ▸ can you tell me the way to the museum? você pode me dizer como a gente faz para chegar no museu? [vosse podjee mee djeezeh komoo a jentchee fash para shegah noo moozew]
  ▸ can you tell me what time it is? pode me dizer que horas são? [podjee mee djeezeh kee orash sowng]

temperature *(meteorological)* a temperatura [temperatoora]; *(fever)* a febre [febree]
  ▸ what's the temperature? qual é a temperatura? [kwal eh a temperatoora]
  ▸ I've got a temperature estou com febre [eeshto kong febree]

ten dez [desh]
  ▸ there are ten of us somos dez [somoosh desh]

tennis o tênis [teneesh]
  ▸ where can we play tennis? onde a gente pode jogar tênis? [ondjee a jentchee podjee jogah teneesh]

tennis racket a raquete de tênis [haketchee djee teneesh]
  ▸ can you rent tennis rackets? dá para alugar raquetes de tênis? [da para aloogah haketcheesh djee teneesh]

tent a barraca [bahaka]
  ▸ I'd like to book space for a tent, please eu queria reservar espaço para uma barraca, por favor [ew keree-a hezeh-var eeshpassoo para ooma bahaka poh favoh]
  ▸ can you put up your tent anywhere? dá para armar a barraca em qualquer lugar? [da para ah-mar a bahaka eng kwowkeh loogah]

tent peg a estaca [eeshtaka]
  ▸ we're short of tent pegs estão faltando estacas [eeshtowng fowtandoo eeshtakash]

terminal *(transportation)* o terminal [teh-meenow]
  ▸ where is terminal 1? onde fica o terminal 1? [ondjee feeka oo teh-meenow oom]
  ▸ is there a shuttle between terminals? tem um serviço de conexão entre os terminais? [teng oom seh-veessoo djee koneksowng entree oosh teh-meenysh]

tetanus o tétano [tetanoo]

> I've been vaccinated for tetanus eu fui vacinado contra o tétano [ew fwee vasseenadoo kontra oo tetanoo]

thank agradecer [agradesseh] ◆ **thanks** obrigado(da) [obreegadoo(da)]

> I can't thank you enough não tem como eu te agradecer o suficiente [nowng teng komoo ew tchee agradesser oo soofeess-yentchee]

> thanks for everything (you've done) obrigado por tudo (o que você fez) [obreegadoo poh toodoo (oo kee vosse fej)]

thank you! obrigado [obreegadoo]

> thank you very much! muito obrigado! [mweentoo obreegadoo]

> thank you for your help obrigado pela ajuda! [obreegadoo pela ajooda]

that *(demonstrative use)* esse(sa) [essee(sa)]; *(in relative clauses)* que [kee] ◆ esse(sa) [essee(sa)]

> who's that? quem é? [keng eh]

> that's right é isso aí [eh eessoo a-ee]

> the road that goes to Curitiba a estrada que vai para Curitiba [a eeshtrada kee vy para kooree-tcheeba]

> I'll have that one eu quero esse [ew keroo essee]

theater *(for plays)* o teatro [tchee-atroo]

> where is there a theater? onde tem um teatro? [ondjee teng oom tchee-atroo]

theft o roubo [hoboo]

> I'd like to report a theft eu queria denunciar um roubo [ew keree-a denoonss-yar oom hoboo]

then *(at a particular time, in that case)* então [entowng]; *(next)* depois [depoysh]

> I'll see you then vejo você depois [vejoo vosse depoysh]

> I'll see you at six then vejo você às seis então [vejoo vosse ash sayz entowng]

---

saying thank you

> thank you obrigado [obreegadoo]
> thanks, that's very kind of you obrigado, muita gentileza de sua parte [obreegadoo mweenta jentcheeleza djee soo-a pah-tchee]
> I can't thank you enough não tem como eu te agradecer [nowng teng komoo ew tchee agradesseh]
> thank you for your help obrigado pela ajuda [obreegadoo pela ajooda]
> I wanted to thank you for inviting me eu queria agradecer por ter me convidado [ew keree-a agradesseh poh teh mee konveedadoo]

there *(in that place)* **lá** [la]
- he's over there **ele está lá** [elee eeshta la]
- there is/are... **há...** [a]
- there's a problem **há um problema** [a oom problema]
- are there any restrooms near here? **tem algum banheiro por aqui?** [teng owgoom banyayroo por akee]
- there you are *(handing over something)* **aqui está** [akee eeshta]

thermometer o **termômetro** [teh-mometroo]
- do you have a thermometer? **tem um termômetro?** [teng oom teh-mometroo]
- the thermometer shows 18 degrees (Celsius) o **termômetro marca dezoito graus (Celsius)** [oo teh-mometroo mah-ka dezoytoo growsh selsee-oosh]

thin *(person)* **magro(gra)** [magroo(gra)]; *(slice, layer, material)* **fino(na)** [feenoo(na)]
- isn't that jacket too thin for a cold evening like this? **essa jaqueta não é muito fina para uma noite fria como esta?** [essa jaketa nowng eh mweentoo feena para ooma noytchee free-a komoo eshta]

thing a **coisa** [koyza]
- what's that thing for? **para que serve esse troço?** [para ke seh-vee essee trossoo]
- I don't know what the best thing to do is **não sei qual é a melhor coisa a fazer** [nowng say kwal eh a melyoh koyza a fazeh]
- could you look after my things for a minute? **você poderia cuidar das minhas coisas por um minuto?** [vosse poderee-a kweedah dash meenyash koyzash por oom meenootoo]

think *(believe)* **pensar** [pensah] ◆ *(use mind)* **achar** [ashah]
- I think (that)... **acho que...** [ashoo kee]
- I thought service charge was included **achei que a taxa de serviço estivesse incluída** [ashay kee a tasha djee seh-veessoo eesh-tcheevessee eenklweeda]
- I don't think so **acho que não** [ashoo kee nowng]

third **terceiro(ra)** [teh-sayroo(ra)] ◆ *(fraction)* o **terceiro** [teh-sayroo]; *(gear)* a **terceira** [teh-sayra]
- this is my third time in Brazil **é a terceira vez que eu venho no Brasil** [eh a teh-sayra vej kee ew venyoo noo brazeew]

thirsty
- to be thirsty **ter sede** [teh sedjee]
- I'm very thirsty **estou com muita sede** [eeshto kong mweenta sedjee]

three **três** [tresh]
- there are three of us **somos três** [somoosh tresh]

throat a **garganta** [gah-ganta]
- I have a fish bone stuck in my throat **estou com uma espinha de peixe presa na garganta** [eeshto kong ooma eeshpeenya djee payshee preza na gah-ganta]

throat lozenge a pastilha para garganta [pashteelya para gah-ganta]
▸ I'd like some throat lozenges eu queria algumas pastilhas para a garganta [ew keree-a owgoomash pashteelyash para a gah-ganta]

thunderstorm o temporal [temporow]
▸ will there be a thunderstorm? vai dar temporal? [vy dah temporow]

Thursday a quinta-feira [keenta-fayra], a quinta [keenta]
▸ we're arriving/leaving on Thursday estamos chegando/saindo na quinta [eeshtamoosh shegandoo/sa-eendoo na keenta]

ticket *(for a bus, a plane, movie theater, the subway)* a passagem [passajeng]; *(for a museum, a sports event)* a entrada [entrada]
▸ I'd like a ticket to... eu queria uma passagem para... [ew keree-a ooma passajeng para]
▸ how much is a ticket to...? quanto custa uma passagem para...? [kwantoo kooshta ooma passajeng para]
▸ a book of 10 tickets, please um talão de dez passagens, por favor [oom talowng djee desh passajengsh poh favoh]
▸ I'd like to book a ticket eu queria reservar uma passagem [ew keree-a hezeh-var ooma passajeng]
▸ I'd like three tickets for... eu queria três entradas para... [ew keree-a trez entradash para]

tide a maré [ma-re]
▸ what time does the tide turn? a que horas muda a maré? [a kee orash mooda a ma-re]

tight *(piece of clothing)* apertado(da) [apeh-tadoo(da)]
▸ these pants are too tight estas calças estão muito apertadas [eshtash kowsash eeshtowng mweentoo apeh-tadash]

time o tempo [tempoo]; *(by clock)* a hora [ora]; *(occasion)* a vez [vej]
▸ do we have time to visit the town? temos tempo para visitar a cidade? [temoosh tempoo para veezeetar a seedadjee]
▸ what time is it? que horas são? [kee orash sowng]
▸ what time do you close? a que horas fecha? [a kee orash fesha]
▸ could you tell me if the bus from Rio is on time? você poderia me dizer se o ônibus que vem do Rio está no horário? [vosse poderee-a mee djeezeh see oo oneeboosh kee veng doo hee-oo eeshta noo oraryoo]
▸ maybe some other time talvez outra hora [tow-vej otra ora]
▸ three times três vezes [tresh vezeesh]
▸ at the same time ao mesmo tempo [ow mejmoo tempoo]
▸ the first time a primeira vez [a preemayra vej]

timetable o horário [oraryoo]
▸ do you have local bus timetables? você tem os horários dos ônibus locais? [vosse teng ooz oraryoosh dooz oneeboosh lokysh]

tipping

Gratuity is included on your check (*a conta*). All Brazilian restaurants include *os 10% do garçom* (10% for the waiter), and you aren't legally obliged to pay it, although everybody does. If you are particularly satisfied with the service or the waiter, you can leave a tip on the table.

tip *(gratuity)* a gorjeta [goh-jeta] ♦ *(give a gratuity to)* dar gorjeta para [dah goh-jeta para]

▸ how much should I leave as a tip? quanto eu devo deixar de gorjeta? [kwantoo ew devoo dayshah djee goh-jeta]

tire *(for a vehicle)* o pneu [pnew]

▸ the tire's flat o pneu está vazio [oo pnew eeshta vazee-oo]
▸ the tire's punctured furou o pneu [fooroo oo pnew]

to para [para]

▸ when is the next bus to Santos? quando sai o próximo ônibus para Santos? [kwandoo sy oo prosseemoo oneeboosh para santoosh]
▸ it's twenty to nine são vinte para as nove [sowng veentche para ash novee]

tobacco store a tabacaria [tabakaree-a]

▸ where is the nearest tobacco store? onde fica a tabacaria mais próxima? [ondjee feeka a tabakaree-a mysh prosseema]

today hoje [ojee]

▸ what's today's date? que dia é hoje? [ke djee-a eh ojee]

toe o dedo do pé [dedoo doo pe]

▸ I think I've broken my toe acho que quebrei o dedo do pé [ashoo kee kebray oo dedoo doo pe]

together junto(ta) [joontoo(ta)]

▸ let's go together vamos juntos [vamoosh joontoosh]

toilet o toalete [twaletchee]

▸ I need to go to the toilet tenho que ir no toalete [tenyoo kee eeh noo twaletchee]
▸ do you have to pay to use the toilet? tem que pagar para usar o banheiro? [teng kee pagah para oozar oo banyayroo]

toilet paper o papel higiênico [papew eej-yeneekoo]

▸ there is no toilet paper não tem papel higiênico [nowng teng papew eej-yeneekoo]

toll *(for a road, a bridge)* o pedágio [pedajyoo]

▸ do you have to pay a toll to use the bridge? tem que pagar pedágio para usar a ponte? [teng kee pagah pedajyoo para oozar a pontchee]

toll-free *(number, call)* gratuito(ta) [gratweetoo(ta)] ◆ *(call)* gratuitamente [gratweeta-mentchee]

▶ there's a toll-free number you can call tem um número gratuito para o qual se pode ligar [teng oom noomeroo gratweetoo para oo kwow see podjee leegah]

tomato o tomate [tomatchee]

▶ a kilo of tomatoes um quilo de tomate [oom keeloo djee tomatchee]

tomato juice o suco de tomate [sookoo djee tomatchee]

▶ I'd like a tomato juice eu queria um suco de tomate [ew keree-a oom sookoo djee tomatchee]

tomorrow amanhã [amanyang]

▶ can you hold my reservation until tomorrow? pode manter minha reserva até amanhã? [podjee manteh meenya hezeh-va a-te amanyang]

▶ I'm leaving tomorrow morning saio amanhã de manhã [sy-oo amanyang djee manyang]

▶ see you tomorrow night te vejo amanhã [tchee vejoo amanyang]

tonight hoje à noite [ojee a noytchee]

▶ do you have any beds available for tonight? tem alguma cama disponível para hoje à noite? [teng owgooma kama djeesh-poneevev para ojee a noytchee]

too *(also)* também [tambeng]; *(excessively)* muito [mweentoo]

▶ enjoy your meal! – you too bom proveito! – para você também [bong provaytoo para vosse tambeng]

▶ she's too tired to... ela está muito cansada para... [ella eeshta mweentoo kansada para]

▶ it's too expensive é muito caro [eh mweentoo karoo]

▶ there are too many people tem gente demais [teng jentchee djeemysh]

tooth o dente [dentchee]

▶ I've broken a tooth quebrei um dente [kebray oom dentchee]

toothache a dor de dente [doh djee dentchee]

▶ I have a toothache estou com dor de dente [eeshto kong doh djee dentchee]

toothbrush a escova de dente [eeshkova djee dentchee]

▶ I forgot my toothbrush esqueci minha escova de dente [eeshkessee meenya eeshkova djee dentchee]

toothpaste a pasta de dente [pashta djee dentchee]

▶ I'd like to buy some toothpaste eu queria comprar pasta de dente [ew keree-a komprar pashta djee dentchee]

top a tampa [tampa] ◆ *(maximum)* máximo(ma) [masseemoo(ma)]

▶ the car drove away at top speed o carro saiu a toda velocidade [oo kahoo sy-oo a toda velossee-dadjee]

tour a viagem [vee-ajeng]

▶ I'm planning to do a two-week tour of the country estou planejando fazer uma viagem de dois dias pelo país [eeshto planejandoo fazer ooma vee-ajeng djee doysh djee-ash peloo pa-eesh]

tourist o(a) turista [tooreeshta] ♦ *(season)* turístico(ca) [tooreesh-tcheekoo(ka)]

▸ do you get many tourists here? vêm muitos turistas aqui? [vayeng mweentoosh tooreeshtaz akee]

tourist attraction a atração turística [atrassowng tooreesh-tcheeka]

▸ what are the main tourist attractions in the area? quais são as principais atrações turísticas da região? [kwyz sowng ash preenseepyz atrassoyngsh tooreesh-tcheekash da hej-yowng]

tourist class a classe turística [klassee tooreesh-tcheeka]

▸ in tourist class, please na classe turística, por favor [na klassee tooreesh-tcheeka poh favoh]

tourist guide o guia turístico [ghee-a tooreesh-tcheekoo]

▸ we have a good tourist guide with a lot of up-to-date information temos um bom guia turístico com um monte de informações atualizadas [temooz oom bong ghee-a tooreesh-tcheekoo kong oom montchee djee eenfoh-massoyngz atwalee-zadash]

tourist office o posto de informações turísticas [poshtoo djee eenfoh-massoyngsh tooreesh-tcheekash]

▸ I'm looking for the tourist office estou procurando um posto de informações turísticas [eeshtoo prokoorandoo oom poshtoo djee eenfoh-massoyngsh tooreesh-tcheekash]

▸ can I get a street map at the tourist office? será que eu consigo um mapa de ruas no posto de informações turísticas? [sera kee ew konseegoo oom mapa djee hoo-ash noo poshtoo djee eenfoh-massoyngsh tooreesh-tcheekash]

tow rebocar [hebokah]

▸ could you tow me to a garage? você poderia me rebocar até uma garagem? [vosse poderee-a mee hebokar a-te ooma garajeng]

toward *(in the direction of)* até [a-te]

▸ we're heading toward Salvador vamos até Salvador [vamooz a-te sow-vadoh]

tow away rebocar [hebokah]

▸ my car's been towed away meu carro foi rebocado [mew kahoo foy hebokadoo]

towel a toalha [twalya]

▸ we don't have any towels não temos toalha [nowng temoosh twalya]

▸ could we have more towels? poderia nos conseguir mais toalhas? [poderee-a nosh konsegeeh mysh twalyash]

tower *(of a church, a castle)* a torre [tohe]

▸ can you visit the tower? dá para visitar a torre? [da para veezeetar a tohe]

town a cidade [seedadjee]

▸ to go into town ir ao centro [eer ow centroo]

town hall a prefeitura [prefaytoora]
- where is the town hall? **onde fica a prefeitura?** [ondjee feeka a prefaytoora]

traffic *(vehicles)* o tráfego [trafegoo]
- is there a lot of traffic on the freeway? **tem muito tráfego na auto-estrada?**
  [teng mweentoo trafegoo na owto-eeshtrada]

traffic circle a rotatória [hotatorya]
- you turn right at the traffic circle **você dobra à direita na rotatória** [vosse dobra a
  djeerayta na hotatorya]

traffic jam o engarrafamento [engahafa-mentoo]
- we got stuck in a traffic jam **ficamos presos num engarrafamento** [feekamoosh
  prezoosh noom engahafa-mentoo]

traffic lights o semáforo [semaforoo]
- turn left at the traffic lights **dobre à esquerda no semáforo** [dobree a eeshkeh-da
  noo semaforoo]

trail *(path)* o caminho [kameenyoo]
- will this trail take us back to the parking lot? **esse caminho nos leva de volta
  para o estacionamento?** [essee kameenyoo nosh leva djee vowta para oo eeshtass-
  yonamentoo]

train o trem [treng]
- is there a train between Rio and São Paulo? **há um trem entre o Rio e São
  Paulo?** [teng oom treng entree o hee-o ee sowng powloo]

tram o bonde [bondjee]
- can you buy tickets on the tram? **dá para comprar passagens no bonde?** [da
  para komprar passajengsh noo bondjee]
- which tram line do we have to take? **que linha de bonde temos que pegar?** [ke
  leenya djee bondjee temoosh kee pegah]

---

getting around town

- which bus goes to the airport? **que ônibus vai até o aeroporto?** [ke oneeboosh
  vy a-te oo a-eropoh-too]
- where does the bus to the station leave from? **de onde sai o ônibus da
  estação?** [djee ondjee sy oo oneeboosh da eeshtassowng]
- I'd like a one-way (ticket) to… **eu queria uma passagem de ida para…** [ew
  keree-a ooma passajeng djee eeda para]
- can I have a book of tickets, please? **poderia me dar um bloco de passagens,
  por favor?** [poderee-a mee dar oom blokoo djee passajengsh poh favoh]
- could you tell me where I have to get off to go to…? **poderia me dizer onde eu
  tenho que descer para ir para…?** [poderee-a mee djeezer ondjee ew tenyoo kee
  desseh para eeh para]

▸ where is the nearest tram stop? onde fica a parada mais perto de bonde? [ondjee feeka a parada mysh peh-too djee bondjee]

transfer *(of money)* a transferência [tranj-ferenss-ya] ◆ *(money)* transferir [tranj-fereeh]

▸ I'd like to transfer some money from my savings account gostaria de transferir dinheiro da minha poupança [goshtaree-a djee tranj-fereeh djeenyayroo da meenya popanssa]

travel a viagem [vee-ajeng] ◆ *(go on a trip)* viajar [vee-ajah]

▸ I'd like a window seat facing the direction of travel eu queria um assento na janela olhando para frente [ew keree-a oom assentoo na janela olyandoo para frentchee]

▸ I'm traveling on my own estou viajando sozinho [eeshto vee-ajandoo sozeenyoo]

travel agency a agência de viagens [ajenss-ya djee vee-ajengsh]

▸ I'm looking for a travel agency estou procurando uma agência de viagens [eeshto prokoorandoo ooma ajenss-ya djee vee-ajengsh]

traveler's check o cheque de viagem [shekee djee vee-ajeng]

▸ do you take traveler's checks? vocês aceitam cheques de viagem? [vossez assaytowng shekeesh djee vee-ajeng]

tree a árvore [ah-voree]

▸ what type of tree is that? que tipo de árvore é esta? [ke tcheepo djee ah-voree eh eshta]

trip *(journey)* a viagem [vee-ajeng]

▸ have a good trip! (tenha uma) boa viagem! [(tenya ooma) boa vee-ajeng]

trouble o problema [problema]

▸ we didn't have any trouble finding the hotel não tivemos problema algum para achar o hotel [nowng tcheevemoosh problema owgoom para ashar oo otew]

▸ I don't want to be any trouble não quero causar nenhum problema [nowng keroo kowzah nenyooom problema]

▸ it's no trouble não tem problema [nowng teng problema]

trunk *(of a car)* o porta-mala [poh-ta-mala]; *(piece of luggage)* o baú [ba-oo]

▸ my things are in the trunk of the car as minhas coisas estão no porta-mala do carro [ash meenyash koyzash eeshtowng noo poh-ta mala doo kahoo]

▸ I've got two small suitcases and a large trunk tenho duas malas pequenas e um baú [tenyoo doo-ash malash pekenaz ee oom ba-oo]

try *(attempt)* tentar [tentah]; *(sample)* provar [provah], experimentar [eeshper-eementah]

▸ I'd like to try the local beer eu queria provar a cerveja local [ew keree-a provar a seh-veja lokow]

try on *(dress, shoes)* experimentar [eeshpereementah]

▸ I'd like to try on the one in the window eu queria experimentar a que está na vitrine [ew keree-a eeshpereementar a kee eshta na veetreenee]

tub *(of ice cream)* a casquinha [kashkeenya]

▸ do you sell tubs of ice cream to take home? vocês vendem casquinha de sorvete para levar? [vossesh vendeng kashkeenya djee soh-vetchee para levah]

Tuesday a terça-feira [teh-sa-fayra], a terça [teh-sa]

▸ we're arriving/leaving on Tuesday estamos chegando/saindo na terça [eeshta-moosh shegandoo/sa-eendoo na teh-sa]

tunnel o túnel [toonew]

▸ is there a toll for using the tunnel? cobram pedágio para passar pelo túnel? [kobrowng pedajyoo para passah peloo toonew]

turn *(in a game, order)* a vez [vej]; *(off a road)* a curva [kooh-va] ◆ *(change direction)* dobrar [dobrah]

▸ it's your turn é a sua vez [eh a soo-a vej]

▸ is this the turn for the campground? esta é a curva para o camping? [eshta eh a kooh-va para oo kampeeng]

▸ turn left at the lights dobre à esquerda no semáforo [dobree a eeshkeh-da noo semaforoo]

▸ you have to turn right você tem que dobrar à direita [vosse teng kee dobrar a djeerayta]

turn down baixar [by-shah]

▸ can we turn the air-conditioning down? podemos baixar o ar-condicionado? [podemoosh by-shar oo ah-kondeess-yonadoo]

▸ how do you turn the volume down? como se baixa o volume? [komoo see by-sha oo voloomee]

turn off *(light, appliance, radio)* desligar [djeej-leegah]; *(cut off electricity)* cortar [koh-tah]; *(tap)* fechar [feshah]

▸ where do you turn the light off? onde se desliga a luz? [ondjee see djeej-leega a looj]

▸ my cell was turned off meu celular estava desligado [mew seloolar eeshtava djeej-leegadoo]

turn on *(light, radio, engine)* ligar [leegah]; *(faucet)* abrir [abreeh]; *(person)* excitar [esseetah]

▸ where do I turn this light on? onde eu ligo essa luz? [ondjee ew leegoo essa loosh]

▸ can you turn on the ignition? você pode dar contato? [vosse podjee dah kontatoo]

turn up *(sound, central heating)* aumentar [owmentah]

▸ how do you turn up the heating? como se aumenta o aquecimento? [komoo see owmenta oo akesseementoo]

TV a tevê [te-ve]

▸ the TV in our room is broken a tevê do nosso quarto está quebrada [a te-ve doo nosso kwah-too eeshta kebrada]

TV lounge a sala de televisão [sala djee televeezowng]

▸ is there a TV lounge? tem uma sala de televisão? [teng ooma sala djee televeezowng]

twelve doze [dozee] ♦ *(noon)* o meio-dia [mayoo-djee-a]; *(midnight)* a meia-noite [maya-noytchee]
▶ there are twelve of us somos doze [somoosh dozee]
▶ it's twelve o'clock *(noon)* é meio-dia [eh mayoo-djee-a]; *(midnight)* é meia-noite [eh maya-noytchee]

twice duas vezes [doo-ash vezeesh]
▶ the ferry runs twice a day a balsa funciona duas vezes por dia [a bowsa foonss-yona doo-ash vezeesh poh djee-a]

twin o gêmeo [jemyoo], a gêmea [jemya]
▶ twin brother irmão gêmeo [eeh-mowng jemyoo]
▶ twin sister irmã gêmea [eeh-mang jemya]

twin beds as camas gêmeas [kamash jemyash]
▶ a room with twin beds um quarto com camas gêmeas [oom kwah-too kong kamash jemyash]

two dois [doysh]
▶ there are two of us somos dois [somoosh doysh]

umbrella o guarda-chuva [gwah-da-shoova]
▶ could you lend me an umbrella? poderia me emprestar um guarda-chuva? [poderee-a mee empreshtar oom gwah-da-shoova]

unacceptable inaceitável [eenassay-tavew]
▶ it's completely unacceptable! isso é totalmente inaceitável [eessoo eh totow-mentchee eenassay-tavew]

underpass a passagem subterrânea [passajeng soob-tehanya]
▶ is the underpass safe at night? a passagem subterrânea é segura à noite? [a passajeng soob-tehanya eh segoora a noytchee]

understand entender [entendeh]
▶ I can understand Portuguese, but I can't really speak it eu consigo entender português, mas não consigo falar [ew konseegoo entendeh poh-toogesh myj nowng konseegoo falah]
▶ I understand a little entendo um pouco [entendoo oom pokoo]
▶ I don't understand a word não entendo uma palavra [nowng entendoo ooma palavra]
▶ do you understand? você entende? [vosse entendjee]

unit *(of condominium complex)* o módulo [modooloo]
▶ we'd prefer a unit with air-conditioning preferimos um módulo com ar-condicionado [prefereemooz oom modooloo kong ah-kondeess-yonadoo]

United States (of America), US(A)

▸ the United States os Estados Unidos [ooz eeshtadooz ooneedoosh]

▸ I'm from the US sou dos Estados Unidos [so dooz eeshtadooz ooneedoosh]

▸ I live in the US moro nos Estados Unidos [moroo nooz eeshtadooz ooneedoosh]

▸ have you ever been to the United States? você já foi para os Estados Unidos? [vosse ja foy para ooz eeshtadooz ooneedoosh]

unleaded *(gas)* sem chumbo [seng shoomboo] ◆ a gasolina sem chumbo [gazoleena seng shoomboo]

▸ do you have premium or just regular unleaded? tem gasolina aditivada ou só sem chumbo? [teng gazoleena adjeetcheevada o so seng shoomboo]

until até [a-te]

▸ I'm staying until Sunday vou ficar até domingo [vo feekar a-te domeengoo]

▸ until noon até o meio-dia [a-te oo mayoo-djee-a]

up *(to a higher position)* para cima [para seema]; *(in a higher position)* em cima [eng seema]

▸ what's up? *(what's wrong)* o que foi? [oo ke foy]; *(as greeting)* e daí? [ee da-ee]

▸ up to now até agora [a-te agora]

▸ what are you up to tonight? o que você pensa em fazer hoje de noite? [oo kee vosse pensa eng fazer ojee djee noytchee]

urgent urgente [ooh-jentchee]

▸ it's not urgent não é urgente [nowng eh ooh-jentchee]

urgently urgentemente [ooh-jentchee-mentchee]

▸ I have to see a dentist urgently tenho que ver um dentista urgentemente [tenyoo kee ver oom dentcheeshta ooh-jentchee-mentchee]

use usar [oozah]

▸ could I use your cellphone? eu poderia usar o seu celular? [ew poderee-a oozar oo sew seloolah]

---

saying that you have understood/not understood

▸ oh, I see...! ah, entendo...! [ah entendoo]

▸ sorry, but I didn't understand desculpe, mas não entendi [djeesh-koowpee myz nowng entendjee]

▸ I'm a little confused... estou um pouco confuso... [eeshto oom pokoo konfoozoo]

▸ I don't understand your question não entendi sua pergunta [nowng entendjee soo-a peh-goonta]

▸ sorry, but I still don't understand desculpe, mas ainda não entendi [djeesh-koowpee myz a-eenda nowng entendjee]

vacancy o quarto livre [kwah-too leevree]
▸ do you have any vacancies for tonight? tem algum quarto livre para esta noite? [teng owgoom kwah-too leevree para eshta noytchee]

vacation as férias [feree-ash]
▸ are you here on vacation? está aqui em férias? [eeshta akee eng feree-ash]
▸ I'm on vacation estou de férias [eeshto djee feree-ash]

valid válido(da) [valeedoo(da)]
▸ is this ticket valid for the exhibit too? esta entrada é válida para a exposição também? [eshta entrada eh valeeda para a eeshpozeessowng tambeng]
▸ how long is this ticket valid for? por quanto tempo vale esta entrada? [poh kwantoo tempoo valee eshta entrada]
▸ my passport is still valid meu passaporte ainda está válido [mew passapoh-tchee a-eenda eeshta valeedoo]

vegetable as verduras [veh-doorash]
▸ does it come with vegetables? vem com verduras? [veng kong veh-doorash]

vegetarian vegetariano(na) [vejetaree-anoo(na)]
▸ I'm a vegetarian sou vegetariano/vegetariana [so vejetaree-anoo/vejetaree-ana]
▸ do you have vegetarian dishes? vocês têm pratos vegetarianos? [vossesh tayeng pratoosh vejetaree-anoosh]

vending machine a máquina de venda [makeena djee venda]
▸ the vending machine isn't working a máquina de venda não está funcionando [a makeena djee venda nowng eeshta foonss-yonandoo]

vertigo a vertigem [veh-tcheejeng]
▸ I suffer from vertigo sofro de vertigem [sofroo djee veh-tcheejeng]

very muito [mweentoo]
▸ I'm very hungry estou com muita fome [eeshto kong mweenta fomee]
▸ very much muito [mweentoo]
▸ very near muito perto [mweentoo peh-too]

view (panorama) a vista [veeshta]
▸ I'd prefer a room with an ocean view eu prefiro um quarto com vista para o mar [ew prefeeroo oom kwah-too kong veeshta para oo mah]

villa a casa de campo [kaza djee kampoo]
▸ we'd like to rent a villa for one week gostaríamos de alugar uma casa de campo por uma semana [goshtaree-amoosh djee aloogar ooma kaza djee kampoo por ooma semana]

virus o vírus [veeroosh]
- I must have picked up a virus devo ter pegado um vírus [devoo teh pegadoo oom veeroosh]

visa o visto [veeshtoo]
- do you need a visa? você precisa de visto? [vosse presseeza djee veeshtoo]

visit a visita [veezeeta] ◆ visitar [veezeetah]
- is this your first visit to Fortaleza? é a sua primeira visita à Fortaleza? [eh a soo-a preemayra veezeeta a foh-taleza]
- I'd like to visit the castle eu queria visitar o castelo [ew keree-a veezeetar oo kashteloo]

voicemail o correio de voz [kohayoo djee vosh]
- I need to check my voicemail preciso verificar meu correio de voz [presseezoo vereefeekah mew kohayoo djee vosh]

voucher o recibo [hesseeboo]
- I haven't received the voucher não recebi o recibo [nowng hessebee oo hesseeboo]

waist a cintura [seentoora]
- it's a little bit tight at the waist me aperta um pouco na cintura [mee apeh-ta oom pokoo na seentoora]

wait esperar [eeshperah]
- have you been waiting long? faz tempo que você está esperando? [faj tempoo kee vosse eeshta eeshperandoo]

waiter o garçom [gah-song]
- waiter, could we have the check, please? garçom, poderia trazer a conta, por favor? [gah-song poderee-a trazer a konta poh favoh]

wait for esperar [eeshperah]
- are you waiting for the bus? está esperando o ônibus? [eeshta eeshperandoo oo oneeboosh]
- I'm waiting for them to call back estou esperando eles ligarem de volta [eeshto eeshperandoo eleesh leegareng djee vowta]
- don't wait for me não espere por mim [nowng eeshperee poh meeng]

waiting room a sala de espera [sala djee eeshpera]
- is there a waiting room near the platform? tem uma sala de espera perto da plataforma? [teng ooma sala djee eeshpera peh-too da platafoh-ma]

waitress a garçonete [gah-sonetchee]
- the waitress has already taken our order a garçonete já levou nosso pedido [a gah-sonetchee ja levo nosso pedjeedoo]

water

A jug of water won't be brought to your table in Brazil as a matter of course. You have to order bottled water: either noncarbonated (*água sem gás*) or sparkling (*água com gás*); you can also ask to have it *com gelo e limão* (with ice and lemon).

wake acordar [akoh-dah]
- could you wake me at 6:45? você poderia me acordar às seis e quarenta e cinco? [vosse poderee-a mee akoh-dar ash sayz ee kwarenta ee seeenkoo]
- I always wake early sempre acordo cedo [sempree akoh-doo sedoo]

wake up acordar [akoh-dah]
- a noise woke me up in the middle of the night um barulho me acordou no meio da noite [oom baroolyoo mee akoh-do noo mayoo da noytchee]
- I have to wake up very early tomorrow to catch the plane tenho que acordar bem cedo amanhã para pegar o avião [tenyoo kee akoh-dah beng sedoo amanyang para pegar oo avee-owng]

walk a caminhada [kameenyada] ♦ *(go on foot)* caminhar [kameenyah] ♦ *(person)* acompanhar [akompanyah]; *(distance)* caminhar [kameenyah]
- are there any interesting walks in the area? dá para fazer alguma caminhada interessante na região? [da para fazer owgooma kameenyada interessantchee na hej-yowng]
- let's go for a walk vamos dar uma caminhada [vamoosh dar ooma kameenyada]
- how long would it take me to walk it? quanto tempo levaria caminhando? [kwantoo tempoo levaree-a kameenyandoo]

walking boots os sapatos de caminhada [sapatoosh djee kameenyada]
- do you need walking boots? você precisa de sapatos de caminhada? [vosse presseeza djee sapatoosh djee kameenyada]

wallet a carteira [kah-tayra]
- I've lost my wallet perdi minha carteira [peh-djee meenya kah-tayra]

want *(wish, desire)* querer [kereh]
- I don't want to go there não quero ir lá [nowng keroo eeh la]

warm quente [kentchee]
- it's warm está quente [eeshta kentchee]
- where can I buy some warm clothing for the trip? onde eu posso comprar uma roupa quente para a viagem? [ondjee ew possoo komprar ooma hopa kentchee para a vee-ajeng]

warn avisar [aveezah]
- no one warned me about that! ninguém me avisou nada! [neengeng mee aveezo nada]

wash lavar [lavah]

- where can I wash my hands? onde eu posso lavar as mãos? [ondjee ew possoo lavar ash mowngsh]

watch o relógio [helojyoo] ◆ *(look at)* olhar [ol-yah]; *(guard)* vigiar [veejee-ah]

- my watch has been stolen roubaram meu relógio [hobarowng mew helojyoo]
- can you watch my bags for a minute? pode vigiar minhas malas por um segundo? [podjee veejee-ah meenyash malash por oom segoondoo]

water a água [agwa]

- could I have some hot water, please? poderia me trazer água quente, por favor? [poderee-a mee trazer agwa kentchee poh favoh]
- there's no hot water não tem água quente [nowng teng agwa kentchee]

water ski o esqui aquático [eeshkee akwatcheekoo]

- can I rent water skis here? dá para alugar esquis aquáticos aqui? [da para aloogar eeshkeez akwatcheekooz akee]

water skiing o esqui aquático [eeshkee akwatcheekoo]

- can I go water skiing anywhere around here? dá para praticar esqui aquático por aqui? [da para pratcheekar eeshkee akwatcheekoo por akee]

wave *(of water)* a onda [onda]

- the waves are very big today as ondas estão bem grandes hoje [az ondaz eeshtowng beng grandjeez ojee]

way *(means)* a forma [foh-ma], o jeito [jaytoo]; *(direction)* a direção [djeer-essowng]; *(route, path)* o caminho [kameenyoo]

- what's the best way of getting there? qual é o melhor caminho para chegar lá? [kwal eh oo melyoh kameenyoo para shegah la]
- which way is it to the station? como se vai para a estação? [komoo see vy para a eeshtassowng]
- I went the wrong way peguei o caminho errado [pegay oo kameenyoo ehadoo]
- is this the right way to the cathedral? este é o caminho certo para a catedral? [esh-tchee eh oo kameenyoo seh-too para a katedrow]

asking the way

- can you show me where we are on the map? você pode me mostrar onde estamos no mapa? [vosse podjee mee moshtrar ondjee eeshtamoosh noo mapa]
- where is the station/the post office? onde fica a estação/agência dos Correios? [ondjee feeka a eeshtassowng/ajenss-ya doosh kohayoosh]
- excuse me, how do you get to Avenida Paulista? desculpe, como se chega na Avenida Paulista? [djeesh-koowpee komoo see shega na aveneeda powleeshta]
- is it far? é muito longe? [eh mweentoo lonjee]
- is it within walking distance? dá para ir caminhando? [da para eeh kameenyandoo]

- ▸ on the way no caminho [noo kameenyoo]
- ▸ all the way *(push)* até o fundo [a-te oo foondoo]
- ▸ no way! nem pensar! [neng pensah]

way out a saída [sa-eeda]
- ▸ where's the way out? onde fica a saída? [ondjee feeka a sa-eeda]

weak fraco(ca) [frakoo(ka)]
- ▸ I feel very weak me sinto fraco [mee seentoo frakoo]
- ▸ could I have a very weak coffee? poderia me servir um café fraco? [poderee-a mee seh-veer oom kaffe frakoo]

wear *(piece of clothing, glasses)* usar [oozah]
- ▸ is what I'm wearing all right? está bem o que eu estou usando? [eeshta beng oo kee ew eeshto oozandoo]

weather o tempo [tempoo]
- ▸ what is the weather like today? como está o tempo hoje? [komoo eeshta oo tempoo ojee]
- ▸ is the weather going to change? será que o tempo vai mudar? [sera kee oo tempoo vy moodah]

weather forecast a previsão do tempo [preveezowng doo tempoo]
- ▸ what's the weather forecast for tomorrow? qual é a previsão do tempo para amanhã? [kwal eh a preveezowng doo tempoo para amanyang]

website address o endereço na Internet [enderessoo na eenteh-netchee]
- ▸ can you give me your website address? você pode me dar o seu endereço na Internet? [vosse podjee mee dar oo sew enderessoo na eenteh-netchee]

Wednesday a quarta-feira [kwah-ta fayra], a quarta [kwah-ta]
- ▸ we're arriving/leaving on Wednesday estamos chegando/saindo na quarta [eeshtamoosh shegandoo/sa-eendoo na kwah-ta]

week a semana [semana]
- ▸ how much is it for a week? quanto custa por uma semana? [kwantoo kooshta por ooma semana]
- ▸ I'm leaving in a week vou embora em uma semana [vo embora nooma semana]
- ▸ two weeks duas semanas [doo-ash semanash]

weekly semanal [semanow]
- ▸ is there a weekly rate? tem uma taxa semanal? [teng ooma tasha semanow]

welcome bem-vindo(da) [beng-veendoo(da)] ♦ as boas-vindas [boash-veendash] ♦ *(person)* dar as boas-vindas a [dar ash boash-veendaz a]
- ▸ welcome! bem-vindo! [beng-veendoo]
- ▸ you're welcome *(in reply to thanks)* de nada [djee nada]
- ▸ you're welcome to join us se quiser se juntar a nós, será bem-vindo [see keezeh see joontar a nosh sera beng-veendoo]

well bem [beng]

- I'm very well, thank you estou muito bem, obrigado [eeshto mweentoo beng obreegadoo]
- get well soon! fique bem logo! [feekee beng logoo]
- well played bem jogado [beng jogadoo]

well done *(steak)* bem passado(da) [beng passadoo(da)]

- well done, please bem passado, por favor [beng passadoo poh favoh]

what o que [oo kee]

- what? *(asking for repetition)* como? [komoo], o quê? [oo ke]
- what is it? *(what's this thing?)* o que é isso? [oo kee eh eessoo]; *(what's the matter?)* qual é o problema? [kwal eh oo problema]
- what's up? *(what's wrong)* o que foi? [oo ke foy]; *(as greeting)* e daí? [ee da-ee]
- what's your name? qual é o seu nome? [kwal eh oo sew nomee]
- what's it called? como se chama? [komoo see shama]
- what time is it? que horas são? [kee orash sowng]
- what day is it? que dia é hoje? [ke djee-a eh ojee]
- what desserts do you have? que sobremesas vocês servem? [ke sobreemezash vossesh seh-veng]

wheel a roda [hoda]

- could you help me change the wheel? poderia me ajudar a trocar a roda? [poderee-a mee ajoodar a trokar a hoda]

when quando [kwandoo]

- when was it built? quando foi construído? [kwandoo foy konshtroo-eedoo]
- when is the next bus to Rio? quando é o próximo ônibus para o Rio? [kwandoo eh oo prosseemoo oneeboosh para oo hee-oo]

where onde [ondjee]

- where do you live? onde você mora? [ondjee vosse mora]
- where are you from? de onde você é? [djee ondjee vosse eh]
- excuse me, where is the nearest bus stop, please? com licença, onde fica a parada de ônibus mais perto, por favor? [kong leessensa ondjee feeka a parada djee oneeboosh mysh peh-too poh favoh]

which que [kee] ◆ *(in questions)* qual [kwow]

- which hotel would you recommend for us? que hotel você nos recomendaria? [kee otew vosse nosh hekomendaree-a]
- which way should we go? qual caminho devemos pegar? [kwow kameenyoo devemoosh pegah]
- which do you prefer? qual você prefere? [kwow vosse preferee]

while enquanto [enkwantoo]

- I'm only planning to stay for a while estou planejando ficar pouco tempo [eeshto planejandoo feekah pooko tempoo]

white *(in color)* branco(ca) *[brankoo(ka)]*
> I need a white T-shirt preciso de uma camiseta branca *[presseezoo djee ooma kameezeta branka]*

white wine o vinho branco *[veenyoo brankoo]*
> a glass of white wine, please uma taça de vinho branco, por favor *[ooma tassa djee veenyoo brankoo poh favoh]*

who quem *[keng]*
> who are you? quem é você? *[keng eh vosse]*
> who should I speak to about the heating? com quem eu tenho que falar sobre o aquecimento? *[kong keng ew tenyoo kee falah sobree oo akesseementoo]*
> who's calling? quem fala? *[keng fala]*

whole inteiro(ra) *[eentayroo(ra)]*
> we spent the whole day walking passamos o dia todo caminhando *[passamooz oo djee-a todoo kameenyando]*
> on the whole we had a good time no geral nos divertimos bastante *[noo jerow nosh djeeveh-tcheemoosh bashtantchee]*

whole-wheat integral *[eentegrow]*
> I'd like some whole-wheat bread eu queria um pão integral *[ew keree-a oom powng eentegrow]*

why por que *[poh ke]*
> why not? por que não? *[poh ke nowng]*

wide *(river, road)* largo(ga) *[lah-goo(ga)]*
> 2 meters wide dois metros de largura *[doysh metroosh djee lah-goora]*

will
> I'll be arriving at six vou chegar às seis *[vo shegar ash saysh]*

win *(competition, race)* vencer *[venseh]*, ganhar *[ganyah]* ♦ *(be ahead)* vencer *[venseh]*, ganhar *[ganyah]*
> who's winning? quem está vencendo? *[keng eeshta vensendoo]*

wind o vento *[ventoo]*
> there's a strong west wind tem um vento oeste forte *[teng oom ventoo weshtchee foh-tchee]*

window *(of a building, of a plane, of a car)* a janela *[janela]*; *(of a store)* a vitrine *[veetreenee]*; *(at a station, in a post office)* o guichê *[ghee-she]*
> I can't open the window não consigo abrir a janela *[nowng konseegoo abreer a janela]*
> I'm cold: could you close your window? estou com frio: poderia fechar a sua janela? *[eeshto kong free-oo poderee-a feshar a soo-a janela]*
> I'd like to see the dress in the window eu gostaria de ver o vestido da vitrine *[ew goshtaree-a djee ver oo vesh-tcheedoo da veetreenee]*
> where's the window for buying tickets? onde fica o guichê para comprar ingressos? *[ondjee feeka oo gheeshe para komprar eengressoosh]*

window seat o assento na janela [assentoo na janela]
- I'd like a window seat if possible eu queria um assento na janela, por favor [ew keree-a oom assentoo na janela poh favoh]

windshield o pára-brisas [para-breezash]
- could you clean the windshield? você poderia limpar o pára-brisas? [vosse poderee-a leempar oo para-breezash]

windsurfing o windsurfe [weendjee-sooh-fee]
- is there anywhere around here I can go windsurfing? tem algum lugar por aqui para praticar windsurfe? [teng owgoom loogah por akee para pratcheekah weendjee-sooh-fee]

windy *(day, weather)* com vento [kong ventoo]
- it's windy tem vento hoje [teng ventoo ojee]

wine o vinho [veenyoo]
- this wine is not chilled enough este vinho não está gelado o suficiente [eshtchee veenyoo nowng eeshta jeladoo oo soofeess-yentchee]

wine list a carta de vinhos [kah-ta djee veenyoosh]
- can we see the wine list, please? podemos ver a carta de vinhos, por favor? [podemoosh ver a kah-ta djee veenyoosh poh favoh]

wish o desejo [dezejoo] ◆ desejar [dezejah]
- best wishes! felicidades! [feleessee-dadjeesh]
- we wish you good luck desejamos boa sorte [dezejamoosh boa soh-tchee]

with com [kong]
- thanks, but I'm here with my boyfriend obrigado, mas estou com o meu namorado [obreegadoo myz eeshto kong oo mew namoradoo]

---

wishes and regrets

- I hope it won't be too busy espero que você não esteja muito ocupado [eeshperoo kee vosse nowng eeshteja mweentoo okoopadoo]
- it'd be great if you stayed seria ótimo se você ficasse [seree-a otcheemoo see vosse feekassee]
- if only I had a car! se ao menos eu tivesse um carro! [se ow menoosh ew tcheevessee oom kahoo]
- unfortunately, we couldn't get there in time infelizmente não conseguimos chegar a tempo [eenfeleej-mentchee nowng konsegeemoosh shegar a tempoo]
- I'm really sorry you couldn't make it lamento muito mesmo você não ter conseguido ir [lamentoo mweentoo mejmoo vosse nowng teh konsegeedoo eeh]

wishing someone something

- Happy Birthday! feliz aniversário! [feleez aneeveh-saryoo]
- Merry Christmas! feliz Natal! [feleej natow]
- Happy New Year! feliz Ano Novo! [feleez anoo novoo]
- enjoy your vacation! aproveite as férias! [aprovay-tchee ash feree-ash]
- enjoy your meal! bom proveito! [bong provaytoo]
- good night! boa noite! [boa noytchee]
- congratulations! parabéns! [parabengsh]

withdraw *(money)* sacar [sakah]
- I'd like to withdraw 100 reais eu queria sacar cem reais [ew keree-a sakah seng hee-ysh]

without sem [seng]
- a chicken sandwich without mayonnaise um sanduíche de frango sem maionese [oom sandweeshee djee frangoo seng my-onezee]

woman a mulher [moolyeh]
- where's the women's changing room? onde fica o vestiário feminino? [ondjee feeka oo vesh-too-aryoo femeeneenoo]

wonderful maravilhoso(sa) [maraveel-yozoo(za)]
- that's wonderful! que ótimo! [ke otcheemoo]
- the weather was wonderful o tempo estava maravilhoso [oo tempoo eeshtava maraveel-yozoo]

word a palavra [palavra]
- I don't know what the word is in Portuguese não sei o que significa essa palavra em português [nowng say oo kee seegneefeeka essa palavra eng poh-toogesh]
- I don't understand a word não entendo nada [nowng entendoo nada]

work *(employment)* o trabalho [trabalyoo] ♦ *(do a job)* trabalhar [trabalyah]; *(function)* funcionar [foonss-yonah]
- to be out of work não ter trabalho [nowng teh trabalyoo]
- I work in marketing trabalho com marketing [trabalyoo kong mah-ketcheeng]
- the heating's not working o aquecimento não está funcionando [oo akessee-mentoo nowng eeshta foonss-yonandoo]
- how does the shower work? como funciona o chuveiro? [komoo foonss-yona oo shoovayroo]

workday o dia útil [djee-a ooteew]
- is tomorrow a workday? amanhã é dia útil? [amanyang eh djee-a ooteew]

world o mundo [moondoo]
- what part of the world are you from? de que parte do mundo você é? [djee ke pah-tchee doo moondoo vosse eh]

worried preocupado(da) [pre-okoopadoo(da)]
- I'm worried about his health estou preocupado com a saúde dele [eeshto pre-okoopadoo kong a sa-oodjee delee]

worry preocupar-se [pre-okoopah-see]
- don't worry! não se preocupe [nowng see pre-okoopee]

worth o valor [valoh]
- how much is it worth? quanto vale? [kwantoo valee]
- it's well worth a visit vale a pena visitar [valee a pena veezeetah]
- what's worth seeing in this town? o que vale a pena ver na cidade? [oo kee valee a pena veh na seedadjee]

wound a ferida [fereeda]
- I need something for disinfecting a wound preciso de alguma coisa para desinfetar a ferida [presseezoo djee owgooma koyza para djeezeenfetar a fereeda]

wrap (up) embrulhar [embroolyah]
- can you wrap it (up) for me? você pode embrulhar para mim? [vosse podjee embroolyah para meeng]

wrist o pulso [poow-soo]
- I've sprained my wrist torci o pulso [toh-see oo poow-soo]

write escrever [eeshkreveh]
- I have some letters to write tenho algumas cartas para escrever [tenyoo owgoomash kah-tash para eeshkreveh]

wrong errado(da) [ehadoo(da)]
- to be wrong *(person)* estar errado [eeshtar ehadoo]
- I'm sorry, but I think you're wrong desculpe, mas acho que você está errado [djeesh-koowpee myz ashoo kee vosse eeshta ehadoo]
- sorry, I dialed the wrong number desculpe, foi engano [djeesh-koowpee foy enganoo]
- you've got the wrong number você discou o número errado [vosse djeeshko oo noomeroo ehadoo]
- this is the wrong bus é o ônibus errado [eh oo oneeboosh ehadoo]
- what's wrong? o que há de errado? [oo kee a djee ehadoo]
- there's something wrong with the switch tem alguma coisa errada com o interruptor [teng owgooma koyza ehada kong oo eente-hooptoh]

X, y, z

X-ray o raio X [hy-oo sheesh]
- do you think I should have an X-ray? acha que eu preciso bater um raio X? [asha kee ew presseezoo bateh oom hy-oo sheesh]

year o ano [anoo]
- we came here last year viemos aqui o ano passado [vee-emooz akee oo anoo passadoo]
- I'm 21 years old tenho vinte e um anos [tenyoo veentchee ee oom anoosh]

yellow amarelo(la) [amareloo(la)]
- the yellow one o amarelo [oo amareloo]

Yellow Pages®
- do you have a copy of the Yellow Pages? tem uma cópia das Páginas Amarelas? [teng ooma kopya dash pajeenaz amarelash]
- why don't you look in the Yellow Pages? por que você não olha nas Páginas Amarelas? [poh ke vosse nowng olya nash pajeenaz amarelash]

yes sim [seeng]
- yes, please sim, por favor [seeng poh favoh]
- it doesn't matter – yes it does! não importa – importa, sim! [nowng eempoh-ta eempoh-ta seeng]

yet ainda [a-eenda]
- I've not been there yet ainda não fui lá [a-eenda nowng fwee la]

yogurt o iogurte [yogooh-tchee]
- do you have any organic yogurt? tem iogurte orgânico? [teng yogooh-tchee oh-ganeekoo]

young man o jovem [joveng]
- who is that young man? quem é aquele jovem? [keng eh akelee joveng]

young person o(a) jovem [joveng]
- are there any discounts for young people? tem algum desconto para jovens? [teng owgoom djeeshkontoo para jovengsh]

young woman a jovem [joveng]
- who is the young woman he's with? quem é a jovem com quem ele está? [keng eh a joveng kong keng elee eeshta]

youth hostel o albergue da juventude [owbeh-ghee da jooven-toodjee]
- I'd like to book two beds for three nights in a youth hostel eu queria reservar duas camas por três noites em um albergue da juventude [ew keree-a hezeh-vah doo-ash kamash poh tresh noytcheez eng oom owbeh-ghee da jooven-toodjee]

zone *(on public transportation)* a zona [zona]
  ▸ I'd like a ticket for zones one to four eu queria uma passagem para as zonas um a quatro [ew keree-a ooma passajeng para ash zonaz oom a kwatroo]

Portuguese language and Brazilian culture

Portuguese around the world: who speaks it and where?

Portuguese is spoken as a first language by over 200 million people worldwide, including over 170 million speakers in Brazil and a further 10 million in Portugal.

The language is also spoken in former Portuguese colonies in Africa, the Far East and Australasia. These include Angola (10 million), Mozambique (18 million), Cape Verde (370,000), Guinea Bissau (980,000) and the islands of Sao Tome and Principe (116,000). In East Timor (950,000), Macao and Goa it is spoken as a second language.

In addition, the language is spoken by Portuguese diaspora communities across the globe, but principally in Europe and North America, with an estimated 500,000 in the US alone.

By contrast, English is spoken as a first language by over 340 million, Spanish by over 350 million and Arabic by over 200 million

Regional variations

There are no dialects of Portuguese in Brazil but several regional variations in accent can be distinguished. Broadly, these variations in accent follow geographic lines: the South, the Southeast, the North, the Northeast and the Central-West.

The Portuguese spoken in the São Paulo and Rio de Janeiro metropolitan areas in the Southeast represent the media standard accents and those to which most foreigners are exposed. The two accents are, however, quite different from one another. To muddy the waters, the accents of these major cities and those of surrounding smaller cities of the respective states are quite distinct. People from the city of São Paulo are known as **paulistas**, while those from cities of the interior are **paulistanos**. A similar distinction exists in the state of Rio de Janeiro: **cariocas** are natives of the city of Rio, while those from the interior of the state are **fluminenses**.

While São Paulo is the economic capital of the country, Rio, as the former political capital, is considered the historical capital and is the most important center for tourism. Increasingly though, the Northeast is developing as a tourist destination and visitors are likely to be exposed to the accent of this region more and more.

Brazil: language and culture

It is important to add that Brazilians of all regions can make themselves understood across the country. Considering the sheer physical size of the country, this is surprising. In this respect, Brazil is similar to the US. Most foreign speakers of Portuguese would probably not be able to distinguish the differences between the regional accents of Brazil.

Brazil also has a number of minority languages which are either indigenous (**Guarani**, **Tupi**, etc.) or have been brought to Brazil by immigrant communities (German, Japanese, Arabic, Polish, etc.). The use of immigrant languages diminishes with the passage of time, except where the language is kept alive by special schools and cultural associations. There are towns in the South where German and Portuguese enjoy equal status in use.

Where did the Portuguese language come from?

The evolution of Portuguese

Portuguese originally evolved from the Latin introduced to the Iberian Peninsula through Roman conquest. Latin (or **Romance**, the regional dialect of formal Latin) continued to be spoken after the end of the Roman Empire, the migration of European tribes across the Pyrenees and the Moorish occupation. The language, in turn, evolved into Iberian, having absorbed these foreign influences.

The Moors introduced many words relating to agriculture, e.g. **arroz** (*rice*), **açúcar** (*sugar*), **café** (*coffee*) and **tâmara** (*dates*). Although Arabic did not replace Iberian, it left a linguistic footprint. Many Portuguese words with the prefix **al-** (which is the definite article 'the' in Arabic) are certain to have their origins in Arabic, e.g. **alface** (*lettuce*), **algodão** (*cotton*), etc.

The emergence of modern Portuguese dates from the 12th century with the expulsion of the Moors and the establishment of Portugal as a state independent of Castilian Spain, which experienced a separate political and linguistic development. Galician, from which both Portuguese and Spanish derive, continues as a dialect of Spanish in the Northwestern corner of Spain.

In the written form, Portuguese and Spanish are broadly similar. However, in the spoken form, the languages contrast sharply, both having distinct cadences and intonation patterns. While Castilian (i.e. European) Spanish is a syllable-timed language, giving rise to a rapid and punchy delivery, Portuguese is a stress-timed language. This produces a slower delivery and a distinctive rise and fall intonation. This is particularly marked in Brazilian Portuguese.

The Portuguese in Brazil

Portuguese was introduced to Brazil through Portuguese colonization from 1500 onwards. The indigenous languages, such as **Tupi** and **Guarani**, were promoted by the Jesuits, and as a consequence widely spoken as the lingua franca. This continued until the late 18th century, when the Jesuits were expelled and the indigenous languages suppressed by Royal decree. However, many indigenous loanwords, principally relating to the natural world, entered usage and remain, e.g. **cajú** (*cashew*), **piranha**, etc. Some of Brazil's most famous place names are indigenous in origin: **Ipanema Beach**, **Itaipu Dam**, and many others. The **ipa-** and **ita-** prefixes mean water and rock respectively and are widespread across the country.

The African linguistic influence on Brazilian Portuguese is principally seen in food (**vatapá**, **caruru**, **dendê**), music (**samba**, **berimbau**) and religion (**candomblé**, **umbanda**). The Africans, of course, did not come to Brazil as immigrants in the strict sense of the word; they were brought forcibly as slaves. This meant that their linguistic input was restricted to the kitchen, to entertainment and to the worship of African deities.

Brazilian and European varieties

It is important to note that Brazilian Portuguese is very distinct from European Portuguese, principally in the spoken form. Brazilians speak with long, languid vowels, while the Portuguese tend to 'eat' their vowels, leaving the words dominated by consonant sounds. In fact, to the non-speaker, European Portuguese can sound almost Slavic in this respect. Brazilians have also simplified the grammar of the language, taking shortcuts through the mass of grammatical rules. A typical example is the exclusion of the object in *he gave it to me*, this translating as **ele me deu**, i.e. *he gave me*, with the object *it* left out. In addition, Brazilian Portuguese has absorbed many words from the numerous linguistic and cultural influences shaping the country's social and economic development. By contrast, Portugal's history has been one of relative economic and cultural isolation. This divergence has been accentuated by Portugal's experience of being, until recently, a net exporter of people, with Brazil being a net importer.

20th century developments

Until the end of the 19th century, the Portuguese represented the most numerous group of immigrants arriving in Brazil, with Rio de Janeiro, then the political capital, being their main destination. Even today, there are remnants of European Portuguese in the **carioca** accent. With the turn of the century came waves of immigration from Europe, the East Mediterranean countries and Japan. Each national group left its imprint on Brazilian Portuguese. The **paulista** accent in particular has been heavily influenced by the Italian language.

The Second World War was a significant watershed for the Portuguese language in Brazil. It marked the arrival of American servicemen to Brazilian shores and Brazil's earliest mass exposure to American music, fashion and products. The period marked the beginning of Brazil's fascination with and admiration for its North America neighbor. Inevitably, with modern marketing has come the language of the medium: English. This process continues unabated today.

Brazilian influences on US culture and the English language

Music

The 1950s was America's decade of rock and roll, with Bill Haley and the Comets, Elvis Presley, Buddy Holly and many others. Few experts predicted the impact of a new kind of music emerging from Brazil: **bossa nova**. The new sound was a synthesis of native elements, such as **samba** and **choro**, and foreign imports, notably jazz. **Bossa nova**'s high-water mark was the 1963 Getz/Gilberto album. The album contained one of the most successful singles of all time, *The Girl from Ipanema*. The song was famously covered by Frank Sinatra, then America's leading male vocalist. Brazil has since produced many fine musicians, but no musical genre has had as much impact as **bossa nova**.

Brazil in the movies

Initial American awareness of Brazil dates from 1930s Hollywood extravaganzas, such as *Road to Rio*. In the 1940s, Brazil's most famous cultural export of the period, Carmen Miranda, embodied Brazilian culture for American audiences. Though criticized in her native Brazil for stereotyping Latin culture, she nevertheless helped popularize

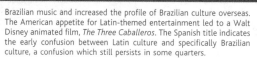

Brazilian music and increased the profile of Brazilian culture overseas. The American appetite for Latin-themed entertainment led to a Walt Disney animated film, *The Three Caballeros*. The Spanish title indicates the early confusion between Latin culture and specifically Brazilian culture, a confusion which still persists in some quarters.

Recent Brazilian film productions, such as *Central Station* and *City of God*, have achieved prominence and Oscar nominations in the US. These films portray the harsh realities of life for Brazil's economic underclass. It is important, nevertheless, to understand this genre of films as one layer of a vast and complex country.

Soccer

The World Cup of 1994, won by Brazil, dramatically raised the profile of soccer in the US, where it had battled with American football, basketball and baseball for American affections. Though soccer is a British invention, the frequency with which Brazil has won the World Cup and its players' distinctive style have made soccer one of Brazil's greatest cultural exports.

Fashion

The world of fashion increasingly has a Brazilian accent. The Brazilian supermodel, Gisele Bündchen, arguably one of the world's leading models, has featured in campaigns promoting that most Brazilian of beach accessories, the *Havaianas*® sandal. The Brazilian 'look,' the product of racial miscegenation, is currently much sought after by international modeling agencies.

Linguistic influences

Brazilian Portuguese has had modest influence on the English language, the main influence being words originated by the indigenous populations to describe the local flora and fauna, e.g. *jaguar*, *piranha*, *cashew* (**cajú**), *manioc* (**mandioca**), *toucan* (**tucano**), etc.

True friends and false friends

The Portuguese and English grammatical systems are both derived from Latin, and the US learner of Brazilian Portuguese soon becomes familiar with the similarities between the languages, particularly with regard to vocabulary. By applying a few rules, the meanings of many Portuguese words can be arrived at.

Clues in word endings

English words ending in *-tion*, such as information, nation, relation, intention, etc. tend to be Latin-derived. The Portuguese equivalents end in **-ção**: *information* - **informação**, *nation* - **nação**, *relation* - **relação**, etc.

For English words ending in *-ing*, e.g. *I am speaking* **eu estou falando**, the Portuguese equivalents end in **-indo**, **-ando** and **-endo**, for infinitives ending in **-ir**, **-ar** and **-er**, respectively. Of course, the meaning of the verb itself is not immediately apparent, but it does give the learner a clue to structure.

For words ending in *-ity* the equivalent would be **-dade**: *city* - **cidade**, *community* - **comunidade**, *tranquility* - **tranqüilidade**, etc.

For adverbs ending in *-ly*, e.g. *really, effectively, efficiently*, etc., the Portuguese equivalent ends in **-mente**: **realmente**, **efetivamente**, **eficientemente**, etc.

For words ending in *-ive*, the Portuguese equivalent is **-ivo/a**: *creative* - **creativo/a**, *imaginative* - **imaginativo/a**, *native* - **nativo/a**, etc.

Words derived from Greek, which in English predominate in medicine and the sciences, tend to be very similar in Portuguese. In addition, there is a pattern in the suffix endings in which *-ist* becomes **-ogo**: *psychologist* - **psicólogo**, *biologist* - **biólogo**, or *-ista*: *dermatologist* - **dermatologista**, *journalist* - **jornalista**. The 'ph' in Greek-derived words in English, becomes an 'f' in Portuguese, for example: *telephone* **telefone**, *phase* - **fase**, *photo* - **foto**, *phrase* - **frase**, etc.

Identical words

Some words are identical: **regular**, **normal**, **final**, **instrumental**, **monumental**, **sentimental**, **musical**, **material**, **face**, **motor** and **banana**, to mention a few. It is important to note that the system of syllable stress differs. Words relating to tourism are also mostly identical: **aeroporto**, **táxi**, **hotel**, **restaurante**, **café**, **bar**, **buffet**, **self-service**, etc.

Brand names

Brand names can become generic for the product in Brazil. A classic example is **gillette**® for a razor blade or shaving razor; the meaning is easily arrived at as the company is well known for this particular product. However, applying this assumption about other products can result in misunderstandings. A good example relates to the leading Brazilian brand of Scotch® tape **durex**®, which means something altogether different in the US. Hence, in Brazil, **durex**® is sold in stationery stores.

Common false friends

The word for '*to pull*' is confusingly **puxar** (*to push* - **empurrar**). If someone declares that they are **constipado**, it does not mean that they are *constipated*, rather they have a cold and their sinuses are blocked. Other confusions arise out of the misuse of: '*actually,*' which translates as **na verdade** and not **atualmente** (*currently*), *library* translates as **biblioteca** and not **livraria** (*bookstore*), **pasta** has nothing to do with Italian food but is actually *paste* (e.g. toothpaste). **Massas** refer to any *pasta* dishes, **pretender** is *to intend* (to do something), **o técnico** in soccer terms is *the manager*, and **um outdoor** is an *advertising billboard* (as seen outdoors!).

English loanwords

The visitor to Brazil will be struck by words which, at first glance, are entirely English in origin, but on closer inspection have been 'Brazilianized' in their spelling and pronunciation.

Food and drink

Food and drink is an area rich in language imported from North America, such as: **hambúrguer**, **cheeseburger**, **sanduíche**, **milkshake**, **drinque**, **coquetel**, **lanche**, **fast food** and many others. Some of these imports now have different (but related) meanings, e.g. **bife** (from *beef*, but meaning steak).

Sports

The national sport and passion, **futebol** (*soccer*), is replete with imported terminology, most notably **gol** (*goal*), enthusiastically yelled by frenzied sports commentators to mark a score. Similarly *to dribble* has become **driblar**, *to shoot* (for goal) has become **chutar**. *Penalty* is corrupted to **pênalti**, while **off-side** remains unchanged. While the influence of soccer cannot be overstated, other popular sports also borrow heavily from English, notably **basquete** (*basketball*) and **vôlei** (*volleyball*), but also **tênis** (*tennis*), **skate** (*skateboarding*), **squash**, **surfe** (*surf*), **bodyboard** and **iatismo** (*yachting*).

English sells

For people committed to the body beautiful, the abundance of **academias de ginástica** (*fitness centers*) and attendant **bodybuilding** and **spin** classes is unsurprising. Many such centers have English-sounding names to generate an upmarket appeal with the public. The same trend can be observed in the retail sector, with terms such as **sales**, **50% off**, **fashion** (*fashionable*) and the spread of **shopping centers**, now commonly referred to as **shopping**. Words like **light**, **clean**, **VIP**, **diet**, **plus** are used as descriptions, marrying with Brazilian expressions: **Coca® light**, **esquema light** (*to do something without stress*), **sala VIP** (*VIP lounge*), **Guara-plus®** (a drink made with **guaraná**, a tropical fruit and an indigenous word), etc.

Clothing

Clothing is another area with a great deal of English penetration: *dinner jacket* - **smoking**, *shorts* - **short**, *Bermuda shorts* - **bermuda**, *jeans* - **calça jeans**, *moccasin shoes* - **mocassim**, *tennis shoes* - **tênis**, etc.

Music

Music is a Brazilian obsession, and this too is heavily influenced by English borrowings, transcribed directly but with a Brazilian pronunciation: **jazz**, **rock**, **reggae**, **musical**, **ir a um show** (*to go to a show*), **videoclipe**, **remix**, etc.

Technology

Technology is probably the principal vector of English loanwords, and this has been accelerated by the increasing pace of Internet penetration. Brazil has the third-highest level of Internet use in the Americas, after the US and Canada. The vast majority of Brazil's urban middle classes have online access; Internet cafes are widespread, and not just in the major cities. Not surprisingly, the Portuguese of IT and Internet borrows heavily from English: **monitor** (*screen/monitor*), **mouse**, **browser**, **site**, **página web** (*webpage*), **cliquar no link** (*to click on the link*), **deletar** (*to delete*), **plugar** (*to plug something*),

disquette (*diskette*), **software**, **upgrade**, **online**, **off-line** and, of course, **internet** and **e-mail**. The borrowings are also found in media jargon: **CD**, **DVD**, **vídeo**, **foto**, **flash**, **slide**, **leiaute** (*layout*) etc. In the office, words such as **fax**, **modem**, **xerox** and **escanear/fazer um scan** (*to scan*) are not uncommon.

Despite being one of the world's leading car manufacturers, Brazilians refer to some vehicles using English terminology instead of workable Brazilian alternatives: **pick-up** (instead of **camionete**), **van** (instead of **furgoneta**). A four-wheel drive vehicle, if specifically designed for off-road use, is a **jipe**, a corruption of Jeep®.

Movies

The titles of many mainstream Hollywood movies are no longer translated, and this is also true of advertising slogans. This means yet more exposure to English for the Brazilian public; **outdoors** (*billboards*) and **pôsters** (*posters*) are highly visible and communicate to all social classes.

At work

The rise of the international MBA and globalization in general has inevitably popularized expressions such as: **estresse** (*stress*), **hora do rush** (*rush hour*), **workshop**, **expert**, **marketing**, **slogan**, **know-how**, **performance**, etc. in professional contexts. The respective meanings generally reflect their usage in English; the structural similarities between Portuguese and English ease this transition.

The backlash

The spread of English in Brazil has recently provoked a backlash against what is perceived in some quarters as a threat to Brazilian culture and a development which socially excludes those who don't speak English. Commercial pressure, however, imposes its own agenda and the onward march of English is unlikely to be stemmed by political or legislative initiatives.

Modern developments in the language

The Portuguese language in Brazil has absorbed influences from diverse cultures through the centuries, from the native indigenous populations, from African slaves, from European immigrants and more recently, from the tremendous impact of the Internet.

Internet and technology

Brazil has one of the world's highest rates of Internet connection and the principal language used is of course English. It is the language used by over 30% of Internet users. When one considers the importance of the Internet to professional and academic development, the extent to which this underpins the demand for English language learning in Brazil is unsurprising. Globalization of the Brazilian economy, the increasing popularity of imported consumer goods and the presence of international advertising are key drivers in this respect.

European and Brazilian Portuguese

These factors have all contributed to distinguish Brazilian Portuguese from the original European Portuguese, and the difference now amounts to about 25% in vocabulary, grammar and pronunciation. This difference is accentuated in the spoken language to the extent that it can be difficult for Brazilians to understand what Portuguese are saying. Brazilian Portuguese tends to simplify the language and the distinction between **tu** and **você** (*you* in the second and third persons, informal and formal respectively) has blurred with the use of **você** for informal address: **ce** in spoken language – **como ce tá?** instead of **como voce está?** (*how are you?*).

Youth culture

Brazilians have readily adopted foreign words instead of translating them. This is illustrated by the slang of Brazilian youth culture. The young, through exposure to popular music and movies, tend to borrow slang from other cultures, e.g. **e aí, brother?** (*what's up, brother?*) but they can also apply Portuguese grammar conventions, so **crowdiar** and **crowdiado** are *to crowd* and *crowded* respectively.

Brazilian culture

Brazil is a land rich in powerful images: Christ the Redeemer, a packed Maracanã stadium, the Rio Carnival, the verdant expanse of the Amazon rainforest, its soccer players celebrating in the distinctive yellow strip, the aggressive modernity of Brasília, and many more too numerous to mention. The global audience may forget names and dates, but images are eternal.

A Cidade Maravilhosa

Rio de Janeiro is arguably one of the most striking cities in the world. Rarely do the forces of nature and man's endeavor combine to create such a dazzling interplay of colors and textures: the long strips of white sandy beaches, the greenery of the forest-clad hillsides rising precipitously from the azure sea, pastel-colored apartment blocks vying for space with the organized chaos of the **favelas** (*slums*). On closer inspection, the visitor will see also decay and disrepair, but this epitomizes the essence of Brazilian culture: the execution of the plan lacks structure and method, but they somehow manage to achieve something beautiful.

Soccer

This approach to getting things done extends to soccer. Armchair admirers of Brazilian soccer should reach consensus on the principal characteristics of the playing style: a contempt for conventions and caution, a celebration of individual skill and exhibition, and, essentially, a desire to enjoy the occasion.

Carnival

The annual Carnival celebrations attract immense interest and huge numbers of foreign visitors. Most visit Rio de Janeiro to view the processions of competing schools of samba: whirling dancers, scantily-clad women and pulsating teams of drummers. It is the Rio Carnival which represents Brazilian Carnival abroad. However, the Carnival celebrated throughout the rest of the country follows a different format. The celebrations are in the street and are more participatory.

Reveillon

Welcoming the New Year on Copacabana Beach is an event familiar to people worldwide thanks to television. Millions throng the beach and adjacent streets to witness the spectacular fireworks display at the stroke of midnight on New Year's Eve. It is an occasion attracting people of all ages, social classes and racial groups. Despite the immense numbers of people crowded into a small area and the easy availability of alcoholic drinks, the event is relaxed and devoid of tension. It is a mirror to the Brazilian personality, described in more depth below. The New Year's celebration is also an opportunity to project aspirations and hopes for the coming year, accompanied by the mantra: **se Deus quiser** – *God willing*.

Lifestyle

Brazil: the immigrant nation

Brazil, like its North American neighbor, the US, is an immigrant nation. Although people arrived in Brazil from a broad spectrum of countries and cultures, the predominant cultural footprint is the Portuguese one. This has its most obvious expression in the language of the country, but also in aspects of everyday life and in the general culture. The next most important influence is African. What distinguishes Brazil from the majority of its South American neighbors, apart from language, is the impact of African slavery on society, people and culture. Of course, there are regions of Brazil where both the Portuguese and African influences on culture are negligible, and examples might include German communities in the South and Japanese communities in São Paulo state. In fact, the latter represent the largest concentration of ethnic Japanese outside Japan.

In general terms, Brazilians have a Latin/Mediterranean outlook: an attachment to family, a respect for elders, the adoration of children, the love of food, of socializing and of leisure. Of course, many Brazilians work long hours for low salaries, and have few opportunities for leisure. However, when the opportunity presents itself, such as at the annual Carnival celebrations, these people surrender themselves wholeheartedly to the occasion.

Family meals on occasions such as Christian festivals, birthdays and Sundays, play a vital role in the cohesion of the extended family. Food is shared and enjoyed, and family members appreciate each other's company.

How Brazilians relate to others

Communication among Brazilians is characterized by generous use of body language, effusive gestures, frequent handshakes and embraces, and repetition of sentiment.

In their personal relationships Brazilians are warm, tactile and spontaneous and open to new friendships. These personal relationships play a key role in 'getting by': finding work, negotiating passage through Brazil's Byzantine bureaucracy, reserving an airline ticket, practically anything, in fact. Closely related to this is the **jeitinho brasileiro** – literally *finding a way*. Brazilians almost never accept 'no' for an answer, nor do they like to give 'no' for an answer. Protecting feelings and honor are paramount, e.g. if a scheduled flight is full, the charm of the passenger and the good nature of the check-in clerk will ensure that a seat is found, albeit on another flight.

Religion

The vast majority of Brazilians are Catholic, and this reflects in an inherent social conservatism; the liberal attitudes for which Brazil is well-known are predominantly found in the big cities. This religiosity can also express itself in fatalism: Brazilians have little faith in the power of planning or decision, rather they hope that destiny will shape events. An obvious reflection of this is in the relaxed Brazilian attitude to timekeeping, and this holds true even in the main economic centers: working lunches can last several hours and meetings rarely start on time.

Catholicism was brought to Brazil by the Portuguese. Historically, their devotion was less dogmatic than that of the Spanish and so absorbed local influences wherever it was established. Recognition, if not the worship, of African deities is not considered eccentric, even among white Brazilians of the professional classes.

Embracing foreign ideas

Brazilians are very open to foreign influences: music, fashion, media, food, etc. However, as soon as these foreign influences are absorbed into mainstream culture, they tend to be 'Brazilianized,' i.e. adapted to local tastes. It is now common for **sashimi** and **sushi** to be served at that most Brazilian of eateries, the **churrascaria**, where they accompany grilled meat and starchy dishes. Similarly, American urban music, such as *hip-hop*, has been absorbed into mainstream Brazilian urban music and has morphed into **funk**.

Two countries: the coast and the interior

The images most foreigners have of Brazil relate to the major cities and the coastal resorts. However, a large proportion of the total population live in small towns and settlements away from the main cities, **o interior**. The culture and lifestyle in these areas are very distinct from those of the main population centers. Though broadcast media in Brazil are very powerful and widespread, the people of the **interior** are less open to foreign influences, and are more conservative and family-oriented.

Brazilians as hosts

A recent survey into levels of friendliness in big cities worldwide rated Rio de Janeiro as one of the friendliest and most welcoming cities in the survey. This has to be viewed in the context of Rio as a major city of nearly 10 million inhabitants, with the attendant problems of rush-hour traffic and stresses of modern life. In recent years it has also been burdened with the notoriety of drugs-fuelled violence in the slums (**favelas**). Yet despite these negative factors, visitors to the city are struck by the essential warmth and gentleness of the people. Bus passengers will surrender their seats to the elderly and expectant mothers, people will offer unsolicited help to lost tourists, and crucially, will advise tourists to be aware of thieves. This welcoming trait is even more accentuated in smaller cities where it is not uncommon for tourists to be invited into homes. The generosity of the welcome can be almost embarrassing for the foreigner.

Leisure

Brazilians love the outdoors. This passion is encouraged by the country's tropical and sub-tropical climates. Brazilians love their long coastline, which includes some of the world's most spectacular beaches, and beach culture is firmly established in the Brazilian psyche. Those who live inland engage in cycling, horse-riding, motocross and extreme sports such as hang-gliding and rock climbing.

The beach

The beach introduces its own language and etiquette. It is common for beaches to be informally divided between different groups of beachgoers: families, teenagers, surfers, gays, etc. The beach is also a popular arena for sports, such as surfing, windsurfing, volleyball, football, jogging and a peculiarly Brazilian take on volleyball, **futevôlei** (a form of volleyball played with the feet). The urban beaches typically have a **calçadão** (*boardwalk*) and an adjacent cycle lane where people run, cycle, power-walk, rollerblade, or simply hang out with friends.

The beach has an unwritten but (largely) respected etiquette: e.g. bikinis are tiny, but always worn, so going topless is frowned upon; any food or drink consumed should be bought on or near the beach; it is considered *déclassé* to picnic on the sand.

Soccer

Inevitably, the game of soccer occupies a lot of Brazilians' spare time. In the urban centers, nearly all Brazilians profess allegiance to a team. Players, performances and refereeing decisions are hotly debated, and the press devotes a significant portion of the front page to soccer news.

In Rio and São Paulo, matches between the leading teams generate huge interest and the teams' respective colors are displayed in windows and on car antennas. This passion for soccer cuts across the (very wide) social and economic divides. Players in the **seleção nacional** (*national squad*) are known by their first names or nicknames: this creates a sense of intimacy between players and the **torcida** (*spectators*) rarely seen in other countries.

Regardless of skill levels, most Brazilian men will play a **pelada**, a spontaneous kick-around held on the beach, the factory shopfloor, the street, anywhere in fact. The sport has recently been attracting the interest of women players.

Friends and family

In Brazil, relationships with family and friends are cherished. The definition of family is broader than that understood in North America and will include distant cousins. Family members keep in regular contact, time and distance permitting, and will get together for occasions such as birthdays, baptisms, Christmas and other religious festivals. Immediate family members will have at least one meal a day together around a table: news and gossip are exchanged and plans discussed. It is also common for friends to visit and to participate in family meals. Brazilians are amazed that people in other countries should value solitude, particularly at mealtimes.

There is no peer or societal pressure for offspring to leave the family home and many continue to live with parents until marriage. By the same token, it is not unusual for the elderly to move in with their children; Brazilians consider it unthinkable to deposit elderly parents in care homes unless there are no viable alternatives.

Movies, theater and music

A popular evening out will include going to the movies, followed by some drinks or a meal out with friends. Movie theaters show the latest Hollywood blockbusters, along with Brazilian productions and art house movies from around the globe. Theater productions are numerous in the major cities and are principally patronized by the middle and upper classes. Concerts and music festivals are also popular and some Brazilian musicians have achieved celebrity status, drawing vast numbers of people to see them play live. Sometimes concerts with internationally known bands and singers are organized – a concert by the Rolling Stones held on Copacabana Beach attracted around 3 million people.

Carnival

Samba is embedded in Brazilian culture and is celebrated with an annual festival for which Brazil is famous worldwide – the Carnival. People from all socio-economic layers take part, either as participants in **desfile de escola de samba** (*the school of samba processions*) in Rio de Janeiro, or by following the Carnival floats (mainly in the Northeast). The preparations for such processions take the whole year and include the production of the costumes and floats, and endless rehearsals. Even people with limited economic means will use whatever money they can save to be able to take part. Carnival is an opportunity for the disenfranchised to take center stage.

Portuguese–English dictionary

a(s) [a(sh)] *art* the ◆ *pron* the one(s) ◆ *prep* to ▸ **a que ...** the one who/that... ▸ **ir a Pernambuco** to go to Pernambuco

à [a] *prep* = a+a ▸ **vamos à praia** let's go to the beach

abacate [abakatchee] *n* avocado

abacaxi [abakashee] *n* pineapple

abadia [abadjee-a] *n* abbey

abafado, da [abafadoo] *adj (weather)* sultry

abaixo [aby-shoo] *adv* below

abarrotado, da [aba-ho-tadoo] *adj* packed

abelha [abelya] *n* bee

aberto, ta [abeh-too] *adj* open

abertura [abeh-toora] *n* opening

abóbora [abobora] *n* pumpkin

aborrecer-se [abo-hesseh-see] *v* to get bored; *(irritated)* to get annoyed

abridor [abreedoh] *n* ▸ **abridor de latas** can opener ▸ **abridor de garrafas** bottle opener

abril [abreew] *n* April

abrir [abreeh] *v* to open

absorvente [absoh-ventchee] *n* pad ▸ **absorvente higiênico** sanitary napkin, pad

acabar [akabah] *v* to end, to finish

açafrão [assafrowng] *n* saffron

acampar [akampah] *v* to camp

acaso [akazoo] *n* chance

aceitar [assay-tah] *v* to accept

acelerador [asseleradoh] *n* accelerator

acender [assendeh] *v* to light

acento [assentoo] *n* accent

acessível [assesseevew] *adj* accessible; *(price)* affordable

acesso [assessoo] *n* access ▸ **acesso proibido** no entry

achar [ashah] *v* to find; *(think)* to think ▸ **(não) acho bom** I (don't) agree ▸ **o que você acha?** what do you think?

acidente [asseedentchee] *n* accident

acima [asseema] *adv* above

acolhedor, ra [akol-yedoh] *adj* welcoming

acompanhar [akompan-yah] *v* to accompany, to go with

acontecer [akontesseh] *v* to happen

acontecimento [akontesseementoo] *n* event

acordar [akoh-dah] *v* to wake up

acostamento [akoshtamentoo] *n (on road)* shoulder

acreditar [akredjeetah] *v* to believe ▸ **não acredito!** I don't believe it!

açúcar [asookah] *n* sugar

adaptador [adaptadoh] *n* adaptor

adega [adega] *n* cellar

adeus! [adewsh] *excl* goodbye!

adiantado, da [adjee-antadoo] *adj* ahead of schedule ▸ **pagar adiantado** to pay in advance

adiante [adjee-antchee] *adv* ahead

admirar [admeerah] *v* to admire

adoçante [adosantchee] *n* sweetener

adoecer [adwesseh] *v* to fall ill, to get sick

adormecer [adoh-messeh] *v* to fall asleep

adulto, ta [adoowtoo] *n* & *adj* adult

aeroporto [a-eropoh-too] *n* airport

afastar(-se) [afashtah-(see)] *v* to move away

afixar [afeeksah] *v* to stick ▸ proibido afixar cartazes post no bills

afogar(-se) [afogah-(see)] *v* to drown

agarrar [aga-hah] *v* to grab

agência [ajensee-a] *n* agency ▸ agência de viagens travel agency

agoniado, da [agon-yadoo] *adj* ▸ estar agoniado to be anguished

agora [agora] *adv* now

agosto [agoshtoo] *n* August

agradar [agradah] *v* to please

agradável [agradavew] *adj* pleasant

agradecer [agradesseh] *v* to thank

agressão [agressowng] *n* aggression

agrião [agree-owng] *n* watercress

água [agwa] *n* water ▸ água benta holy water ▸ água doce fresh water ▸ água sem gás noncarbonated water ▸ água com gás sparkling water ▸ água imprópria para beber/consumo water unfit for drinking, non-potable water ▸ água mineral mineral water ▸ água potável drinking water ▸ água não potável non-potable water ▸ água salgada salt water

aguardar [agwah-dah] *v* to wait ▸ aguarde um momento wait a moment

aguardente [agwah-dentchee] *f* liquor

▸ aguardente de cana rum

agulha [agool-ya] *n* needle

aí [a-ee] *adv* there ▸ aí está o problema that's the problem

ainda [a-eenda] *adv* still

aipo [I-poo] *n* celery

ajuda [ajooda] *n* help

ajudar [ajoodah] *v* to help

albergue [ow-beh-ghee] *n* hostel

▸ albergue da juventude youth hostel

alcachofra [owka-shofra] *n* artichoke

alcaparras [owka-pahash] *npl* capers

álcool [owk-wol] *n* alcohol

aldeia [owdaya] *n* village

alegria [alegree-a] *n* joy

além [aleng] *adv* beyond ▸ além disso besides, in addition

alérgico, ca [aleh-jeekoo] *adj* allergic

alfabeto [owfabetoo] *n* alphabet

alface [owfassee] *n* lettuce

alfândega [owfandega] *n* customs

algarismo [owga-reejmoo] *n* number

algas [owgash] *npl* seaweed

algodão [owgodowng] *n* cotton

alguém [owgeng] *pron* somebody

algum(a) [owgoong(owgooma)] *adj* some ▸ de modo algum in no way

alguns [owgoonsh] *adj* some

alho [alyoo] *n* garlic

alho-poró [alyoo-poro] *n* leek

ali [alee] *adv* there

aliás [alee-ash] *adv* by the way

almoçar [owmosah] *v* to have lunch

almoço [owmosoo] *n* lunch

almofada [owmofada] *n* cushion

almôndega [owmondega] *n* meatball

alojamento [alojamentoo] *n* accommodations

Amazônia

The Amazon region is home to the largest equatorial rain forest in the world, covering almost 5 million square kilometers. This ancient tropical forest makes up a third of Brazil's surface area, and extends into Peru, Colombia and Venezuela. Sadly, this unique ecological site, home to many thousands of species of flora and fauna, is now under threat from multinational timber and subsoil development corporations.

alojar [alojah] *v* to accommodate

alta [owta] *n (in price)* rise ▸ alta dos preços price increase

alto, ta [owtoo] *adj* high; *(voice)* loud ▸ por alto roughly

alugar [aloogah] *v* to rent ▸ alugam-se quartos rooms to rent

aluguel [aloogew] *n* renting

amanhã [aman-yang] *adv* tomorrow ▸ amanhã de manhã/à noite tomorrow morning/night

amar [amah] *v* to love ▸ eu te amo I love you

amarelo, la [amareloo] *adj* yellow

amargo, ga [amah-goo] *adj* bitter

amável [amavew] *adj* friendly

Amazônia [amazonya] *f* ▸ a Amazônia the Amazon region

ambiente [ambee-entchee] *n* environment

ambulância [amboolanss-ya] *n* ambulance

amedrontar [amedrontah] *v* to frighten

ameixa [amay-sha] *n* plum

ameixeira [amay-shayra] *n* plum tree

amêndoa [amendwa] *n* almond

amendoim [amendweeng] *n* peanut

amigo [ameegoo] *n* friend

amor [amoh] *n* love

amora [amora] *n* mulberry

andar [andah] *n* story

andar [andah] *v* to walk ▸ anda! get a move on!

anel [an-ew] *n* ring

anestesia [aneshtezee-a] *n* anesthetic

angina [anjeena] *n* angina

animal [aneemow] *n* animal

aniversário [aneeversar-yoo] *n* birthday

ano [anoo] *n* year

anotar [anotah] *v* to note down

anteontem [antchee-onteng] *adv* the day before yesterday

antes [antcheesh] *adv* before; *(in importance)* rather ▸ antes de before

antibiótico [antcheebee-otcheekoo] *n* antibiotic

antigo, ga [antcheegoo] *adj* old

antiguidades [antcheegwee-dadjeesh] *npl (objects)* antiques

anular [anoolah] *v* to cancel

anúncio [anoonss-yoo] *n* notice; *(TV magazine)* ad

ao [ow] *prep* = a+o ▸ ao(s) domingo(s) on Sunday(s)

apagar(-se) [apagah-(see)] *v (fire)* to put out; *(light)* to turn out ▸ apague o cigarro! put out that cigarette!

apaixonado, da [a-py-shonadoo] *adj* in love

apaixonante [a-py-shonantchee] *adj* exciting

apanhar [apan-yah] *v* to catch; *(get hold of)* to grab

aparelhagem [aparel-yajeng] *n* equipment

aparelho [aparel-yoo] *n* set

apartamento [apah-tamentoo] *n* apartment ▸ **apartamento mobilado** furnished apartment

apelido [apeleedo] *n* nickname

apenas [apenash] *adv* only

apendicite [apendjee-seetchee] *n* appendicitis

aperitivo [apereetchee-voo] *n* aperitif

apertado, da [apeh-tadoo] *adj* tight

apesar [apezah] *prep* ▸ **apesar de** in spite of

apetecer [apetesseh] *v* to be appetizing ▸ **isso te apetece?** would you like that?

apetite [apetcheetchee] *n* appetite

apoiar [apoyah] *v* to support ▸ **apoiar-se em** to lean on

apontar [apontah] *v* to aim ▸ **apontar com o dedo** to point out

aprender [aprendeh] *v* to learn

apresentar [aprezentah] *v* to present

aprovado, da [aprovadoo] *adj* approved

aproveitar(-se) [aprovay-tah-(see)] *v* to take advantage of ▸ **aproveitar a ocasião** to take the opportunity

aproximar(-se) [aprosseemah-(see)] *v* to approach

aquecedor [akessedoh] *n* heater

aquecer [akesseh] *v* to heat

aquecimento [akessee-mentoo] *n* heating

aquela(s) [akella(sh)] *adj & pron* that (those)

aquele(s) [akelee(sh)] *adj & pron* that (those)

aqui [akee] *adv* here ▸ **por aqui** around here ▸ **aqui e ali** here and there

aquilo [akeeloo] *pron* that (thing)

ar [ah] *n* air ▸ **ao ar livre** in the open air

aranha [aranya] *n* spider

arco [ah-koo] *n* arch ▸ **arco-íris** rainbow

arder [ah-deh] *v* to burn; *(sun)* to scorch

areia [aray-a] *n* sand

armário [ah-mar-yoo] *n* wardrobe, armoire; *(in kitchen)* cupboard

armazém [ah-mazeng] *n* store

arrancar [ahankah] *v* to pull off

arranjar [ahanjah] *v* to arrange

arredores [ahedoreesh] *npl* neighborhood

arrendamento [ahenda-mentoo] *n* leasing

arrendar [ahendah] *v* to lease

arroz [ahosh] *n* rice ▸ **arroz com galinha** chicken with rice ▸ **arroz à grega** vegetable risotto

arrumar [ahoomah] *v* to tidy

arte [ah-tchee] *n* art

artesanal [ah-teza-now] *adj* craftwork

artesanato [ah-tezanatoo] *n* craftwork

artigo [ah-tcheegoo] *n* article

árvore [ah-voree] *n* tree

asma [ajma] *n* asthma

aspargos [ashpah-goosh] *npl* asparagus

aspirina [ashpee-reena] *n* aspirin

assado, da [assadoo] *adj* roast ▸ assado na brasa grilled ▸ assado no espeto spit-roasted

assalto [assow-too] *n* attack; *(bank)* raid

assembléia [assemblay-a] *n* assembly

assim [asseeng] *adv & conj* so ▸ assim assim so-so

assinar [asseenah] *v* to sign

assinatura [asseenatoora] *n* signature

assistir [asseeshteeh] *v* to attend

associação [assossee-assowng] *n* associação

assunto [assoontoo] *n* subject; *(matter)* business

atacar [atakah] *v* to attack

atalho [atal-yoo] *v* shortcut

ataque [atakee] *n* attack ▸ ataque cardíaco heart attack

até [a-te] *adv* (up) until ▸ faça isso até amanhã do it before tomorrow ▸ até amanhã! see you tomorrow!

atenção [atensowng] *n* attention

atendente [atendentchee] *n* attendant

atender [atendeh] *v* to attend to; *(care for)* to look after ▸ ninguém atende *(on phone)* there is no answer

atestar [ateshtah] *v* to certify

atirar [atcheerah] *v* to throw

atrás [atrash] *adv* behind ▸ voltar atrás to turn back

atrasado, da [atrazadoo] *adj* late; *(country, custom)* behind the times

▸ estar atrasado to be late

atrasar [atrazah] *v* to delay ▸ atrasar-se to be late

atraso [atrazoo] *n* delay

através [atravesh] *prep* ▸ 'através de' *(via)* through; *(aided by)* by means of

atravessar [atravessah] *v* to cross ▸ 'atravesse na faixa de segurança' 'cross at the crossing'

atrever-se [atreveh-see] *v* to dare ▸ como você se atreve? how dare you!

atropelado, da [atropeladoo] *adj* ▸ ser atropelado to be run over

atum [atoong] *n* tuna

aula [owla] *n* class

auto-estrada [owtoo-eeshtrada] *n* freeway

auxílio [ow-seel-yoo] *n* help ▸ peça auxílio ask for help

avançar [avan-sah] *v* to advance ▸ não avance o sinal! don't run the lights!

avaria [avaree-a] *n* breakdown

ave [avee] *n* bird

avelã [avelang] *n* hazelnut

avenida [aveneeda] *n* avenue

avião [avee-owng] *n* airplane

aviso [aveezoo] *n* warning; *(sign)* notice

azeite [azay-tchee] *n* olive oil

azeitonas [azay-tonash] *npl* olives

azul [azoow] *adj* blue

azulejo [azoolejoo] *n* (decorative) tile

b

bacalhau [bakal-yow] *n* cod

bagagem [bagajeng] *n* luggage ▸ compartimento de bagagens luggage compartment ▸ bagagem de mão carry-on luggage

bagajeiro [bagajay-roo] *n* luggage rack

Bahia [ba-ee-a] *n* Bahia

bairro [by-hoo] *n* neighborhood

baixo, xa [by-shoo] *adj* low; *(person)* short

baixo [by-shoo] *adv* ▸ em baixo down below ▸ por baixo de underneath

balcão [bowkowng] *n* balcony; *(shop)* counter

banana [banana] *n* banana

banco [bankoo] *n* bank; *(seat)* bench

bandeira [banday-ra] *n* flag

banheira [ban-yay-ra] *n* bathtub

banho [banyoo] *n* bath ▸ tomar (um) banho to take a bath ▸ 'é proibido tomar banho' 'no bathing'

barata [barata] *n* cockroach

barato, ta [baratoo] *adj* cheap

barba [bah-ba] *n* beard ▸ fazer a barba to shave

barbeador [bah-bee-adoh] *n* razor

barbear-se [bah-bee-ah-see] *v* to shave

barco [bah-koo] *n* boat ▸ barco de passeio pleasure boat

barragem [bahajeng] *n (barrier in water)* barrage; *(reservoir)* dam

barriga [baheega] *n* bladder

barro [bahoo] *n* clay

barulho [barool-yoo] *n* noise ▸ não faça barulho! stop making a din!

basílica [bazee-leeka] *n* basilica

bastante [bashtan-tchee] *adj & adv* enough

bastar [bashtah] *v* to be enough ▸ basta! that's enough!

batata [batata] *n* potato ▸ batatas fritas fries

Bahia

It is said that in Salvador, the capital of Bahia, a state in the north east of Brazil, there are 365 churches – one for every day of the year. Besides its religious sanctuaries, Bahia is also home to a number of temples to nature, and these extend across the state's one thousand kilometers of beaches, islands and bays. It was in the capital, Salvador, that the African slaves developed their own civilization and culture, most notable for its successful marriage of Catholicism with the religious cults and traditions brought over from Africa.

bater [bateh] *v* to beat ▸ 'bata antes de entrar' 'knock before entering'

batida [batcheeda] *n* (on door) knock

baunilha [bow-neelya] *n* vanilla

bebê [bebe] *n* baby

beber [bebeh] *v* to drink ▸ e para beber? and (what would you like) to drink?

bebida [bebeeda] *n* drink

beijar [bay-jah] *v* to kiss

beijo [bayjoo] *n* kiss

beira-mar [bayra-mah] *n* seaside

belo, la [beloo] *adj* lovely

bem [beng] *n* good

bem *adv* well ▸ tudo bem? everything OK?

bem-vindo, da [beng-veendoo] *adj* welcome

berinjela [bereenjela] *n* eggplant

besta [beshta] *adj* beast; (person) idiot

bica [beeka] *n* spout

bicicleta [beesseekleta] *n* bicycle

bico [beekoo] *n* beak ▸ bico de gás burner ▸ bico do fogão gas ring

bife [beefee] *n* steak

bigode [beegodjee] *n* mustache

bilhete [beel-yetchee] *n* ticket ▸ bilhete de ida one-way ticket ▸ bilhete de ida e volta return ticket ▸ bilhete de avião plane ticket

bilheteria [beel-yeteree-a] *n* ticket office

binóculos [beenokooloosh] *npl* binoculars

biscoito [beesh-koytoo] *n* cookie

bloqueado, da [blok-yadoo] *adj* blocked

boa [boa] *adj* good ▸ boa noite! good night! ▸ a comida está boa? is the food good?

boca [boka] *n* mouth

bocado [bokadoo] *n* bit

boi [boy] *n* ox

bóia [boya] *n* buoy

bola [bolla] *n* ball

bolo [boloo] *n* cake ▸ bolo de chocolate chocolate cake

bolso [bowsoo] *n* pocket

bom [bong] *adj* good ▸ bom dia! good morning!

bomba [bomba] *n* bomb; (machine) pump ▸ bomba de bicicleta bicycle pump ▸ bomba de gasolina gas pump

bombeiros [bombay-roosh] *npl* fire department

bonde [bondjee] *n* streetcar

boné [bo-ne] *n* cap

bonito, ta [boneetoo] *adj* beautiful

borboleta [boh-boleta] *n* butterfly

borbulhar [boh-bool-yah] *v* to bubble

bordados [boh-dadoosh] *npl* embroidery

borracha [bohasha] *n* rubber

bosque [boshkee] *n* wood

bossa [bossa] *f* hump ▸ bossa nova *Brazilian musical movement from the 1960s* ▸ see box on p. 8

botão [botowng] *n* button

botas [botash] *npl* boots

botijão [boteejowng] *n* cylinder ▸ botijão de gás gas cylinder

braço [brassoo] *n* arm

branco, ca [brankoo] *adj* white

Brasil [brazeew] *n* Brazil

brasileiro, ra [brazeelay-roo] *n* Brazilian

Brasília [brazeel-ya] *n* Brasilia ▸ see box on p. 8

breve [brevee] *adj* short ▸ em breve

bossa nova

Bossa nova first appeared toward the end of the 1950s as a jazz-samba fusion. Its syncopated rhythm was made famous by musicians such as João Gilberto and Tom Jobim. The song *Garota de Ipanema* ('The Girl from Ipanema') became such a big international hit that even Frank Sinatra recorded his own cover version, ensuring that the *bossa nova* beat spread across the whole world.

soon ▸ até breve! see you soon!

brigada [breegada] *n* brigade

brincar [breenkah] *v* to play

brincos [breenkoosh] *npl* earrings

brinquedo [breenkedoo] *n* toy

broa [broa] *n* corn bread ▸ broas de mel sweet honey-flavored buns

brócolis [brokoleesh] *npl* broccoli

bronquite [bronkeetchee] *n* bronchitis

bronzeado, da [bronzee-adoo] *adj* tanned

bronzear(-se) [bronzee-ah-(see)] *v* to tan

buraco [boorakoo] *n* hole

burro [boohoo] *n* donkey

buscar [booshkah] *v* to look for

bússola [boossola] *n* compass

buzina [boozeena] *n* horn

buzinar [boozeenah] *n* to honk

Brasília

More than just the capital of Brazil, *Brasília* is a monument to modern architecture. Founded in 1960, it was planned so as to sit in the exact geographical centre of the country. Its palaces and buildings are simple yet elegant, spreading down wide avenues and boulevards in a celebration of speed and efficiency. The central government offices are housed here in the *Palácio do Planalto*, not far from the twin towers of the Brazilian National Congress.

C

caatinga [ka-atcheenga] *n* scrub

cabeça [kabessa] *n* head

cabeleireiro [kabelay-ray-roo] *n* hairdresser

cabelo [kabeloo] *n* hair

caber [kabeh] *v* to fit

cabide [kabeedjee] *n* hanger

cabine [kabeenee] *n* ▶ cabine telefônica phone booth

cabo [kaboo] *n (officer)* corporal; *(grip)* handle; *(electric)* cable

cabra [kabra] *n* goat

caça [kassa] *n (sport)* hunting; *(jet)* fighter

caçador [kassadoh] *n* hunter

cacete [kassetchee] *n* truncheon

cachaça [kashassa] *f* sugar-cane spirit

cachorro [kashohoo] *n (dog)* pup; *(person)* bastard

cada [kada] *adj & pron* each ▶ cada vez mais more and more

cadarço [kadah-soo] *n* shoelace

cadeia [kadaya] *n* chain; *(place)* prison

cadeira [kaday-ra] *n* chair ▶ cadeira de rodas wheelchair

cadela [kadela] *n (dog)* bitch

caderno [kadeh-noo] *n* notebook

caducar [kadookah] *v* to expire

café [kafe] *n* coffee ▶ café com leite coffee with cream ▶ café da manhã breakfast ▶ café preto black coffee

cafeteira [kafetay-ra] *n* coffee pot

caipirinha [ky-peereenya] *f cocktail made of 'cachaça,' lime juice, sugar and ice*

cair [ka-eeh] *v* to fall

cais [kysh] *n* quay

caixa [kysha] *n* box; *(in store)* checkout, registers ▶ caixa automático ATM ▶ caixa de câmbio gearbox

caixote [ky-shotchee] *n* crate

calado, da [kaladoo] *adj* quiet

---

cachaça

Probably Brazil's most famous drink, *cachaça* is a highly alcoholic white rum. It is used in various cocktails such as *caipirinha* (with lime juice and sugar) and *batidas*, blended concoctions of *cachaça*, fruit and occasionally a sprinkle of powdered *guaraná* (a herbal stimulant). If you decide to drink it straight, pouring some on the floor first is said to bring good luck. Look out for the more colorful brand names such as *Levanta-Defunto* (the resurrector), *Mata-Sogra* (mother-in-law killer) and *Xixi-do-Diabo* (devil's pee).

calar(-se) [kalah-see] v to keep quiet

calçar(-se) [kalsah-(see)] v to put on

calças [kalsash] npl pants ▸ calças boca-de-sino bell-bottoms ▸ calças de abrigo jogging pants ▸ calças de brim canvas pants

calções [kalsoynsh] npl shorts ▸ calções de banho swimming trunks

cálculo [kalkooloo] n (math) calculation; (medical) stone

caldo [kaldoo] n broth

calem-se! [kaleng-see] excl be quiet!

calendário [kalendar-yoo] n calendar

calhar [kal-yah] v ▸ isso vem bem a calhar that's just right

calmo, ma [kalmoo] adj calm

calor [kaloh] n heat

cama [kama] n bed

câmara [kamara] n chamber ▸ câmara de ar inner tube ▸ câmara municipal town council

camarão [kamarowng] n prawn

câmbio [kamb-yoo] n change ▸ casa de câmbio currency exchange

caminhão [kameen-yowng] n truck

caminhar [kameen-yah] v to walk

caminho [kameen-yoo] n road

camioneta [kam-yooneta] n van

camisa [kameeza] n shirt

camisola [kameezola] n nightgown

campainha [kampa-eenya] n bell ▸ tocar à campainha to ring the bell

campismo [kampeejmoo] n camping

campista [kampeeshta] n (person) camper

campo [kampoo] n countryside

camponês, esa [kampoonesh] n countryman, countrywoman

canal [kanow] n channel; (waterway) canal

canção [kansowng] n song

candeeiro [kandjee-ayroo] n lamp

canela [kanela] n shin; (spice) cinnamon

caneta [kaneta] n pen

canivete [kaneevetchee] n penknife

canja [kanja] n cinch

cansado, da [kansadoo] adj tired

cansar(-se) [kansah-(see)] v to tire

cansativo, va [kansatcheevoo] adj tiring

cantar [kantah] v to sing

cântaro [kantaroo] n (for water) pitcher

cantiga [kantcheega] n ballad

cantil [kanteew] n flask

---

capoeira

Martial art, dance and game at the same time, *capoeira* was brought to Brazil by African slaves who, when prohibited from taking part in their traditional fighting contests, converted their skill into a dance as a way of keeping a grip on their culture. It is danced in pairs, often to the sound of the *berimbau*, an African stringed instrument. Today, although the spiritual home of *capoeira* is Bahia, it can be learnt in dance schools all over the country.

carnaval

The four-day period before Lent leading up to Ash Wednesday is carnival time in Brazil. Rich and poor alike forget their cares as they party in the streets. Though celebrated across the whole country, the carnival parades in Rio and Salvador are the best known. The Rio carnival is famous for its *escolas de samba* (samba schools), which compete against each other.

---

cantina [kantcheena] *n* canteen

canto [kantoo] *n (music)* song; *(angle)* corner

cantor [kantoh] *n* singer

cão [kowng] *n* dog

capacete [kapassetchee] *n* helmet

capaz [kapash] *adj* ▸ ser capaz de to be capable of

capela [kapela] *n* chapel

capitão [kapeetowng] *n* captain

capoeira [kap-wayra] *f Brazilian fighting dance*

cara [kara] *n* face; *(man)* guy

caracol [karakow] *n* snail

caranguejo [karan-gejoo] *n* crab

caravana [karavana] *n* caravan

cardíaco, ca [kah-djee-akoo] *adj* heart

cardiologista [kah-djee-olojeesta] *n* cardiologist

cárie [karee] *n* tooth decay

carioca [karee-oka] *n (person)* native of Rio de Janeiro

carnaval [karnavow] *n* carnival

carne [kah-nee] *n* meat ▸ carne moída ground beef ▸ carne de porco pork

carneiro [kah-nayroo] *n* lamb

caro [karo] *adj* dear

carona [karona] *n* ▸ andar de carona to hitchhike

carpinteiro [kah-peentay-roo] *n* carpenter

carreata [cahee-ata] *n* motorcade

carregar [kahegah] *v* to load

carrinho [kaheen-yoo] *n* ▸ carrinho de bebê stroller ▸ carrinho de supermercado shopping cart

carro [kahoo] *n* car

carruagem [kah-wajeng] *n* carriage

carta [kah-ta] *n* letter ▸ carta de recomendação reference ▸ carta registrada registered letter

cartão [kah-towng] *n* card ▸ cartão de crédito credit card ▸ cartão de visita business card ▸ cartão telefônico phone card

cartaz [kah-tash] *n* poster

carteira [kah-tayra] *n* wallet ▸ carteira de identidade ID card ▸ carteira de motorista driver's license ▸ see box on p. 12

carteiro [kah-tayroo] *n* letter carrier

carvalho [kah-valyoo] *n* oak

casa [kaza] *n* house ▸ em casa at home ▸ casa de campo country house

casaco [kazakoo] *n* coat

casado, da [kazadoo] *adj* married

casal [kazow] *n* couple

casamento [kazamentoo] *n* wedding

casar(-se) [kazah-(see)] *v* to marry

carteira de identidade

The ID card is the most important official document carried by a Brazilian citizen. It is illegal not to have a valid ID card, and if a Brazilian is stopped by the police and is unable to produce it on the spot, they can be arrested. In Brazil, ID cards are necessary for almost all official procedures, and also function as check guarantee cards. As well as listing place and date of birth, the card also bears a passport photo and a fingerprint.

casca [kashka] *n (tree)* bark; *(fruit)* peel

caso [kazoo] *n* case

castanha [kashtan-ya] *n* chestnut

castanho, nha [kashtan-yoo] *adj* brown

castelo [kashteloo] *n* castle

catapora [katapora] *n* chickenpox

catedral [katedrow] *n* cathedral

caução [kowsowng] *n* bail

causa [kowza] *n* cause

cautela [kowtela] *n* precaution

cavaleiro [kavalay-roo] *n* horseman

cavalo [kavaloo] *n* horse

cavalo-marinho [kavaloo-mareenyoo] *n* seahorse

cebola [sebola] *n* onion

ceder [sedeh] *v* to hand over ▸ 'ceda o lugar' 'please give up your seat'

cedo [sedoo] *adv* soon

cego, ga [segoo] *n & adj* blind

ceia [say-a] *n* supper ▸ A Santa Ceia the Last Supper

celebrar [selebrah] *v* to celebrate

celular [seloolah] *n* cellphone

cemitério [semeetair-yoo] *n* cemetery

cena [sena] *n* scene; *(theater)* stage

cenoura [senora] *n* carrot

centeio [sentayoo] *n* rye

centro [sentroo] *n* center ▸ centro comercial shopping mall ▸ centro da cidade city center

cera [sera] *n* wax

cerâmica [serameeka] *n* pottery

cerca [seh-ka] *n* fence ◆ *adv* near ▸ cerca de around

cercado, da [seh-kadoo] *adj* fenced

cereais [seree-ysh] *npl* breakfast cereals

cérebro [serebroo] *n* brain

cereja [sereja] *n* cherry

cerejeira [serejay-ra] *n* cherry tree

cerimônia [sereemon-ya] *n* ceremony ▸ sem cerimônias informally

cerrado [sehado] *n* scrub

certeza [seh-teza] *n* certainty ▸ com certeza definitely

certo [seh-too] *adj (exact)* correct; *(sure)* certain

cerveja [seh-veja] *n* beer ▸ cerveja preta stout, dark beer

cesto [seshtoo] *n* basket

céu [sew] *n* sky ▸ céu limpo/enevoado/encoberto clear/foggy/overcast sky

cevada [sevada] *n* barley

chá [sha] *n* tea ▸ chá com limão tea with lemon

chama [shama] *n* flame

chamada [shamada] *n* call

chamar(-se) [shamah-(see)] *v* to call ▸ como você se chama? what's your name?

chão [showng] *n* floor

chapéu [shapew] *n* hat

charuto [sharootoo] *n* cigar

chatear(-se) [shatee-ah-(see)] *v* to annoy ▸ não me chateia! leave me alone!

chatice [shateessee] *n* ▸ que chatice! what a drag!

chato, ta [shatoo] *adj* boring

chave [shavee] *n* key; *(electric)* switch ▸ chave de boca wrench ▸ chave de fenda screwdriver ▸ chave inglesa monkey wrench

chaveiro [shavay-roo] *n* key ring

check-in [shek-in] *n* check-in

chegada [shegada] *n* arrival

chegar [shegah] *v* to arrive; *(suffice)* to be enough ▸ já chega! that's enough!

cheio, a [shayoo] *adj* full

cheirar [shay-rah] *v* to smell

cheiro [shayroo] *n* smell

cheque [shekee] *n* check ▸ cheque sem fundo bounced check ▸ cheque pré-datado pre-dated check

cheque de viagem [shekee djee vee-ajeng] *n* traveler's check

chiclete [shee-kletchee] *n* gum

chicória [sheekor-ya] *n* chicory

chinelo [shee-neloo] *n* slipper

chocar [shokah] *v* to shock

chocolate [shokolatchee] *n* chocolate ▸ chocolate ao leite milk chocolate ▸ chocolate amargo dark chocolate

chope [shopee] *n* (draft) beer

choque [shokee] *n* shock; *(automobiles)* crash

chorar [shorah] *v* to cry

chouriço [shoreessoo] *n* blood sausage

chover [shoveh] *v* to rain

chumbo [shoomboo] *n (metal)* lead

churrasco [shoo-hashkoo] *n* barbecue

chuva [shoova] *n* rain

chuveiro [shoovay-roo] *n* shower

cidadão [seedadowng] *n* citizen

cidade [seedadjee] *n* city; *(small)* town

ciência [see-enss-ya] *n* science

cientista [see-entcheeshta] *n* scientist

cima [seema] *n* ▸ de cima from above ▸ em cima de on top of ▸ parte de cima top part ▸ ali em cima up there

cinema [seenema] *n* cinema

cinto [seentoo] *n* belt ▸ cinto de segurança seat belt

cintura [seentoora] *n* waist

cinzeiro [seenzay-roo] *n* ashtray

cinzento, ta [seenzentoo] *adj* grey

circo [seeh-koo] *n* circus

circuito [seeh-kweetoo] *n* circuit

circulação [seeh-koola-sowng] *n* circulation

circular [seeh-koolah] *v* to circulate

círculo [seeh-kooloo] *n* circle

ciúme [see-oomee] *n* jealousy

ciumento, ta [see-oomentoo] *adj* jealous

clara [klara] *n* egg white

claro, ra [klaroo] *adj* clear; *(color)* light ▸ claro! of course!

classe [klassee] *n* class ▸ primeira/segunda classe first/second class ▸ classe executiva business class

clássico, ca [klasseekoo] *adj* classic

cliente [klee-entchee] *n* client

clima [kleema] *n* climate

climatização [kleema-tcheeza-sowng] *n* air-conditioning

coberto, ta [koobeh-too] *adj* covered

cobertor [koobeh-toh] *n* blanket

cobra [kobra] *n* snake

cobre [kobree] *n* copper

cobrir [kobreeh] *v* to cover

código [kodjeegoo] *n* code ▸ código de acesso access code ▸ código pessoal password

coelho [ko-elyoo] *n* rabbit

coentro [ko-entroo] *n* coriander

cogumelo [kogoomeloo] *n* mushroom

coisa [koy-za] *n* thing

cola [kola] *n* glue

colar [kolah] *n* necklace ♦ *v* to glue

colchão [kolshowng] *n* mattress ▸ colchão de ar air mattress ▸ colchão de mola spring mattress

coleção [kolessowng] *n* collection

colega [kolega] *n* colleague

colégio [kolej-yoo] *n* college

colesterol [koleshterow] *n* cholesterol

colete [koletchee] *n* vest ▸ colete salva-vidas life preserver

colheita [kol-yay-ta] *n* harvest

colher [kolyeh] *n* spoon

colina [koleena] *n* hill

colocar [kolokah] *v* to place

colônia [kolon-ya] *n* colony ▸ colônia de férias summer camp

colorido, da [koloreedoo] *adj* multi-colored

com [kong] *prep* with

comando [komandoo] *n* command

combater [kombateh] *v* to fight

começo [komessoo] *n* beginning

comentário [komentar-yoo] *n* comment

comer [komeh] *v* to eat

comerciante [komeh-see-antchee] *n* businessman, businesswoman

comércio [comeh-see-oo] *n* business

comichão [komeeshowng] *n* itch

comida [komeeda] *n* meal

comigo [komeegoo] *pron* with me

comissão [komeessowng] *n* committee

como [komo] *adv* as ▸ tão grande como... as big as ... ▸ como você está? how are you?

cômoda [komoda] *n* bureau

companheiro [kompan-yay-roo] *n* companion

companhia [kompan-yee-a] *n* company

comparar [komparah] *v* to compare

compartimento [kompah-tcheemen-too] *n* compartment

completo, ta [kompletoo] *adj* complete; *(tank)* full

complicado, da [kompleekadoo] *adj* complicated

compota [kompota] *n* fruit compote

compra [kompra] *n* purchase

comprar [komprah] *v* to buy

compreender [kompree-endeh] *v* to understand

comprido, da [kompreedoo] *adj* long; *(person)* tall

comprimido [kompreemeedoo] *n* tablet

computador [kompootadoh] *n* computer

comunicação [komoonee-kassowng] *n* communication

comunicado [komoonee-kadoo] *n* notice

comunidade [komoonee-dadjee] *n* community

concerto [konseh-too] *n* concert

concha [konsha] *n* shell

conclusão [konkloozowng] *n* conclusion

concordar [konkoh-dah] *v* to agree

condição [kondeessowng] *n* condition

condimentado, da [kondeementadoo] *adj* seasoned

conduzir [kondoozeeh] *v* to drive

conferência [konferenss-ya] *n* lecture

confiança [konfee-ansa] *n* confidence

confiar [konfiah] *v* to trust ▸ confiar em alguém to trust somebody

confirmar [konfeeh-mah] *v* to confirm

conforme [konfoh-mee] *conj* as ◆ *prep* according to ▸ conforme o original as in the original

confortável [konfoh-tavew] *adj* comfortable

conforto [konfoh-too] *n* comfort

confusão [konfoozowng] *n* muddle ▸ fazer confusão com to get mixed up with

congelado, da [konjeladoo] *adj* frozen

congelador [konjeladoh] *n* deep freeze

conhaque [konyakee] *n* cognac

conhecer [kon-yesseh] *v* to know

conhecimento [konyesseementoo] *n* knowledge

conjunto [konjoontoo] *n* group

conosco [konoshkoo] *pron* with us

conquista [konkeeshta] *n* conquest

conseguir [konseg-eeh] *v* to achieve ▸ conseguir fazer to manage to do

conselho [konsel-yoo] *n* advice; *(organization)* council

conseqüência [konsekwenss-ya] *n* consequence

conserto [conseh-too] *n* repair ▸ não tem conserto it's beyond repair

conserva [konseh-va] *n* preserves

conservar [konseh-vah] *v* to preserve

consigo [konseegoo] *pron* with him/her/you/them

constipação [konshteepassowng] *n* constipation

constipado [konshteepadoo] *adj* constipated

construção [konshtroossowng] *n* construction

construído, da [konshtroo-eedoo] *adj* ▸ construído em... built in ...

consulado [konsooladoo] *n* consulate

consulta [konsoow-ta] *n* *(medicine)* consultation ▸ marcar uma consulta to make an appointment

consultório [konsoow-toryoo] *n* examining room

consumir [konsoomeeh] *v* to consume ▸ 'consumir antes de.../até...' 'best before ...'

consumo [konsoomoo] *n* consumption

conta [konta] *n* account; *(restaurant)* bill

contador [kontadoh] *n* accountant

contagioso, sa [kontaj-yozoo] *adj* contagious

contar [kontah] *v* to count ▸ contar com to rely on

contatar [kontatah] *v* to contact

contato [contatoo] *n* contact ▸ manter contato to maintain contact ▸ manter-se em contato to keep in touch ▸ mau contato *(electricity)* poor contact

o Corcovado

At the summit of the *Corcovado* (hunchback) mountain, the figure of *Cristo Redentor* (Christ the Redeemer) stands over Rio de Janeiro with welcoming, outstretched arms. The statue is 30 meters tall, and was presented as a gift to the *cariocas* (citizens of Rio) by France to commemorate Brazilian independence. A visit to this landmark affords stunning views over Rio, the *cidade maravilhosa* (marvellous city).

---

contente [kontentchee] *adj* happy

conteúdo [kontchee-oodoo] *n* content

contigo [kontcheegoo] *pron* with you

continuação [konteen-wassowng] *n* continuation

continuar [konteen-wah] *v* to continue

conto [kontoo] *n* story

contra [kontra] *prep* against

contraceptivo [kontra-septcheevoo] *n* contraceptive

contrário, ria [kontrar-yoo] *n & adj* opposite ▸ pelo contrário on the contrary

contrato [kontratoo] *n* contract

contribuir [kontreeb-weeh] *v* ▸ contribuir para to contribute to

controlado, da [kontroladoo] *adj* controlled ▸ 'velocidade controlada por radar' 'speed cameras in operation'

controlar [kontrolah] *v* to control ▸ 'controle a velocidade' 'watch your speed'

controle [kontrolee] *n* control

contudo [kontoodoo] *conj* however

conveniente [konven-yentchee] *adj* convenient

conversa [konveh-sa] *n* chat

conversar [konveh-sah] *v* to chat

convidar [konveedah] *v* to invite

convir [konveeh] *v* ▸ (não) convém fazer... we should (not) do ...

convite [konveetchee] *n* invitation

convívio [konveev-yoo] *n* living together

convulsão [konvoow-sowng] *n* convulsion

cópia [kop-ya] *n* copy

copo [kopoo] *n* glass

cor [koh] *n* color

cor [koh] *adv* ▸ de cor by heart

coração [korassowng] *n* heart

coragem [korajeng] *n* courage

Corcovado *n* ▸ o Corcovado *the Corcovado mountain in Rio de Janeiro*

corda [koh-da] *n* string, rope

cordeiro [koh-dayroo] *n* lamb

cor-de-laranja [koh djee laranja] *adj & n* orange

cor-de-rosa [koh djee hoza] *adj & n* pink

corpo [koh-poo] *n* body

correção [kohessowng] *n* correction

corredor [kohedoh] *n* runner; *(passage)* corridor

correia [kohaya] *n* belt ▸ correia de distribuição/transmissão drive belt

correio [kohayoo] *n* mail ▸ pelo correio by mail ▸ correio eletrônico e-mail

corrente [kohentchee] *n* current; *(on bicycle)* chain

correr [koheh] *v* to run ▸ corram! run!

correspondência [kohesh-pondenss-ya] *n* correspondence

correspondente [kohesh-pondentchee] *adj* corresponding ♦ *n* correspondent

correto, ta [kohetoo] *adj* correct

corrida [koheeda] *n* race

corrigir [koheejeeh] *v* to correct

cortador [koh-tadoh] *n* ▸ cortador de unhas nail clippers

cortar [koh-tah] *v* to cut ▸ cortar-se to cut oneself ▸ cortar em fatias to slice ▸ cortar caminho to take a short cut

corte [koh-tchee] *n* cut

cortiça [koh-tcheessa] *n* cork

cortina [koh-tcheena] *n* curtain

costa [koshta] *n (of country)* coast

costas [koshtash] *npl* back

costeleta [koshteleta] *n* chop

costume [koshtoomee] *n* habit

costura [koshtoora] *n* seam

costurar [koshtoorah] *v* to sew

cotonete [kotonetchee] *n* cotton bud

cotovelo [kotoveloo] *n* elbow

couro [koroo] *n* leather

couve [kovee] *n* spring greens ▸ couve-flor cauliflower

coxa [kosha] *n* thigh

cozer [kozeh] *v* to cook

cozido [kozeedoo] *n* stew

cozinha [kozeen-ya] *n* kitchen; *(making food)* cooking

cozinhar [kozeen-yah] *v* to cook

cravo-da-índia [kravoo-da-eendya] *n* clove

creme [kremee] *n* cream

cremoso, sa [kremozoo] *adj* creamy

crer [kreh] *v* to believe

crescente [kressentchee] *adj* crescent

crescer [kresseh] *v* to grow

crescimento [kresseementoo] *n* growth

criação [kree-assowng] *n* creation; *(of animals)* breeding

criança [kree-ansa] *n* child

cristão, tã [kreeshtowng] *adj & n* Christian

crítica [kreetcheeka] *n* criticism

crustáceos [kroostass-yoosh] *npl* crustaceans

cruz [kroosh] *n* cross

cruzamento [kroozamentoo] *n* junction

cruzeiro [kroozay-roo] *n* cruise

cubo [kooboo] *n* cube ▸ cubo de gelo ice cube

cueca [kweka] *n* underpants

cuidado [kweedadoo] *n* care

cujo [koojoo] *pron* whose

culinária [kooleenar-ya] *n* cookery

culpa [koowpa] *n* blame

culpado, da [koowpadoo] *adj* guilty

cultivar [koow-tcheevah] *v* to grow

cultura [koowtoora] *n* culture

cume [koomee] *n* summit

cumprimentar [koompreementah] *v* to greet

cumprimento [koompreementoo] *n* greeting

cunhada [koon-yada] *n* sister-in-law

cunhado [koon-yadoo] *n* brother-in-law

curar [koorah] *v* to cure

curioso, sa [kooree-ozoo] *adj* curious

curso [kooh-soo] *n* course ▸ fazer um curso de to take a course in

curto, ta [kooh-too] *adj* short

curva [kooh-va] *n* bend

custar [kooshtah] *v* to cost ▸ quanto custa? how much does it cost?

d

da(s) [da(sh)] *prep* = de+a(s)

dados [dadoosh] *n* dice; *(information)* data

damasco [damashkoo] *n* apricot

dança [dansa] *n* dance

dançar [dansah] *v* to dance

daqui [dakee] *adv* from here ▸ daqui a um momento in a while

dar [dah] *v* to give ▸ dá para dois there's enough for two ▸ dar-se bem com alguém to get along well with somebody

data [data] *n* date ▸ data de nascimento date of birth

debaixo [de-by-shoo] *adv* under

debruçar-se [debroossah-see] *v* to bend over ▸ 'não se debruce' 'do not lean out'

decepção [dessepsowng] *n* disappointment

decidido, da [dessee-djeedoo] *adj* resolute

decidir [desseedjeeh] *v* to decide

declaração [deklarassowng] *n* statement

declarar [deklarah] *v* to declare

decoração [dekorassowng] *n* decoration

decote [dekotchee] *n* low-cut neckline

dedicar [dedjeekah] *v* to dedicate

dedicatória [dedjee-kator-ya] *n* dedication

dedo [dedoo] *n* finger; *(on foot)* toe

defeito [defaytoo] *n* defect

defender(-se) [defendeh-(see)] *v* to defend

defesa [defeza] *n* defense

deficiente [defeess-yentchee] *n* & *adj* disabled

degrau [degrow] *n* step ▸ 'cuidado com o degrau' 'watch the step'

deitar [daytah] *v* to throw ▸ deitar de costas to lie down ▸ deitar no chão to lie on the ground

deixar [day-shah] *v* to leave ▸ deixar de fumar to stop smoking

dela [della] *pron* hers

delas [dellash] *pron* theirs

dele [delee] *pron* his

deles [deleesh] *pron* theirs

delícia [deleess-ya] *n* delight ▸ delícias do mar seafood

delicioso, sa [deleess-yozoo] *adj* delicious

demais [djee-mysh] *adv* too much ▸ por demais too

demasiado, da [demazee-adoo] *adj* too much

demitir-se [demeetcheeh-(see)] *v* to dismiss

demolição [demolee-sowng] *n* demolition

demorar [demorah] *v* to delay ▸ isso vai demorar uma hora it will take an hour

dente [dentchee] *n* tooth ▸ dente de alho clove of garlic

os Descobrimentos

The golden age of Portuguese history began in 1415 with the conquest of Ceuta in North Africa. Then, in 1487, Bartolomeu Dias led the first European expedition ever to navigate the Cape of Good Hope successfully, and just a few years later Portuguese ships beat the rest of Europe to both India (Vasco da Gama, 1497) and Brazil (Pedro Alvares Cabral, 1500). It was through Portuguese seafaring expertise and daring that many of the oceans were first charted and trade links with the New World established.

dentista [dentcheeshta] *n* dentist

dentro [dentroo] *adv* inside ▸ aí dentro in there ▸ por dentro inside

depender [dependeh] *v* to depend ▸ depender de algo to depend on something

depilar [depeelah] *v* to depilate, re-move hair

depois [depoysh] *adv* after ▸ depois de amanhã after tomorrow

depósito [depozeetoo] *n* deposit; *(warehouse)* depot ▸ depósito bancário bank deposit

depressa [djeepressa] *adv* quickly

dermatologista [deh-matolo-jeeshta] *n* dermatologist

derretido, da [dehe-tcheedoo] *adj* melted

desagradável [djeez-agradavew] *adj* unpleasant

desaparecer [djeez-aparesseh] *v* to disappear

desastre [djeezashtree] *n* disaster; *(in street)* accident ▸ houve um desastre there's been an accident

descafeinado, da [djeeshkafay-nadoo] *adj* decaffeinated ▸ café descafeinado decaf

descalçar(-se) [djeeshkalsah-(see)] *v* to take off one's shoes

descalço [djeesh-kalsoo] *adj* barefoot

descansar [djeesh-kansah] *v* to rest

descanso [djeesh-kansoo] *n* rest

descarga [djeeshkah-ga] *n* flush ▸ dar a descarga to flush the toilet

descarregar [djeeshkah-gah] *v* to un-load

descartável [djeeshkah-tavew] *adj* dis-posable

descascar [djeesh-kashkah] *v* to peel

descer [desseh] *v* to go down

descida [desseeda] *n* descent

descoberta [djeesh-kobeh-ta] *n* discov-ery

descobrimento [djeeshkobree-mentoo] *n* discovery

descobrir [djeeshkobreeh] *v* to discover

descolar [djeeshkolah] *v* to detach

desconhecido, da [djeeshkon-yessee-doo] *adj* unknown

desconto [djeeshkontoo] *n* discount ▸ fazer um desconto to give a discount

descontrair-se [djeeshkontra-eeh-see] *v* to relax

descuido [djeesh-kweedoo] *n* ▸ por descuido by accident

desculpar(-se) [djeeshkoolpah-(see)] v to forgive ‣ desculpe … forgive … ‣ desculpe! sorry!

desde [dej-djee] *prep* since ‣ desde já right away ‣ desde que as long as; *(in time)* since

desdobrável [djeej-dobravew] n folding

desejar [dezejah] v to wish; *(desire)* to want

desejo [dezejoo] n wish; *(want)* desire

desejos [dezejoosh] *npl* wishes

desembarque [djeeezembah-kee] n disembarkation

desempregado, da [djeez-empregadoo] n & *adj* unemployed

desemprego [djeezempregoo] n unemployment

desenhar [dezen-yah] v to draw; *(technical)* to design

desenho [dezenyoo] n drawing; *(technical)* design

desenroscar [djeezen-hoshkah] v to unscrew

desenvolver(-se) [djeezenvow-veh-(see)] v to develop

desenvolvimento [djeezenvow-vee-mentoo] n development

deserto [dezeh-too] n desert

desfazer [djeesh-fazeh] v to undo

desfeito, ta [djeesh-faytoo] *adj* undone

desfocado, da [djeesh-fokado] *adj* out of focus

desgosto [djeej-goshtoo] n displeasure

desigualdade [djeez-eegwaldadjee] n inequality

desiludido, da [djeez-eeloodeedoo] *adj* disappointed

desinfetar [djeez-eenfetah] v to disinfect

desistir [dezeeshteeh] v to give up

desligado, da [djeej-leegadoo] *adj (electricity)* switched off

desligar [djeej-leegah] v *(machine)* to switch off; *(telephone)* to hang up ‣ não desligue don't hang up

deslocamento [djeej-lokamentoo] n movement

deslocar(-se) [djeej-lokah-(see)] v to move

desmaiar [djeej-my-ah] v to faint

desmontar [djeej-montah] v to dismantle

desodorizante [djeez-odorantchee] n deodorant

despacho [djeesh-pashoo] n offering

despedida [djeesh-pedjeeda] n farewell

despedir-se [djeesh-pedjeeh-see] v to say goodbye

despertador [djeeshpeh-tadoh] n alarm clock

despesa [djeesh-peza] n expense

despir(-se) [djeeshpeeh-(see)] v to undress

desportivo, va [djeeshpoh-tcheevoo] *adj* sports

desporto [djeeshpoh-too] n sports

destinatário [desh-tcheenatar-yoo] n addressee

destino [desh-tcheenoo] n destination; *(future)* destiny ‣ passageiros com destino a… passengers on their way to …

detergente [deteh-jentchee] n detergent

detestar [deteshtah] v to detest

deus [dewsh] n god ‣ Deus do céu! my goodness! ‣ Deus queira que … let's hope that …

devagar [djeevagah] *adv* slowly
dever [deveh] *n* duty ✦ *v* to owe ▸ você deve estar doente you must be ill
devido, da [deveedoo] *adj* due ▸ devido a due to
devolver [devow-veh] *v (hand over)* to return
dezembro [dezembroo] *n* December
dia [djee-a] *n* day ▸ de dia by day ▸ no dia seguinte the next day ▸ dia santo feast day ▸ o dia-a-dia daily routine
diabético, ca [djee-abetcheekoo] *adj* diabetic
diálogo [djee-alogoo] *n* dialogue
diante [djee-antchee] *adv* in front
diário, ria [djee-aryoo] *n & adj* daily
diarréia [djee-ahaya] *n* diarrhea
dicionário [djeess-yonar-yoo] *n* dictionary
diesel [djeezew] *n* diesel
dieta [djee-eta] *n* diet ▸ estar de dieta to be on a diet
diferença [djeeferensa] *n* difference
diferente [djeeferentchee] *adj* different
difícil [djeefee-seew] *adj* difficult
dificuldade [djeefeekoow-dadjee] *n* difficulty
digestão [djeejesh-towng] *n* digestion
digestivo, va [djeejesh-tcheevoo] *n & adj* digestive
diminuir [djeemeen-weeh] *v* to reduce
dinheiro [djen-yayroo] *n* money ▸ trocar dinheiro to change money
direção [djeeressowng] *n* direction ▸ em direção a headed for
direita [djeerayta] *n & adj* right ▸ à direita (de) on the right ▸ siga à direita head right

direito, ta [djeeraytoo] *n & adj* right ▸ ter o direito de... to have the right to ... ▸ direito de resposta right of reply
diretamente [djeereta-mentchee] *adv* straight
direto, ta [djeeretoo] *adj* direct
diretor [djeeretoh] *n* director; *(school)* principal
dirigir(-se) [djeereejeeh-(see)] *v* to direct; *(car)* to drive ▸ dirija-se ao guichê/balcão make your way to the counter
disco [djeeshkoo] *n* disc, disk ▸ disco rígido hard disk
discordar [djeeshkoh-dah] *v* to disagree
discoteca [djeeshko-teka] *n* discotheque
discurso [djeeshkooh-soo] *n* speech
discussão [djeeshkoo-sowng] *n* discussion; *(angry)* argument
discutir [djeesh-kooteeh] *v* to discuss; *(angrily)* to argue
disparar [djeeshparah] *v* to fire
disparate [djeesh-paratchee] *n* nonsense
dispor [djeeshpoh] *v* to arrange
disso [djeessoo] *prep* of that ▸ eu me lembro disso I remember that
distância [djeeshtanss-ya] *n* distance
distinguir [djeesh-tcheen-geeh] *v (see)* to make out
distraído, da [djeeshtra-eedoo] *adj* absent-minded
distrair(-se) [djeeshtra-eeh-(see)] *v* to amuse
distribuir [djeeshtreeb-weeh] *v* to distribute
ditadura [djeetadoora] *n* dictatorship
DIU [diou] *abbr of* Dispositivo Intra–

Uterino n IUD

divertido, da [djeeveh-tcheedoo] adj amusing

divertimento [djeeveh-tcheementoo] n amusement

divertir(-se) [djeeveh-tcheeh-(see)] v to amuse

dívida [djeeveeda] n debt

dividir [djeeveedeeh] v to divide

divisão [djeeveezowng] n division

divorciado, da [djeevoh-see-adoo] adj divorced

dizer [djeezeh] v to say ▸ como é que se diz...,? how do you say ... ?

do [doo] prep = de+o

doce [dossee] n & adj sweet

documento [dokoomentoo] n document ▸ poderia me mostrar os seus documentos? can I see your identity papers please?

doença [dwensa] n illness

doente [dwentchee] adj sick ◆ n patient

doer [dweh] v to hurt ▸ minha cabeça/ garganta/barriga está doendo my head/throat/stomach hurts ▸ isso dói that hurts

doido, da [doy-doo] adj mad

domingo [domeengoo] n Sunday ▸ ao(s) domingo(s) on Sunday(s)

dona [donna] n owner ▸ dona de casa housewife

dono [donoo] n owner

dor [doh] n pain ▸ dor de dente toothache ▸ estar com/ter dor de cabeça to have a headache

dormir [doh-meeh] v to sleep ▸ dormir com to sleep with ▸ dormir ao ar livre to sleep in the open

dos [doosh] prep = de+os

doutor [dotoh] n doctor

droga [droga] n drug

dublado, da [doobladoo] adj (movie) dubbed

ducha [doosha] n shower ▸ tomar uma ducha to take a shower

duplo, pla [dooploo] adj ▸ vidro duplo double glazing

duração [doorassowng] n duration

durante [doorantchee] prep during

durar [doorah] v to last

durex® [dooreks] n Scotch tape®

duro, ra [dooroo] adj hard ▸ o bife está duro the steak is tough

dúvida [dooveeda] n doubt ▸ sem dúvida without a doubt

dúzia [doozee-a] n dozen

e

e [ee] *conj* and

é [e] *v* it is

economia [ekonomee-a] *n* economy

edição [edjeessowng] *n* edition

edifício [edjeefeess-yoo] *n* building

educação [edookassowng] *n* education

educado, da [edookadoo] *adj* polite

educar [edookah] *v* to educate

efeito [efay-too] *n* effect ▸ com efeito indeed ▸ efeitos secundários side effects

eficaz [efeekash] *adj* efficient; *(medicine)* effective

eis [aysh] *adv* here is/are ▸ eis o resultado do problema that's the result of the problem

eixo [ay-shoo] *n* axis; *(of wheel)* axle

ela [ella] *pron* she ▸ é ela it's her

elas [ellash] *pron* they

ele [elee] *pron* he

elegância [eleganss-ya] *n* elegance

eleição [elay-sowng] *n* election

eleitor [elay-toh] *n* elector

elemento [elementoo] *n* element

eles [eleesh] *pron* they

eletricidade [eletreesee-dadjee] *n* electricity

eletricista [eletree-seeshta] *n* electrician

elétrico, ca [eletreekoo] *adj* electric

elevado, da [elevadoo] *adj* high

elevador [elevadoh] *n* elevator

eliminar [eleemeenah] *v* to eliminate

em [eng] *prep* in, on, at ▸ em abril in April ▸ no chão on the floor ▸ estar em casa to be at home

embaixada [em-by-shada] *n* embassy

embarcar [embah-kah] *v* to board

embarque [embah-kee] *n* boarding

embora [embora] *conj* although ◆ *adv* ▸ ir embora to go away

embreagem [embree-ajeng] *n* clutch

embriagado, da [embree-agadoo] *adj* drunk

embrulho [emroolyoo] *n* package

emenda [emenda] *n* correction

emigração [emeegrassowng] *n* emigration

emigrante [emeegrantchee] *n* emigrant

emissão [emeessowng] *n* emission

empate [empatchee] *n* draw

empregado [empregadoo] *n* employee ▸ empregada doméstica maid

emprego [empregoo] *n* job

empresa [empreza] *n* firm

emprestado, da [empreshtadoo] *adj* loaned ▸ pedir emprestado to borrow

emprestar [empreshtah] *v* to lend

empréstimo [empreshteemoo] *n* loan

empurrar [empuhah] *v* to push

encanador [enkanadoh] *n* plumber

encantador, ra [enkantadoh] *adj* charming

encarregado, da [enka-hegadoo] *n*

person in charge ▸ encarregado de negócios chargé d'affaires

encerrado, da [ensehadoo] *adj* closed

encerramento [enseha-mentoo] *n* close

encher(-se) [ensheh-(see)] *v* to fill ▸ encher de ar to inflate

encomenda [enkomenda] *n* order; *(by mail)* package, parcel

encomendar [enkomendah] *v* to order

encontrar(-se) [enkontrah-(see)] *v* to find

encontro [enkontroo] *n* meeting ▸ marcar encontro to make an appointment

endereço [enderessoo] *n* address ▸ endereço eletrônico e-mail address

enervante [eneh-vantchee] *adj* annoying

enervar(-se) [eneh-vah-(see)] *v* to annoy

enevoado, da [enev-wadoo] *n* misty

enfermeira [enfeh-mayra] *n* nurse

enfim [enfeeng] *adv* finally

enganar(-se) [enganah-(see)] *v* to deceive ▸ ele se enganou no número he dialed the wrong number

engarrafamento [engahafa-mentoo] *n* traffic jam

engatar [engatah] *v* to couple up, link together; *(gear)* to engage

engenheiro [enjen-yayroo] *n* engineer

engolir [engoleeh] *v* to swallow

engordar [engoh-dah] *v* to put on weight

engraçado, da [engrassadoo] *adj* amusing

enjoado, da [enj-wadoo] *adj* ▸ estar enjoado to feel sick

enjoar [enj-wah] *v* to feel bored; *(on boat)* to feel sick

enquanto [enkwantoo] *conj* while

ensinar [enseenah] *v* to teach

ensopado [ensopadoo] *n* stew

entalado, da [entaladoo] *adj* stuck

então [entowng] *adv* so; *(time)* then

entender(-se) [entendeh-(see)] *v* to understand ▸ entender-se bem/mal (com alguém) to see/not to see eye to eye (with somebody) ▸ entende? do you understand?

entendido, da [entendjeedoo] *adj (skilled)* expert

entornar [entoh-nah] *v* to spill

entrada [entrada] *n* entry; *(of building)* entrance ▸ boas entradas! Happy New Year!

entrar [entrah] *v* to enter ▸ entre! come in!

entre [entree] *prep* between

entrega [entrega] *n* delivery

entregar [entregah] *v* to deliver

entretanto [entretantoo] *conj* however

entrevista [entreveeshta] *n* interview

entupido, da [entoopeedoo] *adj* blocked

envelope [envelopee] *n* envelope

enviar [envee-ah] *v* to send

enxugar [enshoogah] *v* to dry

epiléptico, ca [epeelep-tcheekoo] *adj & n* epileptic

época [epoka] *n* period

equilíbrio [ekeeleebree-oo] *n* balance

equipe [ekeepee] *n* team

erguer [eh-geh] *v* to raise

errado, da [ehadoo] *adj* wrong ▸ ele está indo pelo caminho errado he's going the wrong way

erro [ehoo] *n* error

erva [eh-va] *n* herb

ervilha [eh-veelya] *n* pea

escada [eeshkada] *n* stairs; *(external)* steps

escalada [eeshkalada] *n* climbing

escaldar [eeshkow-dah] *v* to scald ▸ a água está escaldando the water's scalding hot

escola [eeshkola] *n* school

escolha [eeshkol-ya] *n* choice

escolher [eeshkol-yeh] *v* to choose

esconder [eeshkondeh] *v* to hide

escondido, da [eeshkondjeedoo] *adj* hidden

escova [eeshkova] *n* brush ▸ escova de dentes toothbrush

escovar [eeshkovah] *v* to brush ▸ escovar os dentes to brush one's teeth

escrever [eeshkreveh] *v* to write

escritor [eeshkreetoh] *n* writer

escritório [eeshkreetor-yoo] *n* office

escultor [eeshkoow-toh] *n* sculptor

escultura [eeshkoow-toora] *n* sculpture

escuro, ra [eeshkooroo] *adj* dark

escutar [eeshkootah] *n* to listen ▸ escute! listen

esferográfica [eeshfero-grafeeka] *n* ballpoint pen

esforço [eeshfoh-soo] *n* effort

esfregar [eeshfregah] *v* to scrub

esgotado, da [eej-gotadoo] *adj* exhausted ▸ 'lotação esgotada' 'sold out'

esgoto [eej-gotoo] *n* drain

esmagado, da [eej-magadoo] *adj* crushed

espaço [eeshpassoo] *n* space

espaguete [eeshpa-getchee] *n* spaghetti

especial [eeshpess-yal] *v* special

especialidade [eeshpess-yaleedadjee] *n* speciality

especiaria [eeshpess-yaree-a] *n* spice

espécie [eeshpessee] *n* species

espelho [eeshpel-yoo] *n* mirror ▸ espelho retrovisor rear-view mirror

espera [eeshpera] *n* wait ▸ estar à espera de alguém to be waiting for somebody

esperar [eeshperah] *v* to wait; *(wish)* to hope ▸ espere aí! wait there

esperto, ta [eeshpeh-too] *adj* clever

espetacular [eeshpetakoolah] *adj* amazing

espetáculo [eeshpetakooloo] *n* show

espiga [eeshpeega] *n* ear

espinafre [eeshpeenafree] *n* spinach

espinha [eeshpeenya] *n* pimple; *(fish)* bone

espírito [eeshpeereetoo] *n* spirit

esponja [eeshponja] *n* sponge

esposa [eeshpoza] *n* wife

espreitar [eeshpray-tah] *v* to peep

espuma [eeshpooma] *n* foam ▸ espuma de barbear shaving cream

espumante [eeshpoomantchee] *n* sparkling wine

esquadra [eeshkwadra] *n* fleet

esquecer(-se) [eeshkesseh-(see)] *v* to forget

esquerda [eeshkeh-da] *n* left ▸ vire à esquerda turn left

esquerdo, da [eeshkeh-doo] *adj* left

esqui [eeshkee] *n* ski; *(sport)* skiing ▸ esqui aquático water skiing

esquina [eeshkeena] *n* corner

esquisito, ta [eeshkeezeetoo] *adj* strange; *(taste)* odd

essa [essa] *pron* that

esse [essee] *pron* that

esta [eshta] *pron* this

estabelecimento [eeshtabelessee-mentoo] *n* establishment

estação [eeshtassowng] *n* station; *(period of year)* season ▸ estação de trem train station ▸ estação rodoviária bus station

estacionar [eeshtass-yoonah] *v* to park

estadia [eeshtadee-a] *n* stay

estádio [eeshtad-yoo] *n* stadium

estado [eeshtadoo] *n* state

estágio [eeshtaj-yoo] *n* stage

estalagem [eeshtalajeng] *n* inn

estar [eeshtah] *v* to be ▸ está bem OK ▸ está pronto? are you ready? ▸ (está) tudo bem? (are) you OK?

estátua [eeshtatwa] *n* statue

este [esh-tchee] *pron* this

estender [eeshtendeh] *v* to spread

estendido, da [eeshten-djeedoo] *adj* spread out ▸ estendido no chão lying down

estilo [eeshteeloo] *n* style

estojo [eeshtojoo] *n* case ▸ estojo de lápis pencil case ▸ estojo de unhas manicure set

estômago [eeshtomagoo] *n* stomach

estrada [eeshtrada] *n* road

estragado, da [eeshtragadoo] *adj* ruined

estragar(-se) [eeshtragah-(see)] *v* to ruin

estrangeiro, ra [eeshtran-jayroo] *n* foreigner ◆ *adj* foreign ▸ no estrangeiro abroad

estranho, nha [eeshtran-yoo] *adj* strange

estreito, ta [eeshtray-too] *adj* narrow

estrela [eeshtrella] *n* star

estudante [eeshtoodantchee] *n* student

estudar [eeshtoodah] *v* to study

estúdio [eeshtood-yoo] *n* studio

estupidez [eeshtoopeedesh] *n* ▸ que estupidez! how stupid!

estúpido, da [eeshtoopeedoo] *adj* stupid

eu [ew] *pron* I; *(object)* me

evidente [eveedentchee] *adj* obvious

evitar [eveetah] *v* to avoid

exame [ezamee] *n* examination

exceção [essessowng] *n* exception

excelente [esselentchee] *adj* excellent

excepcional [essepsee-onow] *adj* exceptional

excesso [essessoo] *n* excess ▸ excesso de bagagem excess baggage

exceto [essetoo] *prep* except

excursão [eeshkuh-sowng] *n* trip

exemplo [ezemploo] *n* example

exercício [ezeh-seess-yoo] *n* exercise

exigência [ezeejenss-ya] *n* demand

exigir [ezeejeeh] *v* to demand

existir [ezeesh-tcheeh] *v* to exist

êxito [ezeetoo] *n* success

experiência [eeshperee-enss-ya] *n* experience

experimentar [eeshpereementah] *v* to try

explicar [eeshpleekah] *v* to explain

explorador [eeshploradoh] *n* explorer

exportar [eeshpoh-tah] *v* to export

exposição [eeshpozee-sowng] *n* exhibition

expressão [eeshpressowng] *n* expression

exprimir(-se) [eeshpreemeeh-(see)] *v* to express

exterior [eeshter-yoh] *adj* & *n* outside

f

fábrica [fabreeka] *n* factory

faca [faka] *n* knife

face [fassee] *n* face ▸ face (a) facing

fácil [fasseew] *adj* easy

facilidade [fasseelee-dadjee] *n* ease ▸ facilidades de pagamento easy terms of payment

facilitar [fasseeleetah] *v* to facilitate ▸ 'facilite o troco' 'have your change ready'

faixa [fy-sha] *n* strip ▸ faixa de segurança pedestrian crossing

falar [falah] *v* to speak, to talk

falésia [falez-ya] *n* cliff

falso, sa [fowsoo] *adj* false

falta [fowta] *n* shortage

faltar [fowtah] *v* to be lacking ▸ falta água there's no water

família [fameel-ya] *n* family

famoso, sa [famozoo] *adj* famous

farinha [fareen-ya] *n* cassava flour

farmácia [fah-mass-ya] *n* pharmacy

▸ farmácia de manipulação homeopathic pharmacy

farofa [farofa] *npl fried manioc flour*

farol [farow] *n* ▸ 'acenda os faróis' 'headlights on'

farto, ta [fah-too] *adj* ▸ estar farto (de) to be fed up (with)

fase [fazee] *n* phase

fatia [fatchee-a] *n* slice ▸ em fatias sliced

fato [fatoo] *n* fact ▸ de fato in fact

fatura [fatoora] *n* invoice

favas [favash] *npl* beans ▸ mandar alguém às favas to tell somebody to go away

favela [favella] *f* shantytown, slum

favor [favoh] *n* favor ▸ 'favor fechar a porta' 'please close the door' ▸ por favor please

fazenda [fazenda] *n* ranch

fazer [fazeh] *v* to do, to make ▸ fazer uma pergunta to ask a question ▸ não faz mal never mind

favelas

These shantytowns are the antithesis of the picture-postcard views on sale in all major Brazilian cities. Made up of makeshift shacks, they spread for miles across marginal land in and around the main population centers, painting all too vivid a portrait of the poverty that underpins life for so many Brazilians. The population of some of these *favelas* reaches into hundreds of thousands. Often there is no sanitation, no fresh drinking water and little police protection available for the people living there.

feijoada

Brazilian-style *feijoada* (bean stew) is not only a traditional dish, but also a social event. Made with black beans, salt beef and various cuts of pork, the dish is served with white rice and *farofa* (fried cassava flour), seasoned spring greens and a peeled orange. Often held on Saturdays, *feijoadas* begin at noon and last all day, copious quantities of beer and *caipirinha* (a white rum-based cocktail) being consumed, preferably to the sound of samba!

febre [febree] *n* fever ▸ febre aftosa foot-and-mouth disease ▸ febre amarela yellow fever

fechado, da [feshadoo] *adj* closed ▸ fechado à chave locked

fechar [feshah] *v* to close ▸ fechar-se to shut oneself away

fecho [feshoo] *n* fastener ▸ fecho éclair zipper

feijão [fay-jowng] *n* bean

feijoada [fay-jwada] *n* bean stew

feio, a [fayoo] *adj* ugly

feira [fayra] *n* fair

felicidade [feleessee-dadjee] *n* happiness

feliz [feleej] *adj* happy

feminino, na [femeeneenoo] *adj* feminine

feriado [fer-yadoo] *n* holiday ▸ feriado nacional public holiday

férias [fer-yash] *npl* vacation

ferida [fereeda] *n* wound

ferido, da [fereedoo] *adj* wounded

ferir(-se) [fereeh-(see)] *v* to wound

ferramenta [feha-menta] *n* tool

ferro [fehoo] *n* iron

ferro-velho [fehoo-velyoo] *n* scrap

ferver [feh-veh] *v* to boil

festa [feshta] *n* party

festejar [feshtejah] *v* to celebrate

fevereiro [feveray-roo] *n* February

fiambre [fee-ambree] *n* ham

ficar [feekah] *v* to be; *(to stay)* to remain

fígado [feegadoo] *n* kidney

figo [feegoo] *n* fig

figueira [feegay-ra] *n* fig tree

figura [feegoora] *n* figure

fila [feela] *n* line; row ▸ na primeira fila in the front row ▸ 'aguarde na fila' 'keep in line' ▸ 'não fure a fila' 'don't cut in line' ▸ fila indiana single file

filha [feel-ya] *n* daughter

filho [feel-yoo] *n* son ▸ os filhos the children

filmar [feewmah] *v* to film

filme [feewmee] *n* movie

filtro [feew-troo] *n* filter

fim [feeng] *n* end ▸ fim de semana weekend ▸ estar a fim de to feel like

fino, na [feenoo] *adj* slender; *(clothes)* elegant

fio [fee-oo] *n* thread; *(electrical)* wire ▸ fio dental dental floss ▸ bater um fio to make a call

físico, ca [feezeekoo] *adj* physical

fixar [feeksah] v to fix

flocos [flokoosh] npl flakes ▸ flocos de cereais cornflakes

flor [floh] n flower

floresta [floreshta] n forest

fogão [fogowng] n stove

fogareiro [fogaray-roo] n stove

fogo [fogoo] n fire ▸ fogos de artifício fireworks ▸ você tem fogo? do you have a light?

fogueira [fogay-ra] n bonfire

foguete [fogetchee] n rocket

folclórico, ca [fowk-loreekoo] adj folk

folha [folya] n leaf

fome [fomee] n hunger ▸ estar com/ter fome to be hungry

fonte [fontchee] n fountain

fora [fora] adv outside

força [foh-sa] n force; (power) strength

formidável [foh-meedavew] adj fantastic

formiga [foh-meega] n ant

formulário [foh-moolar-yoo] n form

fornecer [foh-nesseh] v to supply

forno [foh-noo] n oven

forte [foh-tchee] adj strong

fósforo [foshforoo] n match

fotografia [fotografee-a] n photograph ▸ tirar/bater uma fotografia to take a photo

foz [fosh] n (of river) mouth

fraco, ca [frakoo] adj weak

frade [fradjee] n frier

frágil [frajeew] adj fragile

fralda [frowda] n diaper

framboesa [frambweza] n raspberry

franco, ca [frankoo] adj frank

frango [frangoo] n chicken

frasco [frashkoo] n flask

frase [frazee] n sentence

fratura [fratoora] n fracture

freio [frayoo] n brake ▸ freio de mão hand brake ▸ pedal do freio brake pedal

freira [frayra] n nun

frente [frentchee] n front ▸ em frente de in front of ▸ sempre em frente straight ahead ▸ frente fria cold front

fresco, ca [freshkoo] adj fresh

frigideira [freejeeday-ra] n frying pan

frigorífico [freegor-eefeekoo] n fridge

frio, a [free-oo] adj & n cold ▸ está frio it's cold ▸ ter frio to feel cold

fritar [freetah] v to fry

frito, ta [freetoo] adj fried

fronha [fronya] n ▸ fronha (de traveseiro) pillowcase

fronteira [frontay-ra] n border

fruta [froota] n fruit

fruto [frootoo] n fruit

fugir [foojeeh] v to escape

fumante [foomantchee] n smoker ▸ 'fumantes' 'smokers' ▸ 'não fumantes' 'nonsmokers'

fumar [foomah] v to smoke

fumo [foomoo] n smoke

função [foonsowng] n function

funcho [foonshoo] n fennel

fundação [foondassowng] n foundation

fundo, da [foondoo] adj deep ◆ n bottom; (money) fund ▸ no fundo (de) at the bottom (of)

furado, da [fooradoo] adj pierced; (tire) punctured

furar [foorah] v to pierce; (tire) to puncture

furioso, sa [foor-yozoo] adj furious

fusível [foozeevew] *n* fuse

fuso [foozoo] *n* ▸ fuso horário time zone

futebol [footcheebow] *n* football

futuro, ra [footooroo] *adj & n* future

g

gabinete [gabeenetchee] *n* office; *(political)* cabinet

gaiola [guy-ola] *n* cage

gaivota [guy-vota] *n* seagull

galã [galang] *n* playboy

galão [galowng] *n* stripe

galeria [galeree-a] *n* gallery

galeto [galetoo] *n* spring chicken

galinha [galeen-ya] *n* hen

galo [galoo] *n* rooster

gancho [ganshoo] *n* hook

ganhar [gan-yah] *v* to win; *(money)* to earn

garagem [garajeng] *n* garage

garantia [garantchee-a] *n* guarantee

garfo [gah-foo] *n* fork

gargalhada [gah-gal-yada] *n* burst of laughter

garganta [gah-ganta] *n* throat

garoto [garotoo] *n* boy; *small glass of draft beer*

garrafa [gahafa] *n* bottle

gás [gash] *n* gas

gasolina [gazoleena] *n* gasoline ▸ gasolina aditivada premium gasoline

gasoso, sa [gazozoo] *adj* fizzy, carbonated

gastar [gashtah] *v (money)* to spend

gato [gatoo] *n* cat

geada [jee-ada] *n* frost

gel [jew] *n (for hair)* gel

gelado, da [jeladoo] *adj* frozen

gelo [jeloo] *n* ice; *(color)* light gray

gema [jemma] *n* ▸ gema de ovo egg yolk

gêmeo [jem-yoo] *n* twin

gênero [jeneroo] *n* gender

genro [jen-hoo] *n* son-in-law

gente [jentchee] *n* people ▸ toda a gente everybody

geográfico, ca [jee-ografeekoo] *adj* geographical

geração [jerassowng] *n* generation

geral [jerow] *adj* general ▸ em geral in general

gerente [jerentchee] *n* manager

gesso [jessoo] *n* ▸ estar com gesso to be in a cast, to have a cast

gesto [jeshtoo] *n* gesture

gestor [jeshtoh] *n* consultant

gilete [jeeletchee] *n* razor blade

gim [jeeng] *n* gin

ginásio [jeenaz-yoo] *n* gymnasium; *(school)* high school

ginástica [jeenashteeka] *n* gymnastics

ginecologista [jeenekolo-jeeshta] *n* gynecologist

girar [jeerah] *v* to turn

giro [jeeroo] *n* stroll

globo [globoo] *n* globe

gol [gow] *n (sports)* goal

guaraná

A seed which possesses both stimulating and therapeutic properties, *guaraná* was first discovered by the indigenous tribes of the Amazonian rain forests. It is now produced commercially in powder, tablet, liquid and gum form and exported all over the world. It may be taken as a food supplement to help combat a range of complaints, including fatigue, diarrhea and neuralgic pain. It also serves as a base for a popular soda of the same name in Brazil.

golfe [gowfee] *n* golf

golfo [gow-foo] *n* gulf

gordo, da [goh-doo] *adj* fat

gordura [goh-doora] *n* fat

gorjeta [goh-jeta] *n* tip

gorro [gohoo] *n* cap

gostar [goshtah] *v* to enjoy ▸ eu gostaria muito de I'd really like

gosto [goshtoo] *n* pleasure; *(appreciation)* taste

gota [gota] *npl* drop

gótico, ca [goteekoo] *adj* gothic

governo [goveh-noo] *n* government

gozar [gozah] *v* to enjoy; *(make fun of)* to mock

graça [grassa] *n* charm ▸ de graça free

grama [grama] *n (measurement)* gram; *(grass)* grass

gramática [grama-tcheeka] *n* grammar

grande [grandjee] *adj* big

grão [growng] *n* grain; *(coffee)* bean ▸ grão-de-bico chickpea

gratuito, ta [gratweetoo] *adj* free

grau [grow] *n* degree

gravar [gravah] *v* to record

gravata [gravata] *n* tie

grávida [graveeda] *adj* pregnant

grelhado, da [grel-yadoo] *n* grill ◆ *adj* grilled

grilo [greeloo] *n* cricket

gripe [greepee] *n* flu

gritar [greetah] *v* to shout

grito [greetoo] *n* shout

grupo [groopoo] *n* group ▸ grupo sanguíneo blood group

guaraná [gwarana] *n carbonated drink made from guarana seeds*

guarda [gwah-da] *n* care; *(officer)* guard

guarda-chuva [gwah-da-shoova] *n* umbrella

guardanapo [gwah-danapoo] *n* napkin

guardar [gwah-dah] *v* to keep

guarda-sol [gwah-da-sow] *n* parasol

guerra [gue-ha] *n* war

guia [guee-a] *n* guide

guiar [guee-ah] *v (automobiles)* to drive; to guide

guloso, sa [goolozoo] *adj* greedy

h

habitação [abeetassowng] *n* room

habitante [abeetantchee] *n* inhabitant

habitar [abeetah] *v* to live in

hábito [abeetoo] *n* habit

habitualmente [abeet-wow-mentchee] *adv* usually

hambúrguer [ambooh-geh] *n* hamburger

haver [aveh] *v* ▸ haver de to have to ▸ há que esperar you'll have to wait

hemorróida [emohoy-da] *n* hemorrhoid

herança [eran-sa] *n* inheritance

herói [eroy] *n* hero

hesitar [ezeetah] *v* to hesitate ▸ não hesite! don't hesitate!

hipertensão [eepeh-tensowng] *n* high blood pressure

hipótese [eepoteezee] *n* hypothesis

história [eeshtoree-a] *n* history

hoje [ojee] *adv* today

homem [omeng] *n* man

homeopatia [omeopatee-a] *n* homeopathy

homossexual [omosex-wow] *n* homosexual

honesto, ta [oneshtoo] *adj* honest

honra [onra] *n* honor

hora [ora] *n* hour ▸ a que horas? at what time? ▸ às cinco horas at five o'clock

horário [orar-yoo] *n* timetable ▸ horário de verão summer hours

horrível [oheevew] *adj* horrible

horror [ohoh] *n* horror

horta [oh-ta] *n* vegetable garden

hospedaria [oshpedaree-a] *n* guest house

hóspede [oshpedjee] *n* guest

hospedeiro [oshpeday-roo] *n* host

hospital [oshpeetow] *n* hospital

hotel [otew] *n* hotel

humor [oomoh] *n* humor

i

ida [eeda] *v* going

idade [eedadjee] *n* age ▸ que idade você tem? how old are you? ▸ de idade elderly

idéia [eedaya] *n* idea ▸ não faço idéia I can't imagine

identificação [eedentchee-feekas-sowng] *n* identification

idiota [eedjota] *adj* idiotic

igreja [eegreja] *n* church

igual [eeg-wow] *adj* equal

igualdade [eeg-wow-dadjee] *n* equality

ilha [eel-ya] *n* island

iluminação [eeloomee-nassowng] *n* lighting

imenso, sa [eemensoo] *adj* huge

imperfeito, ta [eemperfay-too] *adj* imperfect

império [eempair-yoo] *n* empire

impermeável [eempeh-mee-avew] *n* raincoat ◆ *adj* waterproof

importação [eempoh-tassowng] *n* importation

importância [eempoh-tansee-a] *n* importance; *(money)* sum ▸ não tem importância it doesn't matter

importante [eempoh-tantchee] *adj* important

importar [eempoh-tah] *v* to matter; *(goods)* to import ▸ não se importa de ...? do you mind ... ?

impossível [eemposseevew] *adj* impossible

imposto [eemposhtoo] *n* tax

imprensa [eemprensa] *n* press

impressão [eempressowng] *n* printing; *(emotion)* feeling ▸ ter a impressão de to have the feeling

impressionante [eempress-yonantchee] *adj* impressive

imprimir [eempreemeeh] *v* to print

impróprio, pria [eempropree-oo] *adj* inappropriate ▸ 'água imprópria para consumo' 'non-potable water'

inauguração [eenow-goorassowng] *n* opening

incêndio [eensend-yoo] *n* fire

inchado, da [eenshadoo] *adj* swollen

inclinado, da [eenkleenadoo] *adj* inclined

incluído, da [eenkloo-eedoo] *adj* included

incomodar [eenkomodah] *v* to worry ▸ não incomode do not disturb

incômodo, da [eenkomodoo] *adj* troublesome ◆ *n* trouble ▸ desculpe o incômodo sorry to trouble you

incrível [eenkreevew] *adj* incredible

indeciso, sa [eendesseezoo] *adj* hesitant

independente [eendepen-dentchee] *adj* independent

indicar [een-djeekah] *v* to indicate

indispensável [eendjeesh-pensavew] *adj* essential

indústria [eendooshtree-a] *n* industry

inesquecível [eenesh-kesseevew] *adj* unforgettable

infantil [eenfanteew] *adj* children's; *(immature)* childish

infecção [eenfessowng] *n* infection

infelizmente [eenfeleej-mentchee] *adv* unfortunately

inferno [eenfeh-noo] *n* hell

infiel [eenfee-ew] *adj* unfaithful

inflamação [eenflamassowng] *n* inflammation

influência [eenfloo-ensee-a] *n* influence

informação [eenfoh-massowng] *n* news ▸ informações *(on the phone)* information

infusão [eenfoozowng] *n* herbal tea

íngreme [eengremee] *adj* steep ▸ subida íngreme steep hill

iniciais [eeneessee-ysh] *npl* initials

início [eeneess-yoo] *n* beginning ▸ no início at the start ▸ dar início to start

inimigo [eeneemeegoo] *n* enemy

injeção [eenjessowng] *n* injection ▸ dar uma injeção to give an injection ▸ tomar uma injeção to have an injection

inquietar(-se) [eenkee-etah-(see)] *v* to worry

inscrever(-se) [eensh-kreveh-(see)] *v* to register

inseticida [eensetchee-seeda] *n* insecticide

inseto [eensetoo] *n* insect

insolação [eensolassowng] *n* sunstroke

insônia [eenson-ya] *n* insomnia

instante [eenshtantchee] *n* moment ▸ só um instante just a moment!

instrução [eenshtroossowng] *n* instruc-

tion ▸ 'leia as instruções' 'read the instructions'

instrumento [eenshtroomentoo] *n* instrument

inteiro, ra [eentay-roo] *adj* whole

inteligente [eentelee-jentchee] *adj* intelligent

intenção [eentensowng] *n* intention

interessante [eenteressantchee] *adj* interesting

interior [eenteree-oh] *adj & n* interior

internacional [eenteh-nass-yonow] *adj* international

intervalo [eenteh-valoo] *n* interval

intestino [eentesh-tcheenoo] *n* intestine

intoxicação [eentoxee-kassowng] *n* poisoning

introduzir [eentrodoozeeh] *v* to introduce

inútil [eenoo-teew] *adj* useless

inveja [eenveja] *n* envy

inventar [eenventah] *v* to invent

inverno [eenveh-noo] *n* winter

iogurte [yogooh-tchee] *n* yogurt

ir [eeh] *v* to go ▸ vamos? shall we go? ▸ ir para a praia to go to the beach

irmã [eeh-mang] *n* sister

irmão [eeh-mowng] *n* brother

irritado, da [eehee-tadoo] *adj* irritated

isca [eeshka] *n* bait ▸ iscas naturais live bait

isqueiro [eeshkay-roo] *n* lighter

isso [eessoo] *pron* that (thing) ▸ isso! exactly! ▸ é por isso que... that's why ...

isto [eeshtoo] *pron* this (thing) ▸ isto é namely

j

já [ja] *adv* already ▸ já acabei I've finished now ▸ já vou! coming!

janeiro [janay-roo] *n* January

janela [janela] *n* window

jantar [jantah] *n* dinner ◆ *v* to have dinner ▸ jantar fora to dine out

jardim [jah-djeeng] *n* garden ▸ jardim zoológico zoo ▸ jardim de infância kindergarten

jardineiro [jah-djeenay-roo] *n* gardener

jarra [jaha] *n* carafe

jarro [jahoo] *n* jug ▸ jarro de água jug of water

jato [jato] *n* jet

javali [javalee] *n* boar

joelho [jo-el-yoo] *n* knee

jogador [jogadoh] *n* player

jogar [jogah] *n* to play ▸ jogar bola to play ball

jogging [jogeeng] *n (sports)* jogging

jogo [jogoo] *n* game

jóia [joya] *n* jewel

jornal [joh-now] *n* newspaper

jovem [joveng] *n* youngster

judeu, dia [joodew] *adj* Jewish ◆ *n* Jew

juiz [joo-eesh] *n* judge

juízo [jweezoo] *n* judgment ▸ ter juízo to be sensible

julgar [joow-gah] *v* to judge ▸ julgo que sim I believe so

julho [jool-yoo] *n* July

junho [joon-yoo] *n* June

juntar [joontah] *v* to join, to unite ▸ juntar dinheiro to save money ▸ juntar forças to gather strength

junto, ta [joontoo] *adj & adv* ▸ junto com together with ▸ junto de next to

juntos, tas [joontoosh] *adj* together ▸ vamos todos juntos let's all go together

juro [jooroo] *n (money)* interest ▸ a juros with interest

jus [joosh] *n* ▸ fazer jus a to do justice to

justiça [joosh-teessa] *n* justice

justificar [jooshtee-feekah] *v* to justify

justo, ta [jooshtoo] *adj* fair

juventude [jooven-toodjee] *n* youth

lá [la] *adv* there ▸ lá está ela there she is ▸ para lá de beyond

lã [lang] *n* wool

lábio [lab-yoo] *n* lip

laço [lassoo] *n* bow; *(bond)* tie

lado [ladoo] *n* side ▸ ao lado de beside ▸ em algum lado somewhere

ladrão [ladrowng] *n* thief

ladrar [ladrah] *v* to bark

lago [lagoo] *n* lake

lagoa [lagoa] *n* lagoon

lagosta [lagoshta] *n* lobster

lágrima [lagreema] *n* tear

lama [lama] *n* mud

lambari [lambaree] *n fish similar to shiner*

lamentar [lamentah] *v* to regret ▸ lamento I'm sorry

lâmina [lameena] *n* blade ▸ lâmina de barbear razor blade

lâmpada [lampada] *n* light ▸ lâmpada fluorescente fluorescent light ▸ lâmpada incandescente (light) bulb

lanchar [lanshah] *v* to have a snack

lanterna [lanteh-na] *n* flashlight ▸ lanterna de bolso pocket flashlight

lápis [lapeesh] *n* pencil

lar [lah] *n* home

laranja [laranja] *n* orange ▸ suco de laranja natural fresh orange juice

laranjada [laranjada] *n* orange soda

laranjeira [laranjay-ra] *n* orange tree

lareira [laray-ra] *n* fireplace

largo, ga [lah-goo] *n* square ◆ *adj* wide

largura [lah-goora] *n* width

lata [lata] *n* can

lavadeira [lavaday-ra] *n* washerwoman, laundress

lavanderia [lavanderee-a] *n* laundry

lavar [lavah] *v* to wash ▸ lavar-se to get washed

lavatório [lavator-yoo] *n* cloakroom

lavrador [lavradoh] *n* farmhand

leão [lee-owng] *n* lion

lebre [lebree] *n* hare

legendado, da [lejendadoo] *adj* subtitled

legume [legoomee] *n* vegetable

lei [lay] *n* law

leilão [lay-lowng] *n* auction

leitão [lay-towng] *n* suckling pig

leite [lay-tchee] *n* milk ▸ leite condensado condensed milk ▸ leite desnatado skim milk ▸ leite integral whole milk ▸ leite em pó powdered milk ▸ leite semidesnatado 2% milk

leitura [lay-toora] *n* reading

lembrança [lembransa] *n* souvenir

lembrar [lembrah] *v* to remember; *(bring to mind)* to remind

lenço [lensoo] *n* handkerchief ▸ lenço de papel tissue

lençol [lensow] *n* sheet

lenha [lenya] *n* firewood

lentamente [lentamentchee] *adv* slowly

lente [lentchee] *n (of camera, glasses)* lens ▶ lentes (de contato) duras/gelatinosas hard/soft (contact) lenses

lentilha [lenteel-ya] *n* lentil

lento, ta [lentoo] *adj* slow

leque [lekee] *n* fan

ler [leh] *v* to read

leste [lesh-tchee] *n* east ▶ a leste (de) to the east (of)

letreiro [letray-roo] *n* notice

levantar [levantah] *v* to lift ▶ levantar vôo to take off ▶ levantar-se to get up

levar [levah] *v* to take ▶ levar tempo para to take time to ▶ para levar *(food)* takeout

leve [levee] *adj* light

lhe [l-yee] *pron* to him, to her, to you ▶ eu lhe agradeço muito thank you very much

liberdade [leebeh-dadjee] *n* freedom

lição [leessowng] *n* lesson

licença [lee-sensa] *n* permission; *(permit)* license ▶ com licença! excuse me! ▶ dá licença? may I?

licor [leekoh] *n* liqueur

ligadura [leegadoora] *n* bandage

ligar [leegah] *v* to connect; *(on phone)* to call ▶ não ligue! don't listen!

ligeiro, ra [leejay-roo] *adj* light

lima [leema] *n* file; *(fruit)* lime

limão [leemowng] *n* lemon

limoeiro [leem-wayroo] *n* lemon tree

limonada [leemonada] *f* lemon soda

limpador [leempadoh] *n* cleaner ▶ limpador de pára-brisas windshield wiper

limpar [leempah] *v* to clean

limpa-vidros [leempa-veedroosh] *n* window cleaner

limpeza [leempeza] *n* cleaning ▶ fazer a limpeza to clean

limpo, pa [leempoo] *adj* clean

lindo, da [leendoo] *adj* lovely

língua [leengwa] *n* tongue; *(spoken)* language

linguado [leengwadoo] *n* flounder

linguagem [leengwajeng] *n (polite, foul)* language

lingüiça [leengweessa] *n* sausage

linha [leen-ya] *n* line ▶ linha aérea airline ▶ linha de costura seam ▶ linha cruzada *(on phone)* crossed line ▶ linha férrea/de trem railroad ▶ linha de ônibus bus line

linho [leenyoo] *n* linen

liso, sa [leezoo] *adj (surface)* smooth; *(hair)* straight

lista [leeshta] *n* list ▶ lista telefônica telephone directory

litoral [leetorow] *n & adj* seaboard

litro [leetroo] *n* liter

livraria [leevraree-a] *n* bookstore

livre [leevree] *adj* free

livro [leevroo] *n* book ▶ livro de bolso pocketbook

livro-caixa [leevroo-kysha] *n* cash book

lixo [leeshoo] *n* garbage ▶ pôr no lixo to throw in the can

local [lokow] *n* local ▶ local de nascimento place of birth

logo [logoo] *adv* at once ▶ até logo! see you soon! ▶ logo à noite later this evening

loja [loja] *n* store ▶ loja de departamentos department store

lombo [lomboo] n ▸ lombo de porco pork fillet ▸ lombo de vaca loin of beef

longe [lonjee] adv far

longo, ga [longoo] adj long

louça [lossa] n china ▸ louça de barro earthenware

louco, ca [lokoo] adj crazy ◆ n lunatic

louro, ra [loroo] adj fair ◆ n blond(e)

lua [loo-a] n moon ▸ lua cheia full moon ▸ lua-de-mel honeymoon

luar [loo-ah] n moonlight

lugar [loogah] n place ▸ não conhecer o seu lugar not to know one's place

lula [loola] n squid ▸ lulas à doré calamari

lustrar [looshtrah] v to polish

luto [lootoo] n mourning

luva [loova] n glove ▸ luva de borracha rubber glove

luxo [looshoo] n luxury

luz [looj] n light ▸ acenda/apague a luz turn on/turn off the light

má [ma] adj bad

maçã [massang] n apple

macaco [makakoo] n monkey

macieira [massee-ay-ra] n apple tree

macio, cia [massee-oo] adj soft

maço [massoo] n ▸ maço de cigarros pack of cigarettes

madeira [maday-ra] n wood ▸ de madeira wooden

madrasta [madrashta] n stepmother

madrugada [madroogada] n early morning ▸ de madrugada in the early hours

maduro, ra [madooroo] adj ripe

mãe [myng] n mother

magoar(-se) [magwah-(see)] v to hurt ▸ isso te magoa? does it hurt? ▸ você se magoou? did you hurt yourself?

magro, gra [magroo] adj thin; (meat) lean

maio [my-oo] n May

maionese [my-onezee] n mayonnaise

maior [my-oh] adj bigger ▸ o maior the biggest

maioria [my-oree-a] n majority

mais [mysh] adv more ▸ mais alguma coisa? anything else? ▸ não tem mais... there is no more ...

mal [mow] adv badly; (to answer) rudely ▸ levar a mal to take offense ▸ nada mal not bad ▸ querer mal a alguém to wish somebody ill

mala [mala] n suitcase ▸ mala de mão carry-on luggage

malagueta [mala-geta] n chili pepper

malcriado, da [mow-kree-adoo] adj ill-mannered

mal-educado, da [mow-edookadoo] adj rude

mal-entendido [mow-entendjeedoo] n misunderstanding

malha [mal-ya] n ▸ casaco de malha knitted jacket

maluco, ca [malookoo] *adj* crazy

mamadeira [mamaday-ra] *n* baby bottle

mancha [mansha] *n* stain

mandar [mandah] *v* to order ▸ mandar limpar o carro to have the car cleaned ▸ mandar embora to send away ▸ mandar vir to summon

maneira [manay-ra] *n* manner

manga [manga] *n (of shirt)* sleeve; *(fruit)* mango

manhã [man-yang] *n* morning

manjericão [manjeree-kowng] *n* basil

manta [manta] *n* blanket

manteiga [mantay-ga] *n* butter

manter [manteh] *v* to keep ▸ 'manter fora do alcance das crianças' 'keep out of the reach of children'

mão [mowng] *n* hand ▸ mão dupla two-way ▸ à mão at hand ▸ apertar a mão to shake hands ▸ de segunda mão secondhand ▸ mão na roda great help ▸ mão única one-way

mapa [mapa] *n* map ▸ mapa rodoviário road map

máquina [makeena] *n* machine ▸ máquina de barbear electric shaver ▸ máquina de bebidas *vending machine selling drinks* ▸ máquina fotográfica camera ▸ máquina de lavar washing machine ▸ máquina de lavar louça dishwasher ▸ máquina de secar dryer

mar [mah] *n* sea ▸ mar agitado/calmo rough/calm sea

maravilhoso, sa [maraveel-yozoo] *adj* marvelous

marca [mah-ka] *n* mark ▸ marca registada registered trademark

marcar [mah-kah] *v* to mark ▸ marcar a hora to make an appointment

marcha [mah-sha] *n* gear ▸ marcha a ré reverse gear

marco [mah-koo] *n* landmark

março [mah-soo] *n* March

maré [ma-re] *n* ▸ maré baixa/alta low/high tide

margem [mah-jeng] *n* edge

marido [mareedoo] *n* husband

marinheiro [mareen-yay-roo] *n* sailor

marinho, nha [mareen-yoo] *adj* marine ▸ azul-marinho navy blue

marisco [mareeshkoo] *n* shellfish

marmelada [mah-melada] *n* quince jam

martelo [mah-teloo] *n* hammer

mas [mysh] *conj* but

masculino, na [mashkooleenoo] *adj* male

massa [massa] *n* mass; *(pasta)* dough ▸ massa folhada puff pastry

mastigar [mashteegah] *v* to chew

mata [mata] *n* forest

matar [matah] *v* to kill

matéria [matair-ya] *n* matter

material [materee-ow] *n* material

mato [matoo] *n* scrubland

mau [mow] *adj* bad ▸ está fazendo um mau tempo the weather is bad

máximo, ma [masseemoo] *adj* maximum

me [mee] *pron* me ▸ me dá isso can you give me that? ▸ eu me chamo... my name is...

mecânico [mekaneekoo] *n* mechanic

medalhão [medal-yowng] *n* medallion

média [med-ya] *n* average

medicamento [medjeekamentoo] *n* medicine

médico, ca [medjeekoo] *n* doctor

médio, dia [med-yoo] *adj* average
▸ duração média average duration

medir [medjeeh] *v* to measure

medo [medoo] *n* fear ▸ ter medo (de) to be afraid (of)

meia-noite [maya-noy-tchee] *n* midnight

meia-pensão [maya-pensowng] *n* hotel room with breakfast and a main meal included

meias [mayash] *npl* stockings

meio [mayoo] *adj & n* half ▸ meio litro half a liter ▸ meia hora half an hour ▸ uma hora e meia an hour and a half ▸ meia volta about-face ▸ no meio de in the middle of

meio-dia [mayoo-djee-a] *n* midday

mel [mew] *n* honey

melancia [melansee-a] *n* watermelon

melão [melowng] *n* melon

melga [mew-ga] *n* gnat

melhor [mel-yoh] *adj & adv* better ▸ o melhor the best

melodia [melodjee-a] *n* melody

membro [membroo] *n* member

memória [memoree-a] *n* memory

mendigo [mendjeegoo] *n* beggar

menina [meneena] *n* girl; young lady

menino [meneenoo] *n* boy

menos [menoosh] *adv* less ▸ ao/pelo menos at least ▸ menos do que less than ▸ cada vez menos less and less

mensagem [mensajeng] *n* message

mensal [mensow] *adj* monthly

menstruação [menshtroo-assowng] *n* menstruation

mentir [mentcheeh] *v* to lie

mentira [mentcheera] *n* lie

mercado [meh-kadoo] *n* market

mercadoria [meh-kadoree-a] *n* commodity

mercearia [meh-see-aree-a] *n* grocery store

merenda [merenda] *n* snack

mergulhar [meh-gool-yah] *v* to dive

mergulho [meh-gool-yoo] *n* dip; (*sport*) diving ▸ dar um mergulho to take a dip

mês [mesh] *n* month

mesa [meza] *n* table ▸ mesa de cabeceira bedside table ▸ pôr a mesa to set the table

mesmo, ma [mejmoo] *adv* even ◆ *adj* same, self ▸ mesmo que even though ▸ ele mesmo he himself ▸ agora mesmo right now ▸ mesmo assim even so

mesquita [meshkeeta] *n* mosque

meta [meta] *n* goal; (*race*) finishing line

metade [metadjee] *n* half ▸ pela metade do preço at half price

meter [meteh] *v* to put

metro [metroo] *n* meter

metrô [metro] *n* subway

meu(s) [mew(sh)] *adj* my ◆ *pron* mine

mexer [mesheh] *v* to move ▸ não se mexa! don't move!

mexilhão [mesheel-yowng] *n* mussel

migalha [meegal-ya] *n* crumb

milhão [meel-yowng] *n* million

milho [meel-yoo] *n* corn

militar [meeleetah] *n* soldier ◆ *adj* military

mim [meeng] *pron* me

mingau [meengow] *n* porridge

moeda

Since 1994 the only legal Brazilian currency has been the *real*. The former unit, the *cruzeiro*, and its descendants, the *cruzeiro novo*, the *cruzado*, the *novo cruzado* and others, were all devoured by monstrous hyperinflation. At the end of the 1980s, the Brazilian currency sometimes suffered 90 per cent devaluation within the space of a single calendar month. The *real* is part of a government package aimed to place the country on a course of economic stability.

minha(s) [meen-ya(sh)] *adj* my ♦ *pron* mine

mínimo, ma [meeneemoo] *adj & n* minimum

minuto [meenootoo] *n* minute

miolo [mee-oloo] *n* brains; *(bread)* crumb

miradouro [meeradoroo] *n* viewpoint

miséria [meezair-ya] *n* misery

mistura [meeshtoora] *n* mixture

misturar [meeshtoorah] *v* to mix

miúdo, da [mee-oodoo] *adj* small ♦ *n*
♦ miúdos de galinha chicken giblets

mobília [mobeel-ya] *n* furniture

mobiliado, da [mobeel-yadoo] *adj* furnished

mochila [mosheela] *n* rucksack

moda [moda] *n* fashion ♦ na moda in fashion ♦ fora de moda out of fashion

moderno, na [modeh-noo] *adj* modern

modo [modoo] *n* way

moeda [mweda] *n* coin

moinho [mween-yoo] *n* mill

mole [molee] *adj* soft

molhado, da [mol-yadoo] *adj* wet

molhar(-se) [mol-yah-(see)] *v* to wet

molho [mol-yoo] *n* sauce

momento [momentoo] *n* moment ♦ no momento at the moment

monarquia [monah-kee-a] *n* monarchy

montanha [montan-ya] *n* mountain

montar [montah] *v (on horse)* to ride; *(equipment)* to install

monte [montchee] *n* hill; *(heap)* pile

monumento [monoomentoo] *n* monument

morada [morada] *n* dwelling

morango [morangoo] *n* strawberry

morar [morah] *v* to live ♦ onde você mora? where do you live?

morcela [moh-sela] *n* blood sausage

morder [moh-deh] *v* to bite

moreno, na [morenoo] *adj (skin)* dark-skinned; *(hair)* dark-haired; *(person)* tanned

morno, na [moh-noo] *adj* tepid

morrer [moheh] *v* to die

mortalha [moh-tal-ya] *n* shroud

morto, ta [moh-too] *adj* dead ♦ *n* deceased

mosca [moshka] *n* fly

mosquito [moshkeetoo] *n* mosquito

mostarda [moshtah-da] *n* mustard

mosteiro [moshtay-roo] *n* monastery

mostrar [moshtrah] *v* to show

motocicleta [motosee-kleta] *n* motorcycle

motor [motoh] *n* motor

motorista [motoreeshta] *n* driver

móveis [movaysh] *npl* furniture

movimentado, da [movee-mentadoo] *adj* busy

movimento [moveeementoo] *n* movement; *(activity)* bustle

muçulmano, na [moo-soo-manoo] *adj & n* Muslim

mudar [moodah] *v* to change; *(house)* to move ▸ mudar de roupa to change clothes ▸ mudar de casa to move (to a new house/apartment)

mudo, da [moodoo] *adj* mute

muito, ta [mweentoo] *adv* a lot ◆ *adj* much, many ▸ muitas vezes many times ▸ muito tempo a long time

mulher [mool-yeh] *n* woman; *(spouse)* wife

multa [moow-ta] *n* fine ▸ receber uma multa to be fined

multidão [moow-tcheedowng] *n* crowd

multiplicar [moow-tcheepleekah] *v* to multiply

mundo [moondoo] *n* world

município [moonee-seep-yoo] *n* municipality

muro [mooroo] *n* wall

músculo [moosh-kooloo] *n* muscle

museu [moozew] *n* museum

música [moozeeka] *n* music ▸ ouvir música to listen to music

músico, ca [moozeekoo] *n* musician

n

na [na] *prep* = em+a ▸ na estação at the station

nabo [naboo] *n* turnip

nação [nassowng] *n* nation

nacionalidade [nass-yonalee-dadjee] *n* nationality

nada [nada] *pron* nothing ▸ de nada you're welcome

nadador [nadadoh] *n* swimmer

nadar [nadah] *v* to swim

nádegas [nadegash] *npl* buttocks

namorado, da [namoradoo] *n* boyfriend, girlfriend

namorar [namorah] *v* ▸ namorar com to be going out with

não [nowng] *adv* no, not ▸ não sei I don't know ▸ não é? isn't it so? ▸ também não neither

nariz [nareej] *n* nose ▸ meter o nariz em to stick one's nose into ▸ dar com o nariz na porta to find the doors closed

nascer [nasseh] *v* to be born

nascido, da [nasseedoo] *adj* ▸ nascido a.../em... born on .../in ...

nascimento [nasseementoo] *n* birth

nata [nata] *n* cream

natação [natassowng] *n* swimming

Natal [natow] *n* Christmas

natural [natoorow] *adj* natural ▸ natural de ... native of ...

novela

In recent years, soap operas have become one of Brazil's most profitable exports. Fan clubs for the female stars can be found as far afield as China, due largely to their on-screen antics and romantic liaisons. In Brazil itself a surprisingly large slice of the daily TV schedule is devoted to these shows, which consist of a number of interwoven plots and scandals, usually running every day for about six months.

naturalidade [natooralee-dadjee] *n* ▸ de naturalidade brasileira born in Brazil

natureza [natooreza] *n* nature

navegador [navegadoh] *n* navigator

navegar [navegah] *v* to sail

navio [navee-oo] *n* ship

necessário, ria [nessessar-yoo] *adj* necessary

necessidade [nessessee-dadjee] *n* need ▸ em caso de necessidade if need be

negativo, va [nega-tcheevoo] *adj & n* negative

negociar [negossee-ah] *v* to trade

negócio [negoss-yoo] *n* business ▸ um negócio da China a profitable deal

nem [neng] *adv* nor ▸ nem eu not even I ▸ nem... nem... neither... nor...

nenhum, ma [nen-yoong] *adj* no ◆ *pron* none ▸ em lado nenhum nowhere

nervoso, sa [neh-vozoo] *adj* nervous

neto, ta [netoo] *n* grandson, granddaughter

neve [nevee] *n* snow

nevoeiro [nev-way-roo] *n* fog

ninguém [neengayng] *pron* nobody ▸ não tem ninguém there's nobody there

ninho [neen-yoo] *n* nest

nível [neevew] *n* level

no [noo] *prep* = em+o

nó [no] *n* knot

nobre [nobree] *adj & n* noble

nódoa [nod-wa] *n* stain

noite [noy-tchee] *n* night ▸ à noite at night ▸ esta noite tonight; *(previous)* last night ▸ boa noite! good evening!; *(before going to bed)* good night!

noiva [noy-va] *n* bride ▸ os noivos the bride and groom

nome [nomee] *n* name ▸ nome de família surname, last name ▸ nome de solteira maiden name ▸ nome próprio proper noun

nora [nora] *n* daughter-in-law

normal [noh-mow] *adj* normal

norte [noh-tchee] *n* north

nos [nosh] *pron (object)* us

nós [nosh] *pron (subject)* we

nosso, ssa [nossoo] *adj* our ◆ *pron* ours

nota [nota] *n* note; *(money)* bill

notícia [noteess-ya] *npl* news ▸ ouvir as notícias *(on radio, TV)* to listen to the news ▸ ser notícia to be in the news

noticiário [noteess-yaryoo] *n (on radio, TV)* news bulletin

novela [novella] *n* soap (opera)

novembro [novembroo] *n* November

novidade [novee-dadjee] *n* piece of news

novo, va [novoo] *adj* new ▸ de novo again ▸ Ano Novo New Year

noz [noj] *n* nut ▸ noz moscada nutmeg

nu, a [noo] *adj* naked

nublado, da [noobladoo] *adj* cloudy

▸ céu nublado cloudy sky

número [noomeroo] *n* number; *(referring to clothes)* size

nunca [noonka] *adv* never ▸ nunca mais never again

nuvem [nooveng] *n* cloud

obedecer [obedesseh] *v* to obey

objetivo, va [objetcheevoo] *adj & n* objective

objeto [objetoo] *n* object

obra [obra] *n* work ▸ em obras under repair ▸ obra-prima masterpiece

obrigado, da [obreegadoo] *excl* thank you ▸ muito obrigado/a thank you very much

obrigatório, ria [obreegator-yoo] *adj* obligatory

ocasião [okazee-owng] *n* time; *(opportunity)* chance

oceano [oss-yanoo] *n* ocean

oculista [okooleeshta] *n* optician

óculos [okooloosh] *npl* glasses ▸ óculos escuros sunglasses ▸ óculos de grau prescription glasses

ocupado, da [okoopadoo] *adj* busy

ocupar [okoopah] *v* to occupy ▸ ocupar-se de to look after

odiar [od-yah] *v* to hate

oeste [westchee] *n* west ▸ a oeste (de) to the west (of)

ofendido, da [ofendjeedoo] *adj* offended

oferecer [oferesseh] *v* to offer

oficina [ofee-seena] *n* workshop

oftalmologista [oftow-molojeeshta] *n* ophthalmologist

olá [ola] *excl* hi!

óleo [olee-oo] *n* oil

olhar [ol-yah] *v* to look ▸ olha! look!

olho [ol-yoo] *n* eye

ombro [ombroo] *n* shoulder

onda [onda] *n* wave

onde [ondjee] *adv* where ▸ onde você está? where are you? ▸ onde você vai? where are you going? ▸ de onde você vem? where do you come from?

ontem [onteng] *adv* yesterday ▸ ontem à noite last night ▸ isso é para ontem that's another day

opção [opsowng] *n* choice

operação [operassowng] *n* operation

operado, da [operado] *adj* operated ▸ ser operado to have an operation

operário, ria [operar-yoo] *n* worker

opinião [opeen-yowng] *n* opinion

opor(-se) [opoh-(see)] *v* to oppose

Ouro Preto

Ouro Preto's heyday spanned the 18th century, when it was the wealthiest town in Brazil, thanks to the gold mines of the Minas Gerais region. Now classified as a World Heritage Site by UNESCO, the streets, churches and pumice-stone pavements have been preserved as they were in the days of the gold rush. Ouro Preto is also home to a style of architecture known as *Mineiro Baroque*, whose greatest exponent is widely considered to be the mulatto Aleijadinho.

oposto, ta [oposhtoo] *adj* opposite

ora [ora] *excl* ▸ ora essa! come off it!, stop! ▸ ora bolas! oh, hell!

ordem [oh-deng] *n* order

ordenado [oh-denadoo] *n* salary

orelha [orel-ya] *n* ear

organizar [oh-ganeezah] *v* to organize

órgão [oh-gowng] *n* organ

orgulhoso, sa [oh-gool-yozoo] *adj* proud

orientar(-se) [oree-entah-(see)] *v* to guide

oriente [oree-entchee] *n* East

origem [oreejeng] *n* origin ▸ ser de origem... to be of ... descent

original [oreejeenow] *adj* original

orquestra [oh-keshtra] *n* orchestra

o(s) [oo(sh)] *art* the ◆ *pron* ▸ o que what, the one that/which

osso [ossoo] *n* bone

ostra [oshtra] *n* oyster

ótimo, ma [otcheemoo] *adj* best ◆ *excl* great!

ou [o] *conj* or ▸ ou seja in other words

ourives [oreeveesh] *n* goldsmith

ouro [orou] *n* gold ▸ de ouro gold

Ouro Preto [oroo pretoo] *n* Ouro Preto

ousar [ozah] *v* to dare

outono [otonoo] *n* autumn

outra [otra] *pron* (an)other ▸ outra vez again

outro [otroo] *pron* (an)other ▸ o outro the other one ▸ um após o outro one after the other

outrora [otrora] *adv* in the past

outubro [otoobroo] *n* October

ouvido [oveedoo] *n* ear; *(sense)* hearing ▸ você tem dores de ouvido? do your ears ache? ▸ memorizei a música de ouvido I learned the music by ear

ouvir [oveeh] *v* to hear ▸ está ouvindo? are you listening?

ova [ova] *n* roe ▸ uma ova! no way!

ovelha [ovel-ya] *n* sheep

ovo [ovoo] *n* egg ▸ ovo cozido hard-boiled egg ▸ ovo frito fried egg ▸ ovo estrelado fried egg ▸ ovo quente soft-boiled egg ▸ ovos mexidos scrambled eggs

oxalá [oshala] *excl* let's hope so! ▸ oxalá que chova! I hope it rains!

p

paciência [passee-ensee-a] *n* patience
▸ paciência! it can't be helped!

paciente [passee-entchee] *adj & n* patient

padaria [padaree-a] *n* bakery

padeiro [paday-roo] *n* baker

pagamento [pagamentoo] *n* payment

pagar [pagah] *v* to pay ▸ pagar para ver to demand proof ▸ pagar em dinheiro to pay cash ▸ pagar caro to pay dearly

página [pajeena] *n* page

pago, ga [pagoo] *adj* paid ▸ já está pago it's already paid for ▸ 'entrada paga' 'entry fee'

pai [py] *n* father ▸ os pais the parents

país [pa-eesh] *n* country

paisagem [py-zajeng] *n* scenery

palácio [palass-yoo] *n* palace

paladar [paladah] *n* taste

palavra [palavra] *n* word ▸ palavra de honra word of honor ▸ ele é de palavra he keeps his promises

palavrão [palavrowng] *n* swear word

palha [pal-ya] *n* straw

pálido, da [paleedoo] *adj* pale

palma [pow-ma] *n* ▸ palmas das mãos palms of one's hands

palmeira [pow-may-ra] *n* palm tree

pampa [pampa] *n* pampas

panela [panella] *n* saucepan ▸ panela de pressão pressure cooker

panetone [pan-etonee] *n* panettone

pano [panoo] *n* cloth ▸ pano de pó dust rag ▸ pano de prato tea towel

pantanal [pantanow] *n* wetland

pão [powng] *n* bread ▸ pão amanhecido stale bread ▸ pão de centeio rye bread ▸ pão de forma sliced bread ▸ pão francês small baguette ▸ pão integral whole-wheat bread

pão-de-ló [powng-djee-lo] *n* sponge cake

Papa [papa] *n* Pope

papas [papash] *npl* porridge ▸ não ter papas na língua to be outspoken

---

o Pantanal

The seasonally-flooded plains of the Mato Grosso in western Brazil are inhabited by a huge variety of wildlife, including over 600 species of bird and 350 types of fish, as well as *jacarés* (crocodiles), *capivaras* (enormous rodents), anteaters, ocelots, iguanas, anacondas, cougars, jaguars and black howler monkeys. These wetlands, which extend over 230 square kilometers, are a favorite spot for ecotourism. The best time to visit is between May and September, when the floodwaters are at their lowest.

parques nacionais

Brazil boasts dozens of nature reserves and other environmentally-protected areas where the plants and wildlife are safe from economic exploitation. The most important of these are *Itatiaia* and *Bocaina* in the southeast, the *Pantanal* and *Amazônia*. In the northeast there are two marine reserves, *Fernando de Noronha* and *Abrolhos*.

papel [papew] *n* paper ▸ papel de alumínio tinfoil ▸ papel de embrulho wrapping paper ▸ papel higiênico toilet paper

papelaria [papelaree-a] *n* stationery store

par [pah] *n* pair

para [para] *prep* for ▸ para que in order that ▸ para com towards ▸ para quê? why?

parabéns! [parabengsh] *excl* congratulations! ▸ dar os parabéns to congratulate

pára-brisa [para-breeza] *n* windshield

pára-choque [para-shokee] *n* bumper

parada [parada] *n* stop ▸ parada de ônibus bus stop

parafuso [parafoozoo] *n* screw

paraíso [para-eezoo] *n* paradise

parar [parah] *v* to stop ▸ pára! stop! ▸ sem parar nonstop

parecer [paresseh] *v* to seem ▸ parece que... it appears that ... ▸ o que te parece? what do you think? ▸ parecer-se com to resemble

parede [paredjee] *n* wall

parque [pah-kee] *n* park ▸ parque de diversões amusement park ▸ parque gráfico printer's ▸ parque infantil playground

parte [pah-tchee] *n* part ▸ a maior parte (de) the majority (of) ▸ por toda a parte everywhere ▸ em qualquer parte anywhere

particular [pah-tcheekoolah] *adj* private

partida [pah-tcheeda] *n* departure; *(sport)* game, match

partido, da [pah-tcheedoo] *adj* broken ◆ *n* party

partilhar [pah-tcheel-yah] *v* to share

partir [pah-tcheeh] *v* to break; *(to go away)* to leave ▸ a partir de from

Páscoa [pashk-wa] *n* Easter

passado, da [passadoo] *n & adj* past ▸ no ano passado last year ▸ mal/bem passado rare/well done

passageiro [passajay-roo] *n* passenger

passagem [passajeng] *n* crossing ▸ estar de passagem to be passing through

passaporte [passapoh-tchee] *n* passport

passar [passah] *v* to pass; *(time)* to spend ▸ deixem passar! let me through, please! ▸ passar para trás to dupe ▸ passar desta para melhor to pass away ▸ passem muito bem! have a good time! ▸ passar a ferro to iron

pássaro [passaroo] *n* bird

passas [passash] *npl* raisins

passe [passee] *n (for bus, subway)* pass

passear [passee-ah] *v* to stroll

passeio [passayoo] *n* walk; *(in car, etc.)* ride

passo [passoo] *n* step

pasta [pashta] *n* paste; *(for documents)* briefcase ▸ pasta de dentes toothpaste ▸ pasta de atum tuna spread

pastel [pashtew] *n* pastry ▸ pastel de carne meat pastry ▸ pastel de frango chicken pastry ▸ pastel de queijo cheese pastry

pastelaria [pashtelaree-a] *n* pastry shop

pastilha [pashteel-ya] *n* pill

pata [pata] *n* foot

pátio [patee-oo] *n* patio

pato [patoo] *n* duck

patrão [patrowng] *n* boss

pau [pow] *n* stick

pavimento [paveementoo] *n* story

paz [paj] *n* peace ▸ deixe-me em paz! leave me alone!

pé [pe] *n* foot ▸ a pé on foot ▸ de pé standing ▸ ao pé de beside ▸ dar pé to touch the bottom

peça [pessa] *n* part

pedaço [pedassoo] *n* piece

pedágio [pedaj-yoo] *n* toll

pedestre [pedeshtree] *n* pedestrian ▸ 'rua só para pedestres' 'pedestrians only'

pedir [pedjeeh] *v* to ask for; *(in restaurant)* to order

pedra [pedra] *n* stone

pegar [pegah] *v* to pick up ▸ é pegar ou largar it's take it or leave it

peito [paytoo] *n* chest

peixaria [pay-sharee-a] *n* fish shop

peixe [payshee] *n* fish

pele [pelee] *n* skin

pelo, la [pelloo(pella)] *prep* = por+o(a) ▸ pelo caminho mais curto by the shortest route

pêlo [peloo] *n* hair

pena [pena] *n* penalty; *(of bird)* feather ▸ que pena! what a pity!

pensão [pensowng] *n* boarding house ▸ pensão completa *hotel room with all meals included*

pensar [pensah] *v* to think

pente [pentchee] *n* comb

pentear(-se) [pentchee-ah-(see)] *v* to do one's hair

pepino [pepeenoo] *n* cucumber

pequeno, na [pekenoo] *adj* small

pêra [pera] *n* pear

perceber [peh-sebeh] *v* to understand

percentagem [peh-sentajeng] *n* percentage

percurso [peh-kuh-soo] *n* route

perda [peh-da] *n* ▸ perda de peso weight loss ▸ perda de tempo waste of time

perdão [peh-downg] *n* pardon

perder [peh-deh] *v* to lose; *(bus, subway)* to miss ▸ perder-se to get lost ▸ perder o trem to miss the train

perdido, da [peh-djeedoo] *adj* ▸ estar perdido to be lost

pereira [peray-ra] *n* pear tree

perfeito, ta [peh-faytoo] *adj* perfect

perfume [peh-foomee] *n* perfume

pergunta [peh-goonta] *n* question

perguntar [peh-goontah] *v* to ask

perigo [pereegoo] *n* danger

perigoso, sa [pereegozoo] *adj* dangerous

periódico, ca [peree-odjeekoo] *n* periodical

período [peree-oodoo] *n* period

permanente [peh-manentchee] *adj* permanent

permitido, da [peh-meetcheedoo] *adj* allowed

permitir [peh-meetcheeh] *v* to allow

perna [peh-na] *n* leg

pernil [peh-neew] *n* ▸ pernil de ovelha leg of lamb

pérola [perola] *n* pearl

pertencer [peh-tenseh] *v* to belong

perto, ta [peh-too] *adj* nearby ◆ *adv* near ◆ *prep (in time)* soon

peru [peroo] *n* turkey

pesado, da [pezadoo] *adj* heavy

pesar [pezah] *v* sadness

pesca [peshka] *n* fishing

pescada [peshkada] *n* whiting

pescador, ra [peshkadoh] *n* fisherman, fisherwoman

pescar [peshkah] *v* to fish

pescoço [peshkosoo] *n* neck

peso [pezoo] *n* weight ▸ de peso important

pêssego [pessegoo] *n* peach

péssimo, ma [pesseemoo] *adj* terrible

pessoa [pessoa] *n* person ▸ as pessoas people

piada [pee-ada] *n* joke

picante [peekantchee] *adj* spicy

picar [peekah] *v* to bite ▸ ser picado por to be bitten by

pijama [peejama] *n* pajamas

pilha [peel-ya] *n* battery

pílula [peeloola] *n* pill ▸ pílula do dia seguinte morning-after pill

pimenta [peementa] *n (spice)* pepper

pimentão [peementowng] *n (vegetable)* pepper

pincel [peensew] *n* brush ▸ pincel de barba shaving brush

pinhão [peen-yowng] *n* pine nut

pinheiral [peenyay-row] *n* pine forest

pintado, da [peentadoo] *adj* colored

pintar [peentah] *v* to paint

pintor, ra [peentoh] *n* painter

pintura [peentoora] *n* painting

pior [pee-oh] *adj* worse ▸ o pior the worst

pipa [peepa] *n* barrel

piquenique [peekee-neekee] *n* picnic ▸ fazer um piquenique to have a picnic

pirulito [peerooleetoo] *n* lollipop

pisca-pisca [peeshka-peeshka] *n (on car)* turn signal

piscina [peesseena] *n* swimming pool

piso [peezoo] *n* floor

pista [peeshta] *n* track ▸ pista para ciclistas bicycle path or track (in park) ▸ pista de aterrissagem runway

placa [plaka] *n* plate ▸ placa elétrica hotplate

plano, na [planoo] *n* plan ◆ *adj* flat

planta [planta] *n* plant; *(of city)* map

plástico, ca [plash-tcheekoo] *n & adj* plastic

pneu [pnew] *n* tire

pó [po] *n* dust ▸ limpar o pó to dust

pobre [pobree] *adj* poor

poço [posoo] *n* well

poder [podeh] *n* power ♦ *v* to be able ▸ posso fumar? may I smoke? ▸ não pode ser! that's impossible!

pois [poysh] *conj* well ♦ *excl* ▸ pois é! indeed

polícia [poleess-ya] *n* police; *(agent)* police officer

político, ca [poleetcheekoo] *adj* political ♦ *n* politician

poluição [pol-weessowng] *n* pollution

polvo [powvoo] *n* octopus

pomada [pomada] *n* ointment

pomar [pomah] *n* orchard

pombo [pomboo] *n* dove

ponte [pontchee] *n* bridge

ponto [pontoo] *n* point ▸ três horas em ponto 3 o'clock on the dot ▸ ponto de luz wall socket ▸ ponto morto *(in car)* neutral ▸ ponto de referência point of reference ▸ ponto de vista point of view ▸ pontos cardeais cardinal points

população [popoo-lassowng] *n* population

popular [popoolah] *adj* popular

por [poh] *prep* by, through ▸ por dia/hora daily/hourly

pôr [poh] *v* to put

porcaria [poh-karee-a] *n* filth

porco [poh-koo] *n* pig; *(meat)* pork

porém [poreng] *conj* however

porque [poh-kee] *conj* because ▸ por que não? why not?

porquê [poh-kay] *adv* why

porta [poh-ta] *n* door

porta-bagagem [poh-ta-bagajeng] *n* trunk

portanto [poh-tantoo] *conj* therefore

portátil [poh-tatcheew] *adj & n* portable

porteiro [poh-tayroo] *n* janitor ▸ porteiro eletrônico intercom system

porto [poh-too] *n* port

português, esa [poh-toogesh] *adj* Portuguese

posição [pozeessowng] *n* position

possibilidade [possee-beeleedadjee] *n* possibility

possível [posseevew] *adj* possible ▸ o mais cedo possível as soon as possible

postal [poshtow] *n* postcard

posto [poshtoo] *n* post ▸ posto de saúde health center

potável [potavew] *adj* ▸ água potável drinking water

pouco, ca [pokoo] *adj & n* little ▸ um pouco (de) a little

poupar [popah] *v* to save

pousada [pozada] *n* inn

povo [povoo] *n* people

praça [prassa] *n* square; *(business)* market

praia [pry-a] *n* beach

prancha [pransha] *n* plank ▸ prancha de surf surfboard

prata [prata] *n* silver

prateleira [pra-telay-ra] *n* shelf

praticar [pratcheekah] *v* to practice ▸ praticar alpinismo to go skiing

prático, ca [pratcheekoo] *adj* practical

prato [pratoo] *n* plate ▸ prato do dia dish of the day ▸ prato principal main dish

prazer [prazeh] *n* pleasure ▸ muito prazer! delighted!

precedente [pressedentchee] *adj* preceding ♦ *n* precedent

precioso, sa [press-yozoo] *adj* precious

precisar [presseezah] *v* to need
▸ precisar de to need

preciso, sa [presseezoo] *adj* precise ▸ é preciso... it is necessary ...

preço [pressoo] *n* price

prédio [predjoo] *n* building

preencher [pre-ensheh] *v* to fill in
▸ preencha o formulário fill in the form

preferência [preferenss-ya] *n* preference ▸ de preferência preferably

preferido, da [prefereedoo] *adj* favorite

prego [pregoo] *n* nail; *(shop)* pawnshop

prejudicar [prejoodjeekah] *v* to damage

prenda [prenda] *n* gift ▸ prendas domésticas housework

prender [prendeh] *v* to tie

preocupação [pre-okoopassowng] *n* worry

preocupar(-se) [pre-okoopah-(see)] *v* to worry ▸ não se preocupe! don't worry!

preparar [preparah] *v* to prepare

presente [prezentchee] *adj & n* present

preservado, da [prezeh-vadoo] *adj* preserved

preservativo [prezeh-vatcheevoo] *n* preservative; condom, rubber

pressa [pressa] *n* ▸ estar com pressa to be in a hurry

prestativo, va [preshta-tcheevoo] *adj* helpful

presunto [prezoontoo] *n* ham

preto, ta [pretoo] *adj & n* black

previsões [preveezoynsh] *npl* ▸ previsões meteorológicas weather forecast

primavera [primav-aira] *n* spring

primeiro, ra [preemayroo] *adj & adv* first

primo, ma [preemoo] *n* cousin

principiante [preenseep-yantchee] *n* beginner

princípio [preenseep-yoo] *n* beginning; *(norm)* principle ▸ a princípio at first ▸ em princípio in principle

prisão [preezowng] *n* arrest; *(jail)* prison

privado, da [preevadoo] *adj* private

problema [problemma] *n* problem

procurar [prokoorah] *v* to look for

produto [prodootoo] *n* product

professor, ra [professoh] *n* teacher

profissão [profeessowng] *n* profession

profundo, da [profoondoo] *adj* deep

programa [programa] *n* program

progresso [progressoo] *n* ▸ fazer progressos to make progress

proibido, da [pro-eebeedoo] *adj* forbidden ▸ 'proibido colar cartazes' 'post no bills' ▸ 'proibido o acesso' 'access prohibited'

prometer [prometeh] *v* to promise

pronto, ta [prontoo] *adj* ready ▸ estar pronto to be ready ▸ de pronto promptly

pronunciar [pronoonsee-ah] *v* to pronounce

propor [propoh] *v* to propose

propósito [propozeetoo] *n* purpose ▸ a propósito by the way ▸ de propósito on purpose

proprietário [propree-etaryoo] *n* owner

próprio, pria [propree-oo] *adj* proper; *(belonging to)* own ▸ é próprio para... it is suitable for ...

proteger(-se) [protejeh-(see)] *v* to protect

protestante [protesh-tantchee] *adj & n* Protestant

provar [provah] v to prove; *(food)* to taste; *(dress)* to try on

proveito [provay-too] n ▸ bom proveito! enjoy your food!

próximo, ma [prosseemoo] adj close; *(following)* next ▸ até a próxima! until next time!

prudente [proodentchee] adj cautious

publicidade [poobleessee-dadjee] n publicity

público, ca [poobleekoo] adj & n public

pudim [poodjeeng] n pudding ▸ pudim de leite milk pudding

pulmão [poowmowng] n lung

pulseira [poowsay-ra] n bracelet

pulso [poowsoo] n wrist ▸ tomar o pulso to take the pulse

puro, ra [pooroo] adj pure

puxar [pooshah] v to pull ▸ 'puxe' 'pull'

q

quadril [kwadreew] n hip

quadro [kwadroo] n frame

quais [kwysh] adj & conj which

qual [kwow] adj & conj which

qualidade [kwaleedadjee] n quality

qualquer [kwowkeh] pron any

quando [kwandoo] adv when

quanto [kwantoo] adj how much ▸ quanto é que custa? how much does it cost? ▸ há quanto tempo...? how long ago ... ?

quarta-feira [kwah-ta-fay-ra] n Wednesday

quarteirão [kwah-tay-rowng] n block

quarto [kwah-too] n room; *(amount)* quarter ▸ quarto de hóspedes guest room ▸ um quarto de hora a quarter of an hour

quase [kwazee] adv almost

que [kee] pron that, which, who, what ▸ e que mais? and what else? ▸ o que é que...? what is it ... ?

quê [ke] n ▸ não tem de quê don't mention it

queda [keda] n fall ▸ em queda livre in free fall

queijo [kay-joo] n cheese ▸ queijo prato processed cheese ▸ queijo ralado grated cheese

queima [kay-ma] n *(commerce)* clearance sale

queimada [kay-mada] n burning

queimado, da [kay-madoo] adj burnt

queimadura [kay-madoora] n burn ▸ queimadura de segundo grau second-degree burn

queimar(-se) [kay-mah-(see)] v to burn; *(from sun)* to get sunburnt

queixa [kay-sha] n complaint ▸ apresentar queixa to put in a complaint

queixo [kay-shoo] n chin

quem [keng] pron who ▸ quem é? who is it?

quente [kentchee] adj hot

querer [kereh] v to want ▸ o que vão

querer? what will you be having? ▶ eu queria... I'd like ... ▶ quer dizer in other words ▶ querer dizer to mean ▶ sem querer unintentionally

querido, da [kereedoo] *adj* dear

quilo [keeloo] *n* kilo

quilômetro [keelometroo] *n* kilometer

quinta-feira [keenta-fay-ra] *n* Thursday

r

rã [hang] *n* frog

rabanada [habanada] *n* French toast

raça [hassa] *n* race

radiador [hadjadoh] *n* radiator

rádio [hadjoo] *n* radio

raio [hy-oo] *n* ray

raiz [ha-eesh] *n* root

rajada [hajada] *n* gust

ralado, da [haladoo] *adj* grated

ramo [hamoo] *n* branch ▶ ramo de flores bunch of flowers

rapaz [hapash] *n* boy

rápido, da [hapeedoo] *adj* fast

raramente [haramentchee] *adv* seldom

raro, ra [haroo] *adj* rare

rasgado, da [hajgadoo] *adj* torn

rato [hatoo] *n* rat

razão [hazowng] *n* reason ▶ não tem razão you are wrong

reação [he-assowng] *n* reaction

realidade [he-aleedadjee] *n* ▶ na realidade actually

realizar [he-aleezah] *v* to carry out

rebanho [heban-yoo] *n* herd

reboque [hebokee] *n* tow ▶ a reboque *(car)* in tow

recarregar [heka-hegah] *v* to reload

receber [hessebeh] *v* to receive

receita [hessay-ta] *n* income; *(medical)* prescription

recente [hessentchee] *adj* recent

recepção [hessepsowng] *n* reception desk ▶ na recepção at the reception desk

recepcionista [hessepsee-oneeshta] *n* receptionist

recheado, da [heshee-adoo] *adj* filled

recibo [hesseeboo] *n* receipt

recomendar [hekomendah] *v* to recommend

reconhecer [hekon-yesseh] *v* to recognize

recordação [hekoh-dassowng] *n* memory

recordar(-se) [hekoh-dah-(see)] *v* to remember

recuar [hekoo-ah] *v* to step back ▶ recuem! get back!

recusar [hekoozah] *v* to refuse

redação [hedassowng] *n* essay

rede [hedjee] *n* net; *(for sleeping)* hammock ▶ rede de computadores computer network ▶ rede de distribuição distribution network ▶ rede local local network

redondo, da [hedondoo] *adj* round

redução [hedoossowng] *n* reduction

reduzido, da [hedoozeedoo] *adj* reduced

reduzir [hedoozeeh] *v* to reduce ▸ 'reduza a velocidade' 'slow down'

reembolsar [he-embolsah] *v* to repay ▸ ser reembolsado to be refunded

refeição [hefay-sowng] *n* meal

reforma [hefoh-ma] *n* reform; *(renewal)* repair ▸ reforma agrária agrarian reform

reformado, da [hefoh-madoo] *adj* reformed

refresco [hefreshkoo] *n* drink made from freshly-squeezed fruit

refrigerante [hefree-jerantchee] *n* soda

refúgio [hefooj-yoo] *n* refuge

regar [hegah] *v* to water

região [hej-yowng] *n* region

registrado, da [hejeesh-tradoo] *adj* registered

registro [hejeeshtroo] *n* register ▸ registro civil *office where civil marriages are performed and births, deaths, etc. are recorded*

regra [hegra] *n* rule

regressar [hegressah] *v* to return

regresso [hegressoo] *n* return

relação [helassowng] *n* relationship ▸ ter relações sexuais to have intercourse

relacionar [helass-yonah] *v* to list

relâmpago [helampagoo] *n* lightning

religião [heleej-yowng] *n* religion

relógio [heloj-yoo] *n* clock

remar [hemah] *v* to row

remédio [hemedjoo] *n* remedy

remetente [hemetentchee] *n* sender

renda [henda] *n* income; *(clothing)* lace

rendimento [hendjee-mentoo] *n* profit

reparar [heparah] *v* to repair ▸ mandar reparar to have repaired ▸ reparar em to notice

repatriar [hepatree-ah] *v* to repatriate

repente [hepentchee] *n* ▸ de repente suddenly

repetir [hepetcheeh] *v* to repeat

reportagem [hepoh-tajeng] *n* report

reproduzir [heprodoozeeh] *v* to reproduce

requeijão [hekay-jowng] *n* soft cheese

rescisão [hesseezowng] *n* annulment

reservado, da [hezeh-vadoo] *adj* reserved

reservar [hezeh-vah] *v* to reserve ▸ reservar a passagem to book a ticket

resfriado [heshfree-adoo] *n* cold

residência [hezee-densee-a] *n* residence

residente [hezeedentchee] *adj* & *n* resident

resolver [hezow-veh] *v* to solve; *(resolve)* to decide

respeitar [heshpay-tah] *v* to respect

respiração [heshpeer-assowng] *n* breathing

responder [heshpondeh] *v* to reply

responsabilidade [heshponsa-beelee-dadjee] *n* responsibility

responsável [heshpon-savew] *adj* responsible

resposta [heshposhta] *n* reply

ressaca [hessaka] *n* rough sea

ressoar [hess-wah] *v* to resound

restaurante [heshtow-rantchee] *n* restaurant

resto [heshtoo] *n* rest, remainder ▸ restos mortais mortal remains

rodízio

For the visitor with a healthy appetite, Brazilian *rodízio* restaurants are heaven on earth. For a set price, a whole parade of different meats is served up to the customer, ranging from tongue to the tenderest rump steak. For vegetarians, there are also salad *rodízios*, served – like their meat counterparts – with rice, beans and a special topping called *farofa* (fried cassava flour).

retângulo [hetangooloo] *n* rectangle

retrato [hetratoo] *n* portrait

reumatismo [hewma-tcheejmoo] *n* rheumatism

revelar [hevelah] *v* to reveal ▸ mandar revelar *(photos)* to have developed

revista [heveeshta] *n* magazine; *(inspection)* search

revolução [hevo-loossowng] *n* revolution

riacho [hee-ashoo] *n* stream

rico, ca [heekoo] *adj* rich

ridículo, la [heedjeekooloo] *adj* ridiculous

rim [heeng] *n* kidney ▸ os rins the lower back

rio [hee-oo] *n* river

riqueza [heekeza] *n* wealth

rir [heeh] *v* to laugh

riscar [heeshkah] *v* to scratch

risco [heeshkoo] *n* scratch

rissole [hee-solee] *n* *small cake of seasoned, ground meat or poultry coated in breadcrumbs and egg, then fried* ▸ rissoles de camarão/carne fried shrimp/meat cakes

robe [hobee] *n* dressing gown

rocha [hosha] *n* rock

rochedo [hoshedoo] *n* crag

roda [hoda] *n* wheel ▸ andar à roda to walk around ▸ roda da frente front wheel

rodada [hodada] *n* round (of drinks)

rodeado, da [hodjee-adoo] *adj* surrounded

rodela [hodela] *n* slice

rodízio [hodjeezyoo] *n* restaurant

rojão [hojowng] *n* rocket

rolha [hol-ya] *n* cork

rolo [holoo] *n* roller; *(of paper)* roll

romã [homang] *n* pomegranate

romance [homansee] *n* novel; *(love)* romance

rosa [hoza] *n* rose

rosnar [hojnah] *v* to growl

rosto [hoshtoo] *n* face

roto, ta [hotoo] *adj* torn

rótula [hotoola] *n* label

roubar [hobah] *v* to steal

roupa [hopa] *n* clothes ▸ roupa de baixo underwear

roupeiro [hopay-roo] *n* wardrobe

roxo, xa [ho-shoo] *adj* violet

rua [hoo-a] *n* street

ruído [hweedoo] *n* noise

ruínas [hweenash] *npl* ruins

ruivo, va [hweevoo] *adj* red-haired

rum [hoong] *n* rum

s

sábado [sabadoo] *n* Saturday

sabão [sabowng] *n* soap

saber [sabeh] *v* to know

sabonete [sabonetchee] *n mild soap, often colored and perfumed*

sabor [saboh] *n* taste

saboroso, sa [saborozoo] *adj* tasty

saca-rolhas [saka-hol-yash] *n* corkscrew

saco [sakoo] *n* bag ▶ saco de dormir sleeping bag ▶ saco de lixo garbage bag

sagrado, da [sagradoo] *adj* sacred

saia [sy-a] *n* skirt

saída [sa-eeda] *n* exit ▶ 'saída de emergência' 'emergency exit'

sair [sa-eeh] *v* to go out ▶ sair com alguém to go out with somebody

sal [sow] *n* salt

sala [sala] *n* room ▶ sala de espera waiting room ▶ sala de estar living room ▶ sala de jantar dining room

salada [salada] *n* salad ▶ salada de alface green salad

salário [salar-yoo] *n* wage ▶ salário mínimo minimum wage

saldos [sow-doosh] *npl* sales

salgadinho [sowgadeen-yoo] *n* savory

salgado, da [sow-gadoo] *adj* salted

salmão [sow-mowng] *n* salmon

salpicão [sow-peekowng] *n* smoked sausage

salsa [sowsa] *n* parsley

salsicha [sow-seesha] *n* sausage

saltar [sow-tah] *v* to jump

salto [sowtoo] *n* jump; (*on shoe*) heel ▶ salto em altura high jump ▶ salto de vara pole vault

salvar [sowvah] *v* to save

salva-vidas [sowva-veedash] *n* lifeguard

salvo, va [sowvoo] *adj* safe ◆ *prep* except for

samba [samba] *n* samba

sandália [sandal-ya] *n* sandal

sanduíche [sandweeshee] *n* sandwich

sangrar [sangrah] *v* to bleed

---

samba

Samba has its roots in African drumming and the provocative dancing that accompanies it. The *samba* rhythm springs from a bittersweet mixture of melancholy and joy that seemingly has the power to make almost anybody get up and dance. Whilst there are now numerous different types of *samba*, perhaps the best known is *samba-enredo*, a musical story that livens up Carnival parades.

sangue [sangee] *n* blood

sanitário [saneetar-yoo] *n* bath

santinho [santeen-yoo] *adj* religious figurine

santo, ta [santoo] *adj* holy ♦ *n* saint

são [sowng] *n* Saint

sapataria [sapataree-a] *n* shoe store

sapateiro [sapatay-roo] *n* shoemaker

sapatilha [sapateel-ya] *n* slipper

sapato [sapatoo] *n* shoe ▶ sapatos de salto alto high heels

saquinho [sakeen-yoo] *n* tea bag

sarampo [sarampoo] *n* measles

sardinha [sah-deen-ya] *n* sardine

saudade [sow-dadjee] *n* nostalgia ▶ sentir saudades de alguém to miss somebody

saudável [sow-davew] *adj* healthy

saúde [sa-oodjee] *n* health ▶ estar com boa saúde to be in good health ▶ saúde! cheers!

se [see] *pron* himself, herself, yourself, themselves ▶ se diz que... it is said that ... ▶ cale-se! shut up!

se [see] *conj* if ▶ se quiser if you wish

sé [se] *n* cathedral ▶ a Santa Sé the Holy See

seca [seka] *n* drought ▶ que seca! how boring!

secador [sekadoh] *n* ▶ secador de cabelo hair dryer

seção [sessowng] *n (in shop)* section

secar [sekah] *v* to dry ▶ pôr para secar to put out to dry

seco, ca [sekoo] *adj* dry

secretaria [sekretaree-a] *n* secretary's office

século [sekooloo] *n* century

seda [seda] *n* silk

sede [sedjee] *n* thirst

segredo [segredoo] *n* secret

seguido, da [seg-eedoo] *adj* following ▶ em seguida next

seguinte [seg-eentchee] *adj* following

seguir [seg-eeh] *v* to follow ▶ siga adiante! go straight ahead!

segunda-feira [segoonda-fay-ra] *n* Monday

segundo, da [segoondoo] *n & adj* second ♦ *adv* according to

segurança [segooransa] *n* safety, security

segurar [segoorah] *v* to hold

seguro, ra [segorooo] *adj* safe ♦ *n* insurance ▶ seguro contra roubo insurance against theft ▶ seguro contra terceiros third-party insurance

selecionar [seless-yonah] *v* to select

selo [seloo] *n* stamp

selvagem [sew-vajeng] *adj* wild

sem [seng] *prep* without ▶ sem-teto homeless person

semáforo [semaforoo] *n* traffic lights

semana [semana] *n* week ▶ durante a semana during the week ▶ dia de semana weekday

semanário [semanar-yoo] *n (newspaper)* weekly

semente [sementchee] *n* seed

sempre [sempree] *adv* always ▶ sempre que whenever ▶ nem sempre not always

senão [senowng] *conj* or else

senhor [sen-yoh] *n* gentleman

senhora [sen-yora] *n* lady

sensação [sensa-sowng] *n* feeling

sensível [senseevew] *adj* sensitive

senso [sensoo] *n* sense ▸ ter senso de humor to have a sense of humor

sentar-se [sentah-(see)] *v* to sit ▸ sentem-se sit down

sentido [sentcheedoo] *n* meaning; *(feeling)* sense ▸ os cinco sentidos the five senses ▸ sentido horário clockwise ▸ sentido figurado figurative sense ▸ fazer sentido to make sense

sentir-se [sentcheeh-(see)] *v* to feel; *(be sorry)* to regret ▸ sentir-se bem/mal to feel well/ill

separar(-se) [separah-(see)] *v* to separate

ser [seh] *v* to be ▸ a não ser que unless ▸ é tarde it's late

sério, ria [sair-yoo] *adj* serious

serra [se-ha] *n* mountain range; *(tool)* saw

sertão [seh-towng] *n* wilderness

serviço [seh-veessoo] *n* service ▸ dar serviço to take a lot of effort ▸ 'fora de serviço' 'out of order' ▸ serviço de informações information service ▸ serviço militar military service

servir [seh-veeh] *v* to serve ▸ sirva-se help yourself

sessão [sessowng] *n* performance

sesta [seshta] *n* siesta

setembro [setembroo] *n* September

seu(s) [sew] *pron* his/hers/yours/theirs ◆ *adj* his/her/your/their ▸ é o seu it's his/hers/yours/theirs

sexo [sexoo] *n* sex

sexta-feira [seshta-fay-ra] *n* Friday

sidra [seedra] *n* cider

significado [seegneefee-kadoo] *n (of word)* meaning

significar [seegneefee-kah] *v* to mean

silêncio [seelenss-yoo] *n* silence

sim [seeng] *adv* yes

simpático, ca [seempatcheekoo] *adj* pleasant

simples [seempleesh] *adj* simple

sinagoga [seena-goga] *n* synagogue

sinal [seenow] *n* sign; *(warning)* signal ▸ sinal de pontuação punctuation mark ▸ sinal de trânsito traffic light

sincero, ra [seen-seroo] *adj* sincere

síncope [seen-kopee] *n* fainting spell

sindicato [seendjee-katoo] *n* union

sino [seenoo] *n* bell

sintoma [seentoma] *n* symptom

sistema [seesh-tema] *n* system ▸ sistema nervoso nervous system

sítio [seet-yoo] *n* place

situação [seet-wassowng] *n* situation

só [so] *adj* alone ◆ *adv* only ▸ é só dizer just say the word

sob [sob] *prep* under ▸ sob pena de... on pain of ...

sobrancelha [sobransel-ya] *n* eyebrow

sobrar [sobrah] *v* to be left over

sobras [sobrash] *npl* leftovers

sobre [sobree] *prep* on, over

sobremesa [sobree-meza] *n* dessert

sobrevivente [sobree-veeventchee] *n* survivor

sobrinho [sobreen-yoo] *n* nephew

sociedade [sossee-edadjee] *n* society

sócio [soss-yoo] *n* partner ▸ 'só para sócios' 'members only'

socorro [sokohoo] *n* help ▸ socorro! help! ▸ pedir socorro to ask for help

sofá [sofa] *n* sofa ▸ sofá-cama sofa bed

sofrer [sofreh] *v* to suffer

sogro, gra [sogroo] *n* father-in-law, mother-in-law

sol [sow] *n* sun ▸ ao sol in the sun

sólido, da [soleedoo] *adj* solid

solo [soloo] *n* ground

soltar(-se) [sowtah-(see)] *v* to release

solteiro [sow-tayroo] *n* single

solto, ta [sowtoo] *adj* loose ▸ à solta on the loose

som [song] *n* sound

soma [soma] *n* sum

somar [somah] *v* to add up

sombra [sombra] *n* shadow ▸ à sombra in the shade

sombrio [sombree-oo] *n* shady

sonhar [son-yah] *v* to dream

sonho [son-yoo] *n* dream

sonífero [soneeferoo] *n* soporific

sono [so-noo] *n* sleep ▸ estar com/ter sono to be sleepy

sopa [sopa] *n* soup

sorrir [so-heeh] *v* to smile

sorriso [so-heezoo] *n* smile

sorte [soh-tchee] *n* ▸ boa sorte! good luck! ▸ ter sorte to be lucky

sorvete [soh-vetchee] *n* ice cream; sorbet

sossegado, da [sossegadoo] *adj* quiet ▸ fique sossegado keep calm

sótão [sotowng] *n* attic

sotaque [sotakee] *n* accent

sozinho, nha [sozeen-yoo] *adj* all alone

sua(s) [soo-a] *pron* his/hers/yours/theirs ◆ *adj* his/her/your/their

suar [soo-ah] *v* to sweat

suave [swavee] *adj* smooth

subida [soobeeda] *n* climb

subir [soobeeh] *n* to go up

subsídio [soobseed-yoo] *n* subsidy

subsistência [soobseesh-tenssee-a] *n* subsistence

subsolo [soob-soloo] *n* basement

substituir [soobshtee-tweeh] *v* to replace

subtrair [soobtra-eeh] *v* to steal

subúrbio [sooboorb-yoo] *n* suburb

suco [sookoo] *n* juice ▸ suco de laranja orange juice ▸ suco de limão lemon juice

suficiente [soofeess-yentchee] *adj* enough

sufocar [soofokah] *v* to suffocate

sujar(-se) [soojah-(see)] *v* to dirty

sujeito [soojay-too] *n* person

sujo, ja [soojoo] *adj* dirty

sul [soow] *n* south ▸ a sul (de) to the south (of)

supermercado [soopeh-meh-kadoo] *n* supermarket

suplementar [sooplementah] *adj* extra

suplemento [sooplementoo] *n* supply

suportar [soopoh-tah] *v* to bear

supositório [soopozee-toryoo] *n* suppository

surdo, da [sooh-doo] *adj* deaf ▸ surdo-mudo deaf and dumb

surfar [sooh-fah] *v* to surf

surpresa [sooh-preza] *n* surprise

suspiro [soosh-peeroo] *n* sigh ▸ suspiros meringues

sustar [sooshtah] *v* to stop ▸ sustar um cheque to stop payment on a check

sutiã [sootyang] *n* bra

tabacaria [tabakaree-a] *n* tobacconist

tabaco [tabakoo] *n* tobacco

tabela [tabela] *n* ▸ tabela de preços price list ▸ tabela periódica periodic table

tábua [tabwa] *n* board ▸ tábua da carne cutting board ▸ tábua de passar ironing board

tachar [tashah] *v* to brand as

tainha [ta-een-ya] *n (fish)* mullet

tal [tow] *pron* such ▸ tal e qual just like

talão [talowng] *n* stub ▸ talão de cheques checkbook

talher [tal-yeh] *n* set of cutlery

talho [tal-yoo] *n* cut

talvez [tow-vesh] *adv* perhaps

tamanho [taman-yoo] *n* size

também [tambeng] *adv* also

tamborim [tamboreeng] *n* tambourine

tampa [tampa] *n* lid

tampão [tampowng] *n* tampon

tampo [tampoo] *n* lid

tangerina [tanjereena] *n* tangerine

tanque [tankee] *n* tank ▸ tanque de lavar roupa washtub

tanto [tantoo] *adv* so much

tão [towng] *adv* so

tapar [tapah] *v* to cover; *(reseal)* to close ▸ tapar a vista to block the view

tapete [tapetchee] *n* rug

tarde [tah-djee] *adj* late ◆ *n* afternoon, evening ▸ boa tarde! *(early)* good afternoon!; *(late)* good evening!

tarifa [tareefa] *n* tariff ▸ tarifa normal normal rate ▸ tarifa reduzida reduced rate

tartaruga [tah-tarooga] *n* turtle

taxa [tasha] *n* rate ▸ taxa de aeroporto airport tax ▸ taxa de câmbio exchange rate

te [tchee] *pron* you ▸ eu te amo I love you

teatro [tchee-atroo] *n* theater

tecido [tesseedoo] *n* cloth

tecla [tekla] *n* key

técnico [tekneekoo] *n* technician

teleférico [telefereekoo] *n* cable car

telefonar [telefonah] *v* to phone

telefone [telefonee] *n* telephone

telefonema [telefonema] *n* phone call

telefonista [telefoneeshta] *n (on phone)* operator

telegrama [telegrama] *n* telegram

telejornal [telejoh-now] *n* television news

telenovela [telenovela] *n* soap opera

televisão [televeezowng] *n* television

telhado [tel-yadoo] *n* roof

tema [tema] *n* subject

temperado, da [temperadoo] *adj (weather)* temperate; *(food)* seasoned

temperatura [temperatoora] *n* temperature ▸ medir/tirar a temperatura to take one's temperature

tempero [temperoo] *n* seasoning

tempestade [tempeshtadjee] *n* storm

templo [temploo] *n* temple

tempo [tempoo] *n* time; *(climate)* weather ▶ a tempo on time ▶ há muito tempo a long time ago

temporada [temporada] *n* season

temporal [temporow] *n* storm

temporário, ria [temporar-yoo] *adj* temporary

tenda [tenda] *n* tent

tendão [tendowng] *n* tendon

tenro, ra [ten-hoo] *adj* tender ▶ carne tenra tender meat

tensão [tensowng] *n* tension ▶ alta tensão high voltage ▶ tensão alta high blood pressure ▶ tensão baixa low blood pressure

tenso, sa [tensoo] *adj* tense

tentar [tentah] *v* to try

ter [teh] *v* to have; *(obligation)* to have to ▶ tenho que descansar I have to rest

terça-feira [teh-sa-fay-ra] *n* Tuesday

terminar [teh-meenah] *v* to finish

término [teh-meenoo] *n* end

termo [teh-moo] *n* end; *(of contract)* term

termômetro [teh-mometroo] *n* thermometer

terra [te-ha] *n* land, earth ▶ terra natal land of birth

terraço [tehassoo] *n* terrace ▶ no terraço on the terrace

terreno [tehenoo] *n* ground

território [tehee-toryoo] *n* territory

terrível [teheevew] *adj* terrible

tesoura [tezora] *n* scissors

tesouro [tezoroo] *n* treasure

testa [teshta] *n* forehead

teste [tesh-tchee] *n* ▶ teste do bafômetro Breathalyzer® test

teto [tetoo] *n* ceiling

teu(s) [tew(sh)] *pron* yours ◆ *adj* your ▶ é o teu it's yours

tia [tchee-a] *n* aunt

tigela [tcheejela] *n* bowl

tímido, da [tcheemeedoo] *adj* shy

tinta [tcheenta] *n* paint; *(for writing)* ink ▶ 'tinta fresca' 'wet paint'

tio [tchee-oo] *n* uncle

típico, ca [tcheepeekoo] *adj* typical

tipo [tcheepoo] *n* type

tirar [tcheerah] *v* to take ▶ tirar um dente to pull a tooth ▶ tirar uma cópia to make a copy

toalha [twal-ya] *n* towel

tocar [tokah] *v* to touch; *(instrument)* to play; *(telephone)* to ring ▶ tocar violino to play the violin

todo [todoo] *n* all ▶ todo o dia all day ▶ ao todo *(price)* in all

tolo, la [toloo] *adj* foolish

tom [tong] *n* tone

tomada [tomada] *n* socket

tomado, da [tomadoo] *adj* captured ▶ 'lugar tomado' 'occupied'

tomar [tomah] *v* to take ▶ toma! there you are!

tomate [tomatchee] *n* tomato

tomilho [tomeel-yoo] *n* thyme

tonelada [tonelada] *n* ton

toranja [toranja] *n* grapefruit

torcedor [toh-sedoh] *n* supporter

torcer [toh-seh] *v* to twist ▶ torcer o pé to twist one's ankle

torcicolo [toh-seekoloo] *n* stiff neck

torneio [toh-nayoo] *n* tournament

torneira [toh-nayra] *n* faucet

tornozelo [toh-nozeloo] *n* ankle

Tropicalismo

A cultural movement from the end of the sixties, *Tropicalismo* revolutionized popular music in Brazil, employing debauchery, irreverence and improvisation. It was led by the Bahian musicians Caetano Veloso and Gilberto Gil, who based the movement on a counter-culture which opposed the existing musical norms. Still going strong today, *Tropicalismo* celebrates the fusion of Brazilian culture with foreign influences.

torrada [tohada] *n* toast

tosse [tossee] *n* cough ▸ estar com/ter tosse to have a cough

toucinho [tosseen-yoo] *n* bacon fat

toureiro [toray-roo] *n* bullfighter

touro [toroo] *n* bull

trabalhar [trabal-yah] *v* to work

trabalho [trabal-yoo] *n* work

traço [trassoo] *n* line

tradição [tradeessowng] *n* tradition

tradicional [tradeess-yonow] *adj* traditional

traduzir [tradoozeeh] *v* to translate

tráfego [trafegoo] *n* traffic ▸ 'tráfego interrompido' 'traffic stopped'

tráfico [trafeekoo] *n* traffic ▸ tráfico de droga drug trafficking

traíra [tra-eera] *n* wolf fish

tranqüilizante [trankweelee-zantchee] *n* tranquilizer

tranqüilo, la [trankweeloo] *adj* calm

transferência [transh-ferensee-a] *n (of money)* transfer

transmitir [tranj-meetcheeh] *v* to transmit

transpirar [transh-peerah] *v* to perspire

transportar [transhpoh-tah] *v* to transport

transporte [transhpoh-tchee] *n* transport ▸ transporte público public transport

trás [trash] *prep* & *adv* ▸ para trás backwards ▸ roda de trás rear wheel

tratamento [tratamentoo] *n* treatment

tratar [tratah] *v* to treat ▸ tratar de to try to

trator [tratoh] *n* tractor

travar [travah] *v* to brake

trazer [trazeh] *v* to bring; *(clothes)* to wear ▸ trazer junto to bring along

treinador [tray-nadoh] *n* trainer

treinar [traynah] *v* to train

treino [traynoo] *n* training

trem [treng] *n* train

tremer [tremeh] *v* to tremble

tremor [tremoh] *n* ▸ tremor de terra earth tremor

triângulo [tree-angooloo] *n* triangle

trigo [treegoo] *n* wheat

troca [troka] *n* exchange

trocar [trokah] *v* to change ▸ trocar de roupa to change clothes

troco [trokoo] *n* change ▸ dar o troco to pay back

tronco [tronkoo] *n* trunk

Tropicalismo [tropee-kaleejmoo] *n a blend of Brazilian culture and foreign influences*

trovão [trovowng] *n* thunder

trovoada [trovwada] *n* thunderstorm

truta [troota] *n* trout

tu [too] *pron* you

tua(s) [too-a(sh)] *pron* yours ◆ *adj* your

tubo [tooboo] *n* tube ▸ tubo de escape exhaust pipe

tudo [toodoo] *pron* everything ▸ tudo bem? everything OK?

túmulo [toomooloo] *n* grave

túnel [toonew] *n* tunnel

turista [tooreeshta] *n* tourist

turístico, ca [tooreesh-tcheekoo] *adj* touristic

U

úlcera [oow-sera] *n* ulcer

último, ma [oow-tcheemoo] *adj* last; *(most recent)* latest ▸ no último ano last year ▸ por último finally

ultrapassar [ootrapassah] *v* to overtake

um(a) [oong(ooma)] *art* & *adj* a, an

umas [oomash] *adj* & *pron* some

úmido, da [oomeedoo] *adj* damp

unha [oonya] *n* nail ▸ unha encravada ingrown toenail

união [oon-yowng] *n* union

único, ca [ooneekoo] *adj* single ▸ preço único one price

unidade [ooneedadjee] *n* unit; *(computer)* drive

universidade [oonee-veh-seedadjee] *n* university

uns [oonsh] *adj* & *pron* some ▸ uns aos outros each other

urbano, na [ooh-banoo] *adj* urban

urgência [ooh-jenss-ya] *n* urgency ▸ em caso de urgência in case of emergency

urgente [ooh-jentchee] *adj* urgent

urina [ooreena] *n* urine

urinar [ooreenah] *v* to urinate

usado, da [oozadoo] *adj* worn

usar [oozah] *v* to use; *(clothes)* to wear ▸ usar óculos to wear glasses

uso [oozoo] *n* use ▸ 'fora de uso' 'out of use' ▸ 'para uso externo' 'for external use'

usuário [ooz-waryoo] *n* user

utensílio [ootenseel-yoo] *n* utensil

útil [ooteew] *adj* useful

utilidade [ooteelee-dadjee] *n* usefulness

utilizar [ooteeleezah] *v* to use

uva [oova] *n* grape

vaca [vaka] *n* cow; *(meat)* beef

vacina [vasseena] *n* vaccine

vacinado, da [vasseenadoo] *adj* ▸ estar vacinado contra to be vaccinated against

vagão [vagowng] *n* carriage

vagão-leito [vagowng-laytoo] *n* sleeping car

vaivém [vy-veng] *n* swinging

vale [valee] *n* valley ▸ vale postal postal order

valer [valeh] *v* to be worth ▸ vale a pena it's worth it

validade [valeedadjee] *n* validity

válido, da [valeedoo] *adj* valid

valor [valoh] *n* value

válvula [vow-voola] *n* valve

vantagem [vantajeng] *n* advantage

vapor [vapoh] *n* steam

varal [varow] *n* ▸ varal de roupas clothesline

varanda [varanda] *n* veranda

variado, da [varee-adoo] *adj* varied

variedade [varee-edadjee] *n* variety

varinha [vareenya] *n* ▸ varinha mágica magic wand

vários, rias [var-yoosh] *adj* several

varrer [vaheh] *v* to sweep

vaso [vazoo] *n* vase ▸ vasos sanguíneos blood vessels ▸ vaso sanitário toilet bowl

vassoura [vassora] *n* broom

vazio, zia [vazee-oo] *adj* empty; *(tire)* flat

vegetariano, na [vejetaree-anoo] *adj* & *n* vegetarian

veia [vaya] *n* vein

veículo [ve-eekooloo] *n* vehicle

vela [vela] *n* candle; *(on boat)* sail

velhice [vel-yeessee] *n* old age

velho, lha [vel-yoo] *adj* old

velocidade [veloossee-dadjee] *n* speed ▸ a grande velocidade at high speed

vencedor [ven-sedoh] *n* winner

vencer [venseh] *v* to win

venda [venda] *n* sale ▸ venda a prestações for sale in installments ▸ 'à venda' 'for sale'

vendedor [vendedoh] *n* seller ▸ vendedor de jornais *(person)* news vendor

vender [vendeh] *v* to sell ▸ 'vende-se' 'for sale'

veneno [venenoo] *n* poison

venenoso, sa [venenozoo] *adj* poisonous

vento [ventoo] *n* wind

ventoinha [ventoo-eenya] *n* fan

ventre [ventree] *n* ▸ prisão de ventre constipation

ver [veh] *v* to see

verão [verowng] *n* summer

verdade [veh-dadjee] *n* truth ▸ é verdade it's true

verdadeiro, ra [veh-daday-roo] *adj* true

verde [veh-djee] *adj* green

verificar [vereefeekah] *v* to check

vermelho, lha [veh-melyoo] *adj* red

versão [veh-sowng] *n* ▸ na versão original in the original version

vértebra [veh-tebra] *n* vertebra

vertigem [veh-tcheejeng] *n* dizziness

vespa [veshpa] *n* wasp

vestibular [vesh-tcheeboolah] *n* university entrance exam

vestido [vesh-tcheedoo] *n* dress

vestir [veshteeh] *v* to dress ▸ vestir-se to get dressed

vestuário [veshtoo-ar-yoo] *n* clothing

veterinário [veteree-nar-yoo] *n* veterinarian

vez [vesh] *n* time ▸ às/por vezes at times ▸ em vez de instead of ▸ outra vez once more ▸ era uma vez once upon a time

via [vee-a] *n* track ▸ via aérea by air ▸ em vias de about to

viagem [vee-ajeng] *n* journey ▸ viagem a negócios business trip ▸ viagem de núpcias honeymoon ▸ viagem organizada organized tour

viajar [vee-ajah] *v* to travel

víbora [veebora] *n* viper; snake

vida [veeda] *n* life ▸ vida de cão dog's life ▸ vida fácil easy life

vidro [veedroo] *n* glass

vigilância [veejeelanss-ya] *n* surveillance

vila [veela] *n* town

vinagre [veenagree] *n* vinegar

vinagrete [veena-gretchee] *n* vinaigrette

vindo, da [veendoo] *adj* originating ▸ vindo de... coming from ...

vingativo, va [veenga-tcheevoo] *adj* vindictive

vinho [veenyoo] *n* wine ▸ vinho branco/tinto/rosé white/red/rosé wine

vinícola [veeneekola] *adj* wine-producing

violação [vee-olassowng] *n* rape

violeta [vee-oleta] *adj* violet

vir [veeh] *v* to come ▸ venham conosco come with us

virar [veerah] *v* to turn ▸ vire à esquerda turn left

visita [veezeeta] *n* visit ▸ visita guiada guided tour

visitar [veezeetah] *v* to visit

vista [veeshta] *n* view ▸ até a vista! see you later ▸ golpe de vista glance ▸ vista para o mar sea view

visto, ta [veeshtoo] *n* visa ♦ *adj* seen ▸ visto que seeing as

vitela [veetela] *n* veal

vitral [veetrow] *n* stained-glass window

vitrine [veetreenee] *n* shop window

viúvo, va [vee-oovoo] *adj* & *n* widower, widow

viver [veeveh] *v* to live

vivo, va [veevoo] *adj* alive

vizinho, nha [veezeen-yoo] *n* neighbor

voar [vo-ah] *v* to fly

você(s) [vosse(sh)] *n* you

voleibol [volay-bow] *n* volleyball

volta [vowta] *n* turn ▸ estar de volta to be back ▸ dar uma volta to go for a walk/drive ▸ até a volta until next time

voltar [vowtah] *v* to return ▸ voltar a fazer algo to do something again

vomitar [vomeetah] *v* to vomit

vontade [vontadjee] *n* ▸ ter vontade de to feel like

vôo [vo-oo] *n* flight

votação [votassowng] *n* voting

votar [votah] *v* to vote

voto [votoo] *n* vote

voz [voj] *n* voice ▸ em voz alta/baixa in a loud/low voice

vulcão [voow-kowng] *n* volcano

vulgar [voow-gah] *adj* common

xadrez [shadresh] *n* chess

xale [shalee] *n* shawl

xampu [shampoo] *n* shampoo

xarope [sharopee] *n* syrup

xixi [sheeshee] *n* pee ▸ fazer xixi to have a pee

zangado, da [zangadoo] *adj* angry ▸ ficar zangado to get angry

zangar-se [zangah-see] *v* to get angry

zebra [zebra] *n* zebra

zinco [zeenkoo] *n* zinc

zona [zona] *n* area

zurrar [zuhah] *v* to bray